Why Smart Executives Fail

Why Smart Executives Fail

and What You Can Learn from Their Mistakes

SYDNEY FINKELSTEIN

PORTFOLIO

PORTFOLIO

Published by the Penguin Group

Penguin Group (USA) Inc., 375 Hudson Street, New York, New York 10014, U.S.A.
Penguin Books Ltd, 80 Strand, London WC2R 0RL, England
Penguin Books Australia Ltd, 250 Camberwell Road, Camberwell, Victoria 3124, Australia
Penguin Books Canada Ltd, 10 Alcorn Avenue, Toronto, Ontario, Canada M4V 3B2
Penguin Books India (P) Ltd, 11 Community Centre, Panchsheel Park,
   New Dehli—110 017, India
Penguin Books (N.Z.) Ltd, Cnr Rosedale and Airborne Roads,
   Albany, Auckland, New Zealand
Penguin Books (South Africa) (Pty) Ltd, 24 Sturdee Avenue, Rosebank,
   Johannesburg 2196, South Africa

Penguin Books Ltd, Registered Offices:
80 Strand, London WC2R 0RL, England

First published in 2003 by Portfolio,
a member of Penguin Group (USA) Inc.

10 9 8 7 6 5 4 3 2

Grateful acknowlegdment is made for permission to reprint "Come to the Edge" from *Selected Poems* by Christopher Logue. Reprinted by permission of David Godwin Associates and Faber and Faber Ltd.

Publisher's Note
This publication is designed to provide accurate and authoritative information in regard to the subject matter covered. It is sold with the understanding that the publisher is not engaged in rendering legal, accounting or other professional services. If you require legal advice or other expert assistance, you should seek the services of a competent professional.

LIBRARY OF CONGRESS CATALOGING-IN-PUBLICATION DATA
Finkelstein, Sydney.
   Why smart executives fail and what you can learn from their mistakes / Sydney Finkelstein.
      p.   cm.
   Includes index.
   ISBN 1-59184-010-4
   1. Executive ability. 2. Business failures. 3. Executives—Psychology. 4. Failure (Psychology)
   5. Success in business. I. Title.
HD38.2.F56 2003
658.4'09—dc21   2003042994

This book is printed on acid-free paper. ∞

Printed in the United States of America
Set in Fairfield Light

To my grandfather Leib Dunajec

Acknowledgments

Six years is a long time from when an idea hatches to the point when it is ready to enter the world, and a lot of things have to go right to make that happen. At the top of that list is the commitment of a group of people to support, enable, and energize an intensive research process designed to find the answers to a set of questions that had yet to be explored. This book is the result of such a collaborative effort among a wide-ranging research team having diverse talents but one thing in common: Each person bought into the idea, bringing a sense of passion that has helped to maintain the momentum over a long gestation period.

As a professor at Tuck's School of Business at Dartmouth, I have been incredibly fortunate to work with a Dean's Office that has been supportive from the start. Dean Paul Danos not only pushed me to branch out and take on a challenge of this magnitude, but also backed it up with generous research and moral support, including opening the door for me to spend one uninterrupted year in Paris researching and writing. Associate Dean Bob Hansen and research center directors such as Vijay Govindarajan, Joe Massey, and Espen Eckbo kept writing the checks. Colleagues such as Connie Helfat, Rich D'Aveni, Margie Peteraf, Alva Taylor, Andy King, and Paul Argenti asked questions (sometimes without their even knowing it) that kept me looking for the answers.

My MBA students have been subjected to stories of great corporate mistakes for years, and may well have wondered when I would finally have it all together. Their ideas and critiques helped to sharpen the message, and the participation of a remarkable number of Tuck and Dartmouth students in various parts of the research project was invaluable. Thanks to Tuck students Andrew Brownell, Sherilyn Butler, Fern

Chaddad, Potoula Chresomales, Anna Fincke, Nat Fisher, Sumeet Gugnani, Mark Harvey, Hiroshi Hashiguchi, Iwao Ikeya, Seiji Ikuta, Michael Koester, Nobi Koya, Cathrine Laksfoss, Laura Lovelace, Devin Mathews, Lex Miron, Kazuo Narumiya, Ana Sanchez, Shade Sanford, Jose Santos, Peter Stevens, Ramon Suazo, John Torget, Craig Urch, Suzanne Wilke, and Barry Winer, and to Dartmouth students Adi Herzberg, Catie Huisman, Thomas Kunz, Albert Lee, Jerry Ling, Evan Poon, and David Cahill. In addition, research assistants Leah Dering, Suzan French, Maribeth Gainard, Betty Pak, Gina Rasmussen, and James Yaeger made terrific contributions.

There were three special members of the research team that played central roles. Scott Borg came on in the last eighteen months to play a significant role in helping to make sense of what my research findings were really saying, and it is not an exaggeration to say that without his efforts the finished product would never have turned out the same way. Becky Savage was my secret weapon, hunting down obscure bits of information and talking her way into arranging countless interviews for me. And Alan Elkins, who decided after a long and successful career in medicine to return to Tuck to complete his MBA degree, started working with me as a student and has not stopped since. His multiple roles as chief instigator, conscience of the project, and behind-the-scenes choreographer brought a trifecta of talent to the team. Thank you, Scott, Becky, and Alan.

I had an opportunity to try out some of the ideas in the book in various venues outside of Tuck, and for this I thank Melinda Muth, Lex Donaldson, and Roger Collins for arranging a presentation at the Australian Graduate School of Management, Maurizio Zollo for doing the same at INSEAD, Bente Lowendahl at the Norwegian School of Business, and Costas Markides at the London Business School. Perhaps unsurprisingly, the psychiatry profession took an early interest in this work, resulting in presentations at a Grand Rounds in the Department of Psychiatry at Dartmouth–Hitchcock Medical Center and at the American Psychoanalytic Association annual meeting in New York. Presentations to executive education audiences at Tuck and elsewhere, as well as to Dartmouth alumni in Los Angeles, San Francisco, and Paris, were also helpful in honing the message.

Many academic colleagues were influential in helping to shape my thinking. My collaboration with Ann Mooney into why boards of directors fail yielded important clues; John Slocum's feedback on some of my early writing on dot-com failures triggered new ideas; a second look at Brian Quinn's path-breaking work on intelligent enterprise and innovation helped me to see where so many executive mind-set failures come from; the writings of scholars such as Linda Argote, Amar Bhide, Don Hambrick, Jim March, Charles Perrow, Scott Snook, Barbara Tuchman, Karl Weick, and Abraham Zaleznik all played a role in how these ideas developed.

The book would never have turned out the same way without the cooperation of so many senior executives and others who agreed to be interviewed, sometimes several times. The insights they provided helped me to put together major pieces of the puzzle that I just could not have done otherwise. Several CEOs sat for interviews with the research team more than once, sometimes as often as three or four times, and they deserve special appreciation for dedicating so much time and energy to the project. Here I thank Paul Charron (Liz Claiborne), Robert Galvin (Motorola), Stanley Gault (Rubbermaid and Goodyear Tire & Rubber), Alec Gores (Gores Technology Group), Russell Lewis (New York Times), Leonard Riggio (Barnes & Noble), and Kevin Roberts (Saatchi & Saatchi). All of the people we interviewed are acknowledged in the book, where they would allow it, at the place they are referenced.

Writing about "worst practices," rather than the usual custom of best practices, and writing about failure rather than success, breaks the mold of most books on business, so it takes a special type of person to see its potential. My agent, Helen Reese, saw it instantly and has been a strong advocate for all I've tried to accomplish with this book. It is because of Helen that this book ended up with Adrian Zackheim and his editorial team at Portfolio. He too saw the potential and offered instant insights that strengthened the finished product. Kim Keating, Alicia Green, Andy Steele, and Carol Millay at Tuck all helped behind the scenes.

I was also fortunate to have the support of many friends who seemed always to want to know just what I was learning, and who consistently replied to my rambling answer by saying, "That's interesting." It was clear early on that this book not only is for managers, or investors, or business school students, but can also speak to that large group of people who just want to know, "Why does this happen?"

For the past six years, my wife Gloria and daughter Erica have watched as the book has taken shape. I've managed to work and write in cafes in Hanover and in Paris, on kitchen tables at home, and in airplanes on route to vacations, but in each place I could always count on their love, support, and understanding. Writing a book may be a lonely pursuit, but I was never lonely.

This book is dedicated to my grandfather Leib Dunajec. It is an odd dedication in that I never met him, but the stories of his life have somehow endured over the decades and have penetrated into my conscience. My mother's father lived in a little shetl in Poland; he was not formally educated, and he was extremely poor. Yet he was a scholar, a teacher, a musician, and a leader. Years ago I heard stories of how villagers would press against the window of his home to hear him perform religious services when the house was too full to admit another person. He was the one people would go to if there were problems to solve, and he was the one who would teach children not only to read and write but also to know what was right and what was wrong. It is no doubt a conceit to believe that any of this could have been passed down to me, yet he remains a tremendous influence in my life. This dedication is but a minor gesture in return.

Sydney Finkelstein
Hanover, NH
February 2003

Contents

Why Smart Executives Fail

CHAPTER I

Why Smart Executives Fail

What Can Studying Failure Tell You?

You've seen them on the covers of *Forbes*, *Fortune*, and *BusinessWeek*. You've read about their brilliant and often inspirational leadership. You've listened to business gurus and industry analysts praise their companies as examples to be emulated. You've probably invested in their stock, either directly or indirectly. You may even have seized the chance to work for them or partner with them. These people are among the brightest stars of American and world business. They're business heroes, geniuses, titans.

Yet a few years or even a few months after they were so celebrated, their companies crashed. Key operations were shut down. Workers were laid off. The company's stock plunged. Huge ventures, to which these leaders and their companies were deeply committed, turned out to be almost worthless. When the dust settled, we found out that these leaders had destroyed hundreds of millions or even billions of dollars worth of value.

How is this possible? How can these business leaders fall so far so fast? How can so many people be so disastrously wrong? What can possibly account for the scores of business failures we see every year, in different industries, and even in different countries? And how can we prevent this sort of thing from happening again?

Six years ago I set out to answer these questions in the most extensive investigation ever conducted on this subject. My goal was not only to understand why businesses break down and fail, but to focus on the people behind these failures; not only to understand how to avoid these disasters, but to anticipate the early warning signs of failure. Ultimately,

I wanted to move beyond ad hoc explanations of failure on a case-by-case basis and expose the roots of these breakdowns in a definitive way.

Some of the answers my research team uncovered were as surprising as the sudden fall from grace experienced by many of the business leaders we studied. In fact, many of the qualities that sound like the attributes of a dream enterprise turn out to be the basis for a business nightmare. For managers, many of the qualities we aspire to emulate, or feel guilty for not having, turn out to be ones we're better off without. For investors, many of the signposts of success that we strive to identify turn out to be markers for failure. And for those of us simply fascinated by the world of business, in part because the leaders and executives that run organizations seem so much apart from the rest of us, it turns out that they have the same weaknesses and character flaws, and make the same kinds of mistakes, though perhaps on a grander scale, that we do.

The Causes of Failure

Giant business disasters can be prevented—but only if we start thinking about business leadership and organizations in strikingly new ways. For starters, this means putting aside the easy answers and looking intently at the real causes of business failures—the people who create, manage, and lead the company.

Journalists, employees, business gurus, other managers, investors, members of the general public—everyone has an opinion on how a top executive managed to turn an apparently successful enterprise into a corporate catastrophe. In fact, there are seven theories usually cited for executive failure. But how many are correct?

1. The Executives Were Stupid

The most common explanation for a business failure is to say that the CEO and other senior executives were stupid and incompetent. We point to their incredibly stupid mistakes and conclude that if management could do such stupid things, the executives involved must be stupid people.

But is this true? Are major business failures ever *really* due to stupidity or lack of talent? The reality is that people who become CEOs of large corporations are almost always remarkably intelligent. *Every* failed executive who was interviewed for this book was extremely articulate, perceptive, and knowledgeable. No one who talked with these executives for even a few minutes could fail to be impressed with their intelligence. Does anyone really think that former Rubbermaid CEO Wolfgang Schmitt, who was known as an innovative genius and had a knack for knowing the right answers before most people even recognized the critical issues, is lacking in raw intelligence or talent? Does anyone really think that Wang Labs founder An Wang, who earned a Ph.D. from an Ivy League university, owned several patents in his own name, and created a billion-dollar company, was lacking in raw intelligence or talent?

Nearly all of these people reached the top because executives and shrewd investors repeatedly chose them over their fellow managers for being the *most* able and *most* competent. Many of them graduated from the world's most selective and demanding schools. In the earlier stages of their careers, they were the managers who turned crises into triumphs. Once they got to the top, they were often able to hang on to their positions long enough to shape the fate of their enterprises, because corporate boards and business partners were utterly confident of these executives' ability to make truly intelligent decisions. Nobody wants to entrust the fate of a large corporation to somebody who isn't very, very smart, so as a rule, they don't.

Despite these executives' general intelligence, could the major business failures nevertheless be due to ignorance of the industry or a lack of relevant knowledge or experience?

This possibility isn't very plausible either. The people responsible for major business disasters almost always have terrific track records in their relevant areas of business. They tend to be enormously knowledgeable about everything that seems likely to affect their company. If they come upon something they *don't* know, they generally make a point of catching up right away. These people are usually recognized as the top authorities on whatever type of business they are in.

In sum, managers are far from stupid. We cannot understand corporate failure by resorting to the cop-out excuse of poor managerial quality. No, we'll need to look elsewhere for an explanation.

2. *The Executives Couldn't Have Known What Was Coming*

The second most common way of explaining business disasters is to acknowledge that while the executives were intelligent, they were caught by events they couldn't have foreseen. Even the best executives might be expected to fail when business conditions suddenly shift in unpredictable ways.

The only problem with this explanation is that *none* of the business disasters we investigated turned out to be due to executives being caught by unforeseeable events. In company after company, regardless of industry, time period, or even country, the managers had every opportunity to see the important changes that were coming to their industry. In most cases, the executives possessed all the necessary facts. In many cases, people tried to tell them what these facts meant.

Executives at the Schwinn Bicycle Company knew all about mountain bikes and the other new designs that would threaten their brand. They had even received presentations on these designs and turned them down. Motorola knew all about the digital cell phones that would cut into its analog sales. Motorola was collecting royalties on them. When the Internet changed the PDA market that General Magic was going after, it was a development that some of General Magic's own people had predicted. In each of these cases and many others, the relevant change in business conditions was foreseen and discussed—and then disregarded.

3. *It Was a Failure to Execute*

Recently, it has become fashionable to claim that the executives of failed companies probably had the right policies, but that their companies didn't carry out the policies well enough. If the managers and employees at all levels had only done their jobs better and not messed up the details, everything would have been fine. This certainly sounds like an appealing explanation. It implies that the senior managers got the big things right and only slipped up on the little ones. It suggests that a few improvements in "execution" are all that would be necessary to put everything right again.

Yet attributing business failures to "a failure to execute" is a bit like attributing business bankruptcies to insufficient money. Every business failure can be described as a failure to execute because the business ultimately failed to do what it set out to do: create value for its employees, customers, and stockholders. Furthermore, by the time the business as a whole has broken down, many of its operations will also have broken down. Show me a business that has failed, a business guru might proclaim, and I'll show you a failure to execute.

But how often is the *root* cause of a business breakdown simply a failure to execute? Major business and engineering schools turn out competent management and operations experts by the thousand. Tell these experts exactly what you want to do, and they'll set up a reasonably efficient and reliable system for doing it—usually in a matter of weeks. Major consulting firms can deliver impressive operations expertise to companies in a matter of days. Given the availability of this expertise, no one can realistically claim that an inability to execute operations effectively is the *main* reason a business fails. If execution were the core problem, all a CEO would have had to do to save his or her company would have been to pick up the phone.

A closer look at companies that underwent major breakdowns makes this explanation even less plausible. In many cases, the businesses that suffered huge losses were typically performing all sorts of operations brilliantly. Even when some kind of operational breakdown was at the heart of a company's problems, it was never where the problems began. What could be more operational than computer glitches that throw data on billing, costs, and internal metrics into turmoil? But the real reasons Oxford Health Plans struggled so mightily in 1997 with operational breakdown had much more to do with fundamental misconceptions about the marketplace and the underlying culture at the company. If we conclude that it's all execution, how do we ever get behind the curtain to tackle the real underlying problems? Operational breakdowns in today's business world are seldom the true cause of failure; they are invariably a symptom of something else.

4. *The Executives Weren't Trying Hard Enough*

Some would say that if the top executives had the necessary skills and the necessary information, then they must have been asleep at the switch, goofing off. Lower-level employees are especially prone to conclude that senior managers were fiddling while the company burned.

Is the problem, then, that the people responsible aren't trying hard enough? If the top executives were somehow motivated better, would this make them do a better job?

No one who has looked at the daily schedule of a top executive of a major corporation would believe this for a minute. People in these jobs work extraordinarily long hours, most of their activities away from work are work-related, and they stand to profit hugely if their company gains in value. Their whole self-image is often wrapped up with their success at their job. Most of these executives are willing to risk their health, their marriages, their reputations, and practically everything else in their drive to make their companies more successful. To hear some of the executives we interviewed describe the ordeal they went through when disaster struck would be enough to dispel anyone's naïve assumptions about lack of motivation.

5. The Executives Lacked Leadership Ability

Is it possible that the executives responsible for major business failures have difficulty getting people to follow the course they have set?

Anyone who has met the people involved in these disaster stories knows that lack of leadership ability isn't the problem. Most of these executives are strikingly forceful personalities with an enormous amount of charm and charisma. They all command attention and respect. Although their personal styles vary widely, these are people who have all demonstrated an impressive ability to get other people to do what they want. What's more, these are managers who, in most cases, had a clear vision of their company's future.

If we conceive of leadership ability as some combination of talent and force of personality that enables someone to build a cadre of followers who are prepared to go to battle for the leader, we need look no farther than Jeffrey Skilling, the former CEO at Enron. By all accounts, Skilling had the ability to set a dynamic and clear vision, empower his people to reach that target, and create an environment where excellence in reaching those goals was highly rewarded. Much the same could be said of former Tyco CEO Dennis Kozlowski, among others who are profiled in this book. The idea that weak leadership accounts for failure doesn't hold up to close scrutiny.

6. *The Company Lacked the Necessary Resources*

OK, if major business disasters aren't due to any obvious qualities of the business leaders, are they then due to some obvious limitation or defect on the part of the larger business enterprise?

Perhaps a lack of technological resources, capabilities, or assets?

This explanation doesn't work either. Companies that manage to fail on a large scale also have resources that are large in scale. Many of these companies that have failed so spectacularly were technological power-houses. Furthermore, most of the companies that have survived their business disasters remain technological powerhouses to this day, even though in other respects they may be pale shadows of their earlier selves.

How about financial causes then? Are major business failures due to an inability to pay for the resources and expertise that were necessary for success? Were there simply insufficient funds to put the executives' vision into operation?

No. These businesses were able to lose huge amounts of money because they had huge amounts of money to lose. We're talking about monster companies that possessed or acquired tremendous resources and yet still managed to fail spectacularly. And even the dot-coms we studied were generously funded—probably too generously.

7. *The Executives Were Simply a Bunch of Crooks*

Is the problem, finally, that the top executives were simply crooks? Were the senior managers so greedy that they let the whole company go under while they stripped the business of assets?

That idea doesn't hold up either. Contrary to the recent impression created by a few spectacular scandals, the clear majority of CEOs who preside over major business disasters are scrupulously honest.

But even when the CEOs *are*, in fact, crooks, this begs the question of why they became crooks. After all, these are people whose salaries alone would make them rich by any ordinary standards. Why, having reached that level of success, would they suddenly decide to start stealing?

Some people claim that it was "just their nature," that some managers are irrationally driven to steal, that dishonesty was part of their charac-ters all along. But even if some of these top executives were always crooks, this still doesn't explain much. What was it about the companies in question that caused them to put crooks into their top positions? And why weren't the crooks promptly exposed and ousted when their behavior began to threaten the company's ability to succeed?

Finally, there is the awkward fact that the sums stolen, while disgustingly large, were not, in most cases, large enough to bring these companies down.

The Failure to Understand Failure

All seven of these standard explanations for why executives fail are clearly insufficient. Understanding why smart executives fail would be much easier if we could rely on these explanations, but we can't.

The faulty theories don't begin to address the overall syndromes associated with major business failures. Even more puzzling than the fact that brilliant managers can make such bad mistakes is the way they so often magnify the damage by making additional ones. Truly colossal blunders don't come in isolation; they come in clusters. Once a company has made a really bad misstep, it often seems as though it can't do anything right. How does this happen? Why, instead of fixing their mistakes, do business leaders regularly make them worse?

The general question of why successful businesses suddenly fail leads to a number of other, more specific questions. How do leaders who have been successful for years suddenly start getting everything wrong? Why do business leaders sometimes do things that seem completely irrational? How do they manage to ignore conspicuous evidence that their policies aren't working? Why do organizations fall into the same traps again and again? Why are safeguard procedures often suspended at the very moment when they are most needed? How can corporate boards sit back and watch all these things happen? Above all, what can company leaders do in advance to guard against making major corporate mistakes? This book is an attempt to answer these questions and more.

The Research Behind the Book

The questions and puzzles raised by studying mistakes and failure required a special kind of research program. The kind of investigations that once led to *In Search of Excellence* and its many successors were vitally important, but they needed to be supplemented by equally penetrating investigations *in search of failure*—or, more precisely, *in search of the causes of failure.*

For six years my research team at the Tuck School of Business at Dartmouth carried out an extensive investigation on business break-downs. We started off by identifying some forty companies that had gone through a major business failure. The size of the resulting loss in earn-ings and destruction of market value in absolute terms were less impor-tant than that the loss relative to the size of the company was "major." In practice, the magnitude of the loss was usually in the hundreds of mil-lions of dollars, often in the billions of dollars. A number of the compa-nies we studied went bankrupt, but the majority were robust enough to lick their billion-dollar wounds and move on.

A second criterion for selection was to ensure that we were building a sample of companies from many different industries and even some dif-ferent countries. This criterion was easily met.

Third, we wanted a balance between new and fresh cases on the one hand, and some classic stories of failure on the other. So, for example, General Motors' robotics strategy of the 1980s is a dated story, yet a clas-sic one that still holds relevant lessons for managers today. That's why we took another look at the rise and fall of John DeLorean and his namesake automobile, RJ Reynolds' Project Spa designed to produce a "smokeless" cigarette, Wang Labs' failed quest to destroy IBM, and the Boston Red Sox's decision to field an all-white baseball team after every other major league organization had integrated African-Americans onto their roster.

The research project was first conceived in 1997, so it was natural to look at some of the most interesting failures of the 1990s, including Johnson & Johnson's fall from the top of the cardiovascular stent busi-ness, Motorola's failure to shift from analog to digital cell phones, Irid-ium's even more disastrous foray into the satellite-based cell phone business, Fruit of the Loom's delayed response to the North American Free Trade Act that made it cost-prohibitive to manufacture underwear in the U.S., Rubbermaid's ruinous battle of wills with Wal-Mart, Target, and other megaretailers, and the implosion of advertising industry heavy-weight Saatchi & Saatchi.

In truth, that was to be all of it—some classic stories of failure, some more contemporary business breakdowns—in a book that perhaps would have been published a year or two earlier. But two events occurred that made us rethink our research strategy. First, the Internet bubble burst, scattering hundreds of defunct companies across the business landscape, and, second, the business world was rocked by an incredible series of scandal-driven failures that continue to make front-page news. It wasn't possible to close down the research program and call it a day when two such dramatic and impactful developments exploded on the business scene in relatively quick succession.

The result was a significant delay in completing the research project, but, much more importantly, an opportunity to try to understand the underlying reasons for failure in these two apparently very different arenas, and how the causes of failure differed from the more "traditional" case histories that made up the earlier part of the research. So the sample expanded to accommodate companies such as eToys, Power-Agent, Boo.com, Webvan, Enron, WorldCom, Tyco, Rite Aid, Adelphia, and ImClone.

In the end, our sample consisted of fifty-one companies that we investigated in detail. In addition, perhaps another dozen or so other companies and organizations were studied briefly. Together, this represents the largest and most comprehensive study of business failures ever conducted.

The Data

To really understand what happened in the companies we studied, we wanted to try to put ourselves in the shoes of the key decision makers at the time that things went bad. When you do this, one of the first things you realize is that many great corporate mistakes were due to managerial inaction as much as to inappropriate managerial action. And this makes sense, of course. Companies as diverse as Rubbermaid, Schwinn, Encyclopedia Britannica, and the Boston Red Sox fell into serious trouble precisely because they didn't respond to critical challenges when they had the opportunity.

But how can anyone really put themselves in the shoes of key decision makers when the events of interest may have taken place a decade ago? This is where we had one advantage over historians, whose research tactics are similar to ours—at almost each company we were able to interview people who could give us first-hand accounts that inevitably went far beyond the original press reports we also consulted. So, for example, when we investigated the reasons why Motorola refused to shift from analog to digital cell phones in the mid-1990s, we interviewed three former Motorola CEOs, two former midlevel managers, and two executives who held senior positions at the Bell operating company that kept asking Motorola to sell them digital cell phones. There were other companies we studied where fewer interviews were conducted, but overall the interviews played a major role in our ability to distill the lessons from the past.

Altogether, we conducted 197 interviews. In the companies that suffered severe breakdowns, our interviews often included CEOs, former CEOs, other executives, and midlevel managers. Occasionally, successive CEOs from the same company were interviewed. Sometimes, we interviewed competitors, journalists, industry experts, investment bankers, insurance underwriters, and others. In most cases, the subjects of the interviews allowed their answers to be taped, ensuring accuracy and verifiability. We took extensive notes when taping wasn't allowed. Thus, documentation of the interviews was substantial.

In every case, the extensive direct interviews were supplemented with large quantities of information collected from financial statements, news stories, published analyses, press releases, and company reports. This made it possible for us to check out many of the claims made by the people interviewed and to put their comments into a broader context. The fact that a major business failure had occurred in each case we studied was beyond dispute: The hard, verifiable numbers demonstrated in each instance that something had gone badly wrong. In every case, for example, the business failure in question had a large adverse effect on the business's shareholder value. What was nonetheless missing, until our research team put the pieces together, was enough information and insights from enough sources to uncover exactly what happened and why.

As we learned more about what was really going on in these companies, our assumptions changed dramatically. For example, we didn't think that we'd find that executives expressly chose not to respond to change even when they knew it was happening. But at Motorola, our interviews revealed that key decision makers had an abundance of information on the public's preference for digital cell phones, and each of the former CEOs we interviewed confirmed that Motorola executives saw the change happening but chose not to respond. Why they didn't respond is a fascinating story with relevance not just for managers and investors, but even for people who deal with the same challenge of facing unwanted truths in their everyday lives.

By the same token, as we collected more information we also revised our initial ideas on whether a company really did make a huge corporate mistake that led to failure. For example, many people have suggested that IBM made a major blunder in its development of the original PC in 1979 by relying on Microsoft for the operating system and Intel for the microprocessor. While it's certainly true that the operating system and the microchip hold the lion's share of value in this industry, it doesn't seem particularly reasonable to expect IBM to have figured this out almost twenty-five years ago. Few of us, anywhere, have that type of crystal ball. In addition, IBM's strategy to outsource the operating system and microprocessor—both areas that were beyond its core competence in hardware—mirrors the same tight focus that is the hallmark of leading companies such as Honda, Dell, and Nike today. So if you want to critique IBM for its PC strategy, you've got to also argue against state-of-the-art strategy thinking circa 2003.[1]

The Range of Companies Investigated

The range of companies we investigated is wide enough to include almost everyone's business and investment interests. It includes car companies, entertainment companies, food and drink companies, consumer electronics companies, fashion houses, financial service companies, computer companies, drug companies, communications companies, electronic equipment manufacturers, retail chains, insurance companies, an HMO, a toy company, an advertising agency, a publisher, a restaurant chain, a cigarette company, a plastic container company, a baseball franchise, a cable company, a bicycle company, an energy company, a company that manufacturers landscaping tools and machines, dot-coms, and a conglomerate.

In addition, while American businesses dominate the list of companies in the sample, we also studied four Japanese companies (Sony, Nissan, Firestone, and Snow Brand Milk), four British companies (Saatchi & Saatchi, Marks & Spencer, DeLorean, and Boo.com[2]), and one company each from South Korea (Samsung), Germany (DaimlerChrysler), Singapore (Barings Bank/ING), and Australia (AMP).

Among the companies whose breakdowns were examined in considerable detail are the following:

AMP	eToys	Oxford Health Plans
Adelphia	Firestone	PowerAgent
Advanced Micro	Food Lion	Quaker/Snapple
Devices	Ford	Rite Aid
Bankers Trust	Fruit of the Loom	RJ Reynolds (Project
Barings/ING	General Magic	Spa)
Barneys	General Motors	Rubbermaid
Boo.com	ImClone	Saatchi & Saatchi
Boston Market	Iridium	Samsung Motors
Boston Red Sox	Johnson & Johnson	Schwinn
Bristol-Myers Squibb	(Cordis)	Snow Brands
Cabletron	L.A. Gear	Sony (Columbia
Coca-Cola (Belgian	Levi Strauss	Pictures)
contamination)	LTCM	Toro
Conseco	Marks & Spencer	Tyco
DaimlerChrysler	Mattel	Wang Labs
DeLorean	Mossimo	Webvan
Encyclopedia Britannica	Motorola (cell phones)	WorldCom
Enron	Nissan	

The Interview Process

When we spoke to the Hollywood executive, he was driving down Santa Monica Boulevard with the top down, telling us how sunny it was in L.A. that day.

When we talked to the former CEO who saw his company self-destruct under the watch of his successor, there was a palpable sense of anger in his voice as he gave us his account.

When we chatted with the son of the founder of a company that no longer exists, he shared stories of what it was like to live with his hyper-ambitious dad.

What we discovered in the interview process could not have been predicted, but stands as a fascinating side note to the entire process. For many of the key executives we spoke to, despite the fact that we were interested in uncovering the mistakes and lessons from often painful episodes in a career, it was almost as if they were waiting by the phone for our call. Not all of the people we interviewed, to be sure, but a surprisingly large proportion really wanted to tell their side of the story.

Why were most of the executives who have been widely blamed for business disasters so willing to be interviewed for this book? In many cases, they believe that the very same facts that others think show their weaknesses can exonerate them. It's also because they believe that a deeper analysis, capturing more of the complexities they confronted, presents them in a more favorable light than the relatively superficial coverage they've received in newspapers and magazines. In fact, some of the leaders who presided over the worst disasters seemed almost desperate to announce that they were right all along and to blurt out information that they believed would support their case. "What makes you think the Sony acquisition of Columbia Pictures was a corporate blunder?" asked Mickey Schulhof, former president of Sony USA, despite the fact that Sony took a $3.2 billion write-off in connection with this acquisition.

While the vast majority of people we asked for an interview said yes, there were some who didn't. Those whom we did interview, however, always had a chance to review their comments and even rescind them if they wanted. That this seldom happened is another remarkable sidelight.

In sum, despite a perceived risk to their reputation, many people almost felt compelled to talk to us. It made for fascinating discussions and gave us terrific insight, although one CEO finished the interview by saying, "I hope you are kind to me."

A Book About People

Ultimately, this book is about people. People who run organizations, and run organizations into the ground, but people nonetheless. And just as you and I behave badly or act irrational at times, so too do the people in this book. The difference is, the people we write about have primary responsibility for million-dollar products, billion-dollar divisions, and multibillion-dollar companies, and when they act in seemingly irrational ways, the collateral damage can be immense.

There's the young entrepreneur who makes it big and then proceeds to destroy everything he's built when he becomes convinced that he has all the right answers. There's the established big-time CEO who invests billions in a venture not because there's a truly compelling case for the venture, but because he wants to. There's the leadership team so in love with their product that they refuse to listen when their customers tell them, and tell them again, that something must change. There's the CEO who pursues acquisition after acquisition unencumbered by such pedestrian concerns as strategic logic and integration. There's the group of executives who persist in self-destructive behavior, despite considerable evidence that such behavior can be toxic.

These people don't do these bad things on purpose. They want nothing more than to be successful, and oftentimes some of them were, to a grand degree.

They also don't do these bad things by accident. Their actions, and inactions, while not intended to yield the disastrous results that they do, are also not random. It is not so-called "acts of God" that account for the stories of failure in this book, but rather "acts of men and women."

And they don't do these bad things because they're not very smart. No, they are very smart, and very talented—often remarkably so—but bad things they do nonetheless.

How to explain such calamities and collapses if not for these reasons? That is the question we set out to answer.

The Patterns of Failure

We didn't start out with crystal-clear hypotheses on what patterns of failure we would see, or even whether definitive patterns could be identified. Rather, our major findings and conclusions emerged from the data over time. We were looking for two things.

First, we wanted to get as close to the "inside story" as possible for each case history, and the interviews were the key to connecting the facts collected from publicly available documents. In addition, the study of one company often informed our understanding of another as the data we gathered via interviews and other sources helped to make sense of what we were observing.

Second, while analyzing each company in the sample, we looked for the patterns. Gradually, the pieces of the puzzle began to come together as the lessons from the case histories coalesced around a small set of themes. Over time, it became clear just how deep-rooted and relatively small in number the causes of failure actually were. Businesses that seemed at first to have nothing in common turned out to have failed for exactly the same reasons and in much the same way. Even the excuses that we heard from failed managers turned out to be the same in case after case. Despite the vast numbers of things that could go wrong in something as complex as business enterprises, the really devastating failures turned out to have a surprisingly limited number of causes.

This is one of the major findings of the study. Patterns of failure emerged that could be applied not only to the scores of classic, almost common business breakdowns—think Rubbermaid, L.A. Gear, Barneys—but also to the Internet one-year wonders and the rogue companies that have dominated the news over the past two years.

The case histories and results from our research are laid out in three sections: "Great Corporate Mistakes," "The Causes of Failure," and "Learning from Mistakes."

The Results

Part I: Great Corporate Mistakes

When we considered all of the companies together, we realized that most of them failed during four major business passages: creating new ventures, dealing with innovation and change, managing mergers and acquisitions, and addressing new competitive pressures. These are multifaceted events that involve some degree of corporate transformation, and are very complex, so it's probably not that surprising that we find these stages of business especially perilous. Instead of bringing out the hidden strengths of a business, each of these challenges tends to bring out the hidden weaknesses.

In Part I we describe these four business passages and explain why they represent periods of increased vulnerability for any business. More important, we show why the conventional wisdom about these stages of business is inadequate.

Why was each of these stages so dangerous for these companies? What were the great corporate mistakes they made? What pitfalls exist for executives as they take their own organizations through each of these transitions, and what can they do about it? The answers to these questions reveal why the conventional wisdom about these key chapters in a business life is inadequate.

Part II: The Causes of Failure

Part II looks across all fifty-one companies studied and across the four critical transitions described in Part I where executives tend to stumble, and it identifies the key underlying reasons for failure that we saw again and again.

We discovered that precipitous business failures are caused by four destructive patterns of behavior that set in, without anyone noticing them, well before a business goes under. These four syndromes involve (1) flawed executive mind-sets that throw off a company's perception of reality, (2) delusional attitudes that keep this inaccurate reality in place, (3) breakdowns in communications systems developed to handle potentially urgent information, and (4) leadership qualities that keep a company's executives from correcting their course. Long before there are obvious danger signs, several of these syndromes can take hold of executive behavior. While the business might appear outwardly healthy, the inner mechanisms are breaking down. Examining these interrelated behavior patterns, one at a time, makes it chillingly clear how each one can set a business up for collapse. Together they provide a framework on how to think about business failure.

Part III: Learning from Mistakes

In Part III we reveal our third and final set of research results—how board members, CEOs, executives, lower-level managers and employees, investors, and other interested stakeholders can learn from the mistakes of others, so as to avoid and prevent the disastrous outcomes we document in this book.

We address these issues in two ways. First, we identify a set of early warning signs of failure that executives and investors alike need to watch out for. And second, we present ways to diagnose business mistakes as they are happening, and provide tools to help people learn from their own mistakes. These last two chapters, then, offer a set of ideas and tools that readers can use to help avoid and sometimes even predict business failure.

By studying the great corporate mistakes made by executives struggling with the key challenges of new venture creation, innovation and change, mergers and acquisitions, and competitive rivalry, we gain insight not just about what not to do, but about what you should do. By studying the destructive syndromes behind failure—executive mind-set failures, delusional attitudes, communication systems breakdowns, and unsuccessful leadership habits—you learn not just what not to do, but what you should do. And by studying early warning signs and how to diagnose and prevent business mistakes, you learn not just what not to do, but what you should do. By trying to solve the problem of how smart executives fail, I hope, in the end, that what I've actually done is shown how smart executives can succeed.

PART I

GREAT CORPORATE MISTAKES

In Part I we focus on four different business challenges: creating successful new ventures, managing mergers and acquisitions, coping with innovation and change, and developing winning strategies in the face of new competitive pressures. These are all fundamental, and sometimes daily, tests for executives, yet in contrast to what you might read in most business books, there aren't so many happy endings. By digging into the detailed case histories of thirteen companies as well as shorter vignettes of more than two dozen others, you'll discover just why executives and the companies they work for falter when engaging in these demanding transitions of organizational life.

These stories of failure offer us an opportunity to learn from the experiences of other companies and other executives from the safety of our desks or armchairs. But don't get too comfortable. I wouldn't be surprised if you see worrisome parallels between the failing companies we profile and your own.

CHAPTER 2

New Business Breakdowns

Stories of New Ventures That Don't Work . . . and Why

Take the best and the brightest (though not quite modest and rather fond of hype), add money (with strings attached), key partners (who perhaps care more about their own businesses than yours), and a terrific idea (yes, competitors have noticed too), and mix. Result. General Magic. A technology powerhouse tackles a glorious technological challenge by investing billions of dollars to solve a problem that, as it turns out, few customers need solved. Result: Iridium. One of the largest conglomerates in the world decides—or more precisely, its chairman and CEO decides—to enter a highly competitive, capital-intensive business because, well, because he wants to. Result: Samsung Motors. Louis Borders of big-bookstore fame asks, "Why can't we deliver anything to anyone?" This question takes him and a billion dollars of start-up costs to the frontier of retailing—the "last mile" between store and customer. Result: Webvan.

Four stories from four very different companies, but with two things in common: All were entrepreneurial ventures that started out with tremendous advantages, and all have failed. The business of new businesses creation has one of the highest mortality rates of any stage of corporate life, yet each of these companies was not your run-of-the-mill start-up. These aren't stories of shoestring budgets and inexperienced founders but of deep-pocketed talent gone bad, each of which makes us ask, "What went wrong?" Making new ventures work is tough, and there are many things that must go right. Yet, what's fascinating is that despite the diverse industries, people, and challenges these new ventures involved, several common patterns emerge when they are considered together. As you read each of these stories, look for the clues that point out the wider insights into what goes wrong in new ventures. Think about what you would have done had you been at the helm. What you may discover is that there are a remarkably small number of fundamental mistakes that happen again and again. Stop those mistakes and maybe the odds will shift in your favor.

Venturing into PDA: The General Magic Story

Computers that fit in the palm of your hand were all the rage in the early 1990s. Not that any of them existed yet, but the promise of beeper-sized personal digital assistants didn't seem far away. Led by consumer product expert John Sculley, Apple Computer was a palm-computing pioneer and in 1990 it handpicked its brightest stars to attack the PDA market by setting them up in a top-secret company called General Magic. In the five years prior to its 1995 IPO, General Magic raised $90 million in venture capital from a collection of the greatest consumer electronics and telecommunications companies in the world. The PDA market was crowded, but among the many competitors, General Magic had the most money, the best talent, and the strongest relationships. Despite these advantages, the company's magicians never delivered on their promises, and either quit out of frustration or were fired soon after the IPO. How did a company with such promise, such strong support, and such an early and clear vision of the future perform such a disappearing act?

The Secret Start-Up

No one wants to talk about General Magic Inc. Not the founders. Not the investors. Not even the company spokeswoman hired last August, presumably, to talk. In fact, so hush-hush are the goings-on at this 18-month-old startup that Apple Computer Inc. Chairman John Sculley sidesteps questions with this whispered response: "What's General Magic?"

—BusinessWeek, December 23, 1991

By the time the personal computer (PC) established its permanence in American homes and offices in the late 1980s, futurists were already looking toward the next big thing. It was a time of high-technology convergence. Cellular phone service went from sideshow to "must have," PCs were starting to talk to each other across local- and wide-area networks, and the next frontier was miniaturization, portability, and mobility. In a March 1991 speech to the Software Publisher's Association, Apple CEO John Sculley described a hand-held device with built-in communications capabilities, including FAX, pager, and cellular telephone that would move data via wireless networks.

Like its computer industry rivals, Apple was feverishly working on a portable, hand-held computer. Unlike its rivals, however, the company initially decided not to take on this challenge from within. So, in July 1990, Apple Computer gave birth to a company called General Magic, put $10 million in its bonnet, and sent it on its way to capitalize on the emerging hand-held computer market. Apple retained a minority stake in General Magic and held the first (but not exclusive) right to license the company's technology for future Apple products.

General Magic assembled a "dream team" at the top. CEO Marc Porat had been John Sculley's technical guru and head of business development for Apple's Advanced Technology Group. The "interface ninjas of our time"[1]—Mac designers Bill Atkinson (MacPaint and HyperCard author) and Andy Hertzfeld (the spiritual leader known as Yoda around the office) headed up development. Susan Kare, creator of Apple's signature icons such as the desktop trash can, joined on as a designer. Rich Miller and Jim White (the "father of email") came on board shortly thereafter, bringing with them what would become the core of the fledgling company—an agent software language called Telescript. Both Hertzfeld (Apple employee number twelve) and Atkinson (Apple employee number fifty-one) invested $1 million in the new venture, and Apple CEO John Sculley joined the board of directors.

Despite, or perhaps because of, the project's "secrecy," it didn't take long for word to spread about this all-star team and their secret directive. Marc Porat could be found in every magazine and on every news show touting the future that General Magic would soon bring to the masses. Financial analysts even gushed about the private company, stating that General Magic's communication language had the potential to become the digital version of English.

Jumping on the Bandwagon

Along with the hype and expectation came money and partnerships. General Magic never had to look too far for cash—the Apple connection opened the door to a slew of high-profile companies that wanted a piece of the action. In November 1991, Sony and Motorola joined the General Magic family, each purchasing 5 percent stakes in the company for $5 million. AT&T followed two months later with a similar investment. At the end of 1992, Matsushita signed on, followed by Northern Telecom, NTT, Cable & Wireless, Sanyo, and Philips. By 1994, General Magic had raised over $90 million in venture capital and license agreements.

General Magic's investors had big plans for the company. Most had failed to grab a major share of profits from the PC revolution of the 1980s and they weren't going to let the hand-held market pass them by. Each was either manufacturing hand-helds for the consumer market or providing the telecommunications network over which PDA data would be transmitted. Each had a lot to gain from mass adoption of this new technology. Because General Magic could potentially become the industry standard, hardware manufacturers and telecommunications providers flocked to support the company. In fact, every General Magic investor committed to use Telescript as its common network language. In 1992, AT&T launched a new group that constructed a nationwide Telescript messaging service from the ground up called PersonaLink. AT&T expected to derive billions of dollars of revenue through this network once the PDA market exploded. Around the same time, Motorola started building the Envoy, a wireless two-way communicator that relied on General Magic's software. The Envoy communicator (though not actually released until 1996) was seen as a major driver of network traffic through which millions of dollars of revenue would flow. And Apple was about to launch the Newton, its first hand-held computer/organizer/communicator.

Sony was even more optimistic. Mickey Schulhof, president of Sony Software Corp and a Ph.D. in solid-state physics, told a colleague, "Sony has failed three times in the computer business. This is our last chance and I think it's a winner."[2] Sony set out to create its own hand-held computer called Personal Link based on General Magic's technology. Schulhof stated in 1992 that he saw no obstacles to Telescript becoming a world standard. The possibilities seemed endless.

The Company Unveiled, Unfortunately

On February 8, 1993, the company held a press conference to finally announce its products, its blue-chip investors, and its global consumer electronics and telecommunications partners. The press conference was lavish, but once the hoopla died down, there was little to evaluate.

General Magic was developing two products: Magic Cap and Telescript. Magic Cap was an ultra–user-friendly operating system for PDAs and other non-PC devices. Telescript was a communications language that provided secure mobile agent hosting that ran over proprietary networks allowing any computer or communicator to talk to other devices on any kind of network using Telescript. The lack of such a common language had stunted PC growth for years and General Magic's advances were considered vital to the widespread use of PDAs. As impressive as these products were, however, neither the company's software nor the devices required to run the software were available yet (nor would they be for at least two more years).

Following the grand press conference, General Magic was quickly stung with charges of favoritism. The primary attraction of Telescript was General Magic's pledge of a totally open industry standard for wireless data communications. At the press conference, however, General Magic revealed that it had signed an exclusive arrangement giving AT&T the use of Telescript in its telecommunications network for 2½ years before directly competitive carriers such as MCI Communications, Sprint Corp., or private data networks could install it. This arrangement not only endangered a deal with IBM, which was considering an investment in General Magic, but, more importantly, damaged the credibility of the venture.

Despite these rumblings, the promise of a digital secretary kept the financial community breathlessly awaiting General Magic's next step. In 1994, after four years of work, General Magic released the Magic Cap operating system and a rudimentary version of Telescript to Sony and Motorola. CEO Porat—described in news stories as "a sort of silver-tongued devil"[3] and "God's gift to headline writers"[4]—was soon making the news circuit again, culminating in a 1995 IPO that raised an additional $82 million for the company. At the time of the IPO, General Magic had burned through $53 million developing and promoting the technology, yet brought in only $2.5 million in revenue.

Not long after the IPO, General Magic announced a series of product delays. Rumors began to surface that its products were failing to live up to the hype—in fact, they might not even work. There were also consumer complaints about the cost of the PDAs that actually made it to market. The original designs cost upwards of $3,000 though prices eventually dropped to around $1,000. Given the lack of available software and the limitations of a communicator that had no one else with whom to communicate, market acceptance was slow. General Magic's product delays and telecom providers' inability to equip their global networks with a robust communications language severely stunted market penetration. Apple was the first to abandon the company when it decided to develop its own operating system for the Newton. Then, in early 1996, a frustrated AT&T announced that it was abandoning PersonaLink, the worldwide Telescript network. Did this call for a new strategy? If so, what would it be?

As early as 1994, General Magic knew that the Internet would impact its future, but developing products that ran on the Internet would be in direct conflict with strategies of its partners (especially France Telecom, Northern Telecom, NTT of Japan, and AT&T) for proprietary data communications networks. These partners were in the midst of developing private networks based on the promise of General Magic's Telescript language. If General Magic became an Internet company, there would be nothing proprietary about its offering. Suddenly, the company's blue-chip (and disgruntled) partnerships became a major liability. In 1996, faced with an Internet-accelerated extinction, General Magic finally scrapped its device strategy and refocused its business entirely on the Internet.

The Wheels Finally Come Off

The Internet came along and broadsided the company. We immediately added a browser and we made Telescript an open language rather than proprietary, but it was too late. Palm came in and took the market for hand-helds. And Java took the market for networking. Had we started the company in 1994 instead of 1991, we would have ridden the crest of the Internet. Timing in this business is everything.

—Marc Porat, former chairman and CEO, General Magic, interviewed April 16, 2001

General Magic found itself in a strategic "no-man's land." Delays, criticism, and the daily grind of developing products for an increasingly skeptical market began to take its toll. Less than a year after its IPO, chief scientist and cofounder Bill Atkinson took a leave of absence from the company, never to return. Other senior executives followed, including CEO Marc Porat, who was forced to relinquish control of General Magic although he remained on the board to advise the company. In a last-ditch effort to save the company's development efforts and to demonstrate support for the new management, the company's investors agreed to commit an additional $75 million to the company in late 1996.

Probably the biggest casualty was the business itself. With its failure to develop the software to run PDAs (Palm's OS software became the early industry standard instead) and the rise of the Internet quickly relegating proprietary networks to the sidelines, General Magic scrambled to pull a rabbit out of its hat. The bunnies that emerged—browsers, email software, and a search engine—each proved ineffective as they brought the company face-to-face with the real heavyweights of the industry, including Sun, Netscape, Microsoft, and 3Com's Palm Computing.

By June of 1999, Goldman Sachs, General Magic's IPO underwriter, dropped research coverage, and analyst James Cramer "shamefacedly confess[ed] that he'd been one of those suckered in by the company's hype machine."[5] While General Magic's stock had become a penny stock, just a few years later the handheld computer market exploded with the introduction of 3Com's Palm Pilot in 1995. Since its introduction, over twenty million units have sold worldwide[6] and its simple interface and lean operating system have influenced other manufacturers to develop similar products. Finally, the vision of a personal digital assistant was a reality, though not for General Magic.

Around the same time that General Magic was being spun out of Apple, Motorola was creating Iridium and embarking on its own journey to stardom.

Iridium: Shooting for the Stars

Where do revolutionary ideas come from? For Motorola engineer Bary Bertiger, it was from listening to his wife complain that she couldn't reach

clients via her cell phone while on vacation in the Caribbean. After coming home, Bary and two other engineers working at Motorola's Satellite
Communications Group in Arizona hit upon the Iridium solution—a
constellation of sixty-six low–Earth-orbiting (LEO) satellites that would
allow subscribers to make phone calls from any global location.

Communications satellites, in use since the 1960s, were typically geo-
stationary satellites that orbited at altitudes of more than 22,000 miles.
Satellites at this altitude meant large phones and annoying quarter-
second voice delays. Comsat's Planet 1 phone, for example, weighed in
at a computer-case–sized 4.5 pounds. Iridium's innovation was to use a
large constellation of low-orbiting satellites (approximately 400–450 miles
in altitude). Because Iridium's satellites were closer to earth, the phones
would supposedly be much smaller and the voice delay imperceptible.

Was the idea a good one? While Bertiger's immediate superiors nixed
the project, Motorola Chairman Robert Galvin liked what he saw and
gave the go-ahead. To Robert, and later his successor and son Chris
Galvin, Iridium held the potential for greatness, a symbol of Motorola's
technological prowess that was too exciting to give up. For the engineers
at Motorola, the challenge of launching Iridium's constellation was classic "techtosterone"[7] eventually driving them toward initial service in 1998
for a price tag of $5 billion plus.

The business officially started in 1991, when Motorola established
Iridium LLC as a separate company, investing $400 million in exchange
for an equity stake of 25 percent, and six of twenty-eight seats on Iridium's board. Motorola also made loan guarantees to Iridium of $750 mil-
lion, with Iridium holding an option for an additional $350 million loan.
For its part, Iridium agreed to $6.6 billion in contracts with Motorola
that included $3.4 billion for satellite design and launch, and $2.9 billion for operations and maintenance. Iridium also exposed Motorola to
developing satellite technology that was expected to provide the latter
with significant expertise in building satellite communications systems.

As Iridium came closer to the anticipated launch, Edward Staiano
came on board as CEO. Prior to joining Iridium, Staiano had worked for
Motorola for twenty-three years, during which time he developed a
reputation for being hard-nosed and unforgiving. In leaving Motorola's
payroll for Iridium's, Staiano gave up a $1.3 million per year contract
with Motorola for a $500,000 base salary plus 750,000 Iridium stock op-

tions that vested over a five-year period. If Iridium made money, Staiano would hit paydirt.

Service Launch

We're a classic MBA case study in how not to introduce a product. First we created a marvelous technological achievement. Then we asked how to make money on it.
—John Richardson, Iridium CEO, *Washington Post,* May 24, 1999

On November 1, 1998, after launching a $180 million advertising campaign and an opening ceremony where Vice President Al Gore made the first phone call using Iridium, the company launched its satellite phone service, charging $3,000 for a handset and $3–$8 per minute for calls. The results were devastating. By April 1999, the company had only ten thousand subscribers. Facing negligible revenues and a debt interest of $40 million per month, the company came under tremendous pressure. In April, two days before Iridium was to announce quarterly results, CEO Staiano quit, citing a disagreement with the board over strategy. John Richardson, an experienced insider, immediately replaced Staiano as interim CEO, but the die was cast.

In June 1999, Iridium fired 15 percent of its staff, including several managers who had been involved in designing the company's marketing strategy. By August, Iridium's subscriber base had grown to only twenty thousand customers, significantly less than the fifty-two thousand necessary to meet loan covenants. Two days after defaulting on $1.5 billion in loans—on Friday, August 13, 1999—Iridium filed for Chapter 11 bankruptcy protection.

The Autopsy

There is still debate on whether Iridium was doomed from the start. While some insiders remained true believers in the concept even after the bankruptcy, outsiders were caustic, calling Iridium "the fantasy of Motorola. It's like a sexual obsession. Anyone who brings up economic reality is not a true believer—it's in the category of the Taliban."[8] What really happened?

Cellular build-out dramatically reduced the target market's need for Iridium's service. Iridium knew its phones would be too large and too expensive to compete with cellular service, forcing the company to play in areas where cellular was unavailable. With this constraint in mind, Iridium sought a target market by focusing on international business executives who frequently traveled to remote areas where cellular phone service wasn't available. Although this market plan predated the rise of cell phones, Iridium remained focused on the business traveler group through the launch of its service. As late as 1998, CEO Staiano predicted that Iridium would have 500,000 subscribers by the end of 1999.

One of the main problems with Iridium's offering was that terrestrial cellular had spread faster than the company had originally expected. In the end, cellular *was* available. Due to Iridium's elaborate technology, the concept-to-development time was eleven years—during this period cellular networks spread to cover the overwhelming majority of Europe and even migrated to developing countries such as China and Brazil. In short, Iridium's marketing plan targeted a segment—business travelers—whose needs were increasingly being met by cell phones that offered significantly better value than Iridium.

Iridium's technological limitations and design stifled adoption. Because Iridium's technology depended on line-of-sight between the phone antenna and the orbiting satellite, subscribers were unable to use the phone inside moving cars, inside buildings, and in many urban areas. Moreover, even in open fields users had to align the phone just right in order to get a good connection. As a top industry consultant told us, "You can't expect a CEO traveling on business in Bangkok to leave a building, walk outside on a street corner, and pull out a $3,000 phone." Even former Motorola CEO George Fisher acknowledged in an interview that "Not having a very small phone and not having in-building coverage were not part of the original concept and for whatever reason it was done hurt the concept a lot."[9]

There were other technological bugs that couldn't be fixed. Iridium lacked adequate data capabilities, an increasingly important feature for business users. Making matters worse were annoyances such as the fact that battery recharging in remote areas required special solar-powered accessories. These limitations made the phone a tough sell to Iridium's target market of high-level traveling businesspeople.

The design of Iridium's phone also hampered adoption. In November 1997, John Windolph, Iridium's director of marketing communications, described the handset in the following manner: "It's huge! It will scare people. If we had a campaign that featured our product, we'd lose."[10] Yet a year later Iridium went forward with essentially the same product. The handset, although smaller than competitor Comsat's Planet 1, was still literally the size of a brick. In the end, however, this was one mistake too many for the venture to overcome.

Iridium was an idea that got a lot of people very excited at Motorola. The next company we profile in the new-venture business—Samsung—developed an idea that got hardly anyone excited. Samsung is particularly interesting because it is the only Korean company we studied, and is a terrific example of that country's fascination with chaebols (conglomerates). Is it possible that a company from a different part of the world, with different corporate governance mechanisms and particularly strong connections among bankers, government, and private enterprise, can make some of the same mistakes made by Internet start-ups and corporate spin-offs? In a word, yes.

Against All Odds: The Tale of Samsung Motors

We are launching Samsung Motors for the sake of the nation. As Samsung contributed to the national development with electronics in 1970s and with semiconductors in 1980s, we should lead the national economy with cars in 1990s.

—Kun-Hee Lee, chairman of Samsung, biographical essay, 1997

The announcement from Samsung Group Chairman Kun-Hee Lee regarding the company's entry into the motor vehicle business sent a ripple through the public and private sectors of the industry. Korea's auto industry had not had a new entrant in decades and was an oligopoly made up of three major carmakers: Hyundai Motors, Daewoo Motors, and Kia Motors.

At the time of the announcement in 1995, Samsung Group was riding high on the soaring memory-chip profits of the electronics division, and had earned a reputation for being a leader in nearly every sector it competed in, despite being a late-mover. Still, many questioned Lee's decision to enter the automobile business. It was no secret that he was a car enthusiast with a lifelong dream to build cars. Hence, business leaders, the press, and even Samsung's own managers speculated that the Group's decision to enter the motor vehicle industry was perhaps more a result of Lee's passion than a sound business decision. According to one Samsung manager, "Kun-Hee Lee, chairman of the Samsung Business group, has been known by his love with cars. Many believed that there were more and better investment opportunities, and that the motor business was not a good choice at all. Of course there were a lot of objections."[11]

Despite these objections, Samsung Motors pushed forward with its plan. The company's first cars were unveiled in March 1998, amidst a great deal of controversy. The astounding impact of the Group's motor business, however, would shock the world. No one—neither the venture's fiercest proponents nor its sharpest critics—could have predicted the effect the venture would have on Samsung's bottom line and its future direction.

What Is Samsung?

Samsung was founded in 1938 as a noodle-making company by the late Chairman Byong Chull Lee, with only 30,000 won (U.S. $30) in capital. The company's early business development plan mirrored that of other Korean chaebols in that it entered into trading businesses requiring minimal investment and soon expanded into manufacturing and sales.

The company grew tremendously during the 1950s and 1960s, again via the classic chaebol pattern of venturing into any industry where an opportunity arose. In the following decades the company continued to enter new markets, and built its reputation as a corporate leader in Korea, eventually becoming a world-leading semiconductor and electronics manufacturer.

Kun-Hee Lee succeeded his father as chairman when the elder Lee passed away in 1987. During a celebration of Samsung's fiftieth anniversary in 1988, the new chairman declared the "second founding" of the Group and announced his intention to expand Samsung into a leading world-class corporation of the twenty-first century. Indeed, by 1999, Samsung had grown to be the second largest corporation in Korea with forty-seven companies in five broad industry categories (electronics, machinery and heavy industries, chemicals, financial services, and others such as hotels, department stores, and a theme park) 161,000 employees,[12] and total revenues of $93.5 billion.

The Controversy That Was Samsung Motors

Chairman Lee may have dominated Samsung, but the gods of business were not so accommodating. Let's look at the landscape Lee was facing as he bulldogged into the car business. South Korea was on the verge of a deep recession—indeed, by late 1997 an economic crisis of unprecedented scale had hit the entire region. As a result, Korea's currency, the won, had depreciated substantially, sharply increasing the cost of imported raw materials. Further, the growth of domestic demand for passenger cars was projected to slow significantly, from a record-high annual growth of 13 percent (1990 to 1995) to 4 percent. The industry was already suffering from overcapacity with local carmakers rolling out more than 2.4 million units to their factory lots annually, even though the Korean auto market could consume only 1.6 million passenger cars per year. It was predicted at the time that this market saturation would cause the factory utilization rates of all Korean carmakers to fall below 60 percent after the year 2000.[13] For Samsung to be competitive, its annual production capacity would have to be at least 240,000 units;[14] however, the company didn't have enough capital to achieve such capacity without adversely affecting its finances. Even well-established automakers such as Nissan and Mazda were in serious financial trouble due to declining sales and eroding market share.

Obtaining government approval for the new business was critical to Samsung. To finance the venture, the company had to borrow huge amounts of capital from banks that, in turn, needed approval from the government to issue such large loans. However, the government had initiated an industry policy restricting conglomerates' expansion into new businesses to prevent excess competition and to maintain a balanced business portfolio for the entire economy. There was intense political pressure on Samsung, specifically, to improve efficiency by dumping unfeasible ventures and trimming its size; therefore, the company's decision to add a new business unit directly opposed these initiatives and caused intense friction with government officials.

Samsung's first attempt to garner approval was unsuccessful and the request was denied. Chul-Soo Kim, minister of trade, industry, and energy, held a firm position against Samsung's entry into the motor business, pointing out the pervasive warning signs such as excessive competition and slow market growth. Lee, however, was determined and played the "Pusan card" during negotiations.[15] Pusan was the power base of then-President Young-Sam Kim and locating a factory there was a tremendous economic proposition for Pusan residents. After two months of negotiations and intense pressure from local townspeople, President Kim finally relented, and Samsung Motors was born.

The political ploy proved costly for Samsung, as Pusan was a less-than-ideal construction site due to the high cost of real estate. Consequently, the plan consumed a tremendous amount of capital, resulting in an unworkable investment of 26.2 million won (U.S. $21,825) per car, compared to Hyundai's and Daewoo's total investments of 2.4 million won and 3.3 million won per car, respectively. Additionally, Samsung had entered into a highly disadvantageous licensing agreement with Nissan Motors, which further burdened the company. Samsung agreed to license core components of Nissan and pay a high 1.6–1.9 percent of sales turnover as royalty. At the time, Korean carmakers' average return on sales was only around 1 percent.[16]

In the face of so many drawbacks, it would have taken a miracle for the car business to work. Indeed, the cars themselves were impressive, pointing out how execution and product quality are necessary, but not sufficient, requirements for business success. Despite rave reviews, Samsung Motors sold fewer than fifty thousand cars (mostly to employees), even though the $3 billion Pusan plant was able to produce more than 240,000 per year. During the first half of 1998, Samsung Motors posted a net loss of 156 billion won and its debt surged to 3.6 trillion won compared to 2.6 trillion won at the end of 1997. Many observers believed that Lee had no choice but to give up his car-making aspirations. In early 1999, Samsung Motors went into a bank receivership and sought ways to salvage the business.

What Went Wrong?

Like Iridium, Samsung Motors was an extremely low-probability venture. The deck was stacked against the venture from the start. The so-called "chill" of the International Monetary Fund (IMF) bailout program had frozen the Korean domestic market. Demand for cars nose-dived to a mere 35 percent of the previous year's sales, leaving production lines virtually idle. When competitors acquired two of the other weak players in the Korean auto business, Samsung was left to its own resources, which proved insufficient. Despite efforts to revitalize itself, in May 2000, Samsung Motors' creditors agreed to sell 70.1 percent equity to Renault, a French automaker, for $560 million. Industry analysts considered the deal a bargain, given Samsung's estimated $5 billion investment in the venture, including the $3 billion Pusan factory.[17] Though Samsung managers opposed the deal, company creditors saw no alternatives, since further delay would have caused successive bankruptcies for parts suppliers. (Because Hyundai and Daewoo had discouraged their key suppliers from selling parts and components to Samsung Motors, Samsung Motors had to establish its own supplier network. Thus, these parts suppliers would have gone bankrupt unless the company resumed operation.)

It is clear that Samsung should not have gone into autos in the mid-1990s at the peak of the local and global glut. The impact of the economic crisis combined with the failed motor vehicle venture forced Samsung Group to undergo a painful, corporatewide restructuring to survive. To improve the soundness of its financial structure, the company was compelled to sell ten affiliated companies and reduce its labor force by fifty thousand.

In the end, Samsung was almost fortunate. For a company that could never fail, this very public failure was a shot across the bow, and a warning of what can happen when a large, resource-rich company is dominated by a primary owner-manager. Has the lesson been learned? Despite major corporate restructuring in 2001, Jae-Yong Lee, the thirty-four-year-old son of Chairman Kun-Hee Lee, was appointed assistant managing director at Samsung Electronics, the largest promotion ever at the company.[18] The jury is still out. . . .

Our analysis of new ventures wouldn't be complete without considering at least one of the online failures, Webvan. We're already seeing in business school new students who almost don't believe the stories of Internet failure; they are asking, "That couldn't really have happened, could it?" Well, it could, and it did.

Webvan and the New Grocery Revolution

In contrast to the preceding stories of corporate entrepreneurship, Webvan was an independent firm, and a company that fit the model of online start-up during the Internet boom. Backed by such prestigious investors as venture capital firms Sequoia Capital and Benchmark Capital, as well as Goldman Sachs and Yahoo!, the highly anticipated launch of the Internet grocer Webvan was to have marked a revolution in the grocery industry. Webvan exists as an extreme example of an online retailer gone wrong. Although this story has an ending not remarkably different from that of other dot-com companies, the factors leading to Webvan's demise were more spectacular than the factors for many other Internet firms. Just twenty-five months after its founding, the company was forced to file for Chapter 11, leaving its loyal customers with only a large billboard on the outfield wall of San Francisco's Pac Bell Park and Webvan stickers attached to the cup holders of thirty thousand of the stadium's 41,341 seats to remind them of another promising dot-com turned sour. The lessons from this case, however, extend well beyond Internet firms to the General Magics, Iridiums, and Samsungs of the world.

The Founding of Webvan: Bookseller Louis Borders Dips His Hand into the Grocery Bag

Louis Borders, the cofounder and former chairman of Borders Books, first conceived of Webvan in 1996 under the rubric "Intelligent Systems for Retail." The goal? To deliver anything to anyone anywhere. Although Webvan was not actually the first to market—companies such as Peapod, NetGrocer, and Streamline came online earlier—its complex distribution system was expected to revolutionize the Internet grocery business. Huge distribution and warehouse facilities located around the country would serve as hubs to offer delivery of groceries and other products to homes in the surrounding area in a classic hub-and-spoke alignment.

By April 1999, more than one month before the launch of its Web site, Webvan had already raised $120 million. Borders claimed that he could be profitable in the industry by approaching problems differently than other entrants. Instead of having individual "shoppers" walk through a warehouse or grocery store and fill orders by hand, he devised a complex mechanized warehouse in which machines filled orders with very little human intervention, eliminating store costs and the need for stock clerks and multiple warehouses. In one hour, a single Webvan worker would pack 450 items for grocery shoppers, amounting to ten times the productivity of the traditional "shopper" model. Once assembled, the products would be delivered to consumers in refrigerated vans marked with the Webvan logo. Delivery time ranged from the same day to the next day. Turning the stereotypical "cable guy" delivery incompetence on its head, consumers would be able to select a thirty-minute window when their groceries would be delivered. Webvan predicted that automated warehouses would give the company a ten-percentage–point edge in profit margins over traditional supermarkets. This margin would allow Webvan to keep prices low while covering delivery costs to avoid surcharges for customers.

The Build-Out

The creation of 26 distribution centers—each one bigger than 18 conventional supermarkets—will take costs out of the equation.
   —George Shaheen, chairman and CEO, Webvan, Forbes.com, October 18, 1999

Borders founded Webvan on a "go big or go home" philosophy to attract investors and seize the opportunity to raise significant capital to quickly grow the business. He felt that delaying expansion to ensure profitability in the initial market would only detract from Webvan's advantage in automated distribution. So big it went: On July 10, 1999, Webvan placed a $1 billion order with Bechtel for the construction of massive distribution and delivery centers in twenty-six markets. Borders contended that the initial center in Oakland, California, would be profitable within six to twelve months, and that additional Webvan warehouses would face shorter lead time, possibly breaking even in as little as sixty days. In a classic prognosis, Borders said, "I don't see any reason why an Internet company should take five to ten years to be profitable."[19]

   To make the project work, Borders turned to George Shaheen, who resigned from Andersen Consulting on September 21, 1999, to become CEO of Webvan. This was big. Shaheen was high profile, a thirty-year veteran of Andersen Consulting (now Accenture) who served as CEO and managing partner from 1989 on. During his tenure as CEO of Andersen, revenues increased from $1.1 billion to more than $8.3 billion. He was also the driving force behind the successful spin-off of Andersen Consulting from the now infamous, and departed, parent Arthur Andersen.

Shaheen was a believer. He gave up a hefty retirement package at Andersen that would have kicked in ten months later for an opportunity to create what can only be called "family wealth." And who are we to quibble? When Webvan went public on November 5, 1999, Shaheen's stock and options were worth $285 million. Said he, "Webvan was all about leveraging technology and reinventing the grocery business, just as Andersen had reinvented consulting . . . [Webvan will] set the rules for the largest consumer sector in the economy."[20]

From Theory to Practice

Webvan sounded good for a relatively long time. But eventually the cracks in what was a fatally flawed business model began to show.

There is a difference between a "good idea" and a "good business idea." In a word—profitability. Even as Webvan was going down the drain, articles appeared in the business press by smart people lauding the company for fighting the good fight, and, but for the grace of God knows what, it would have worked. It should have worked. Even today, writing about Webvan, it's easy to get excited by the vision. But the business model was fatally flawed from the start.

The supermarket business is notoriously low-margin to start with, so where was the money going to come from? No matter how many distribution centers were constructed and how efficient they were, the ability to squeeze out margins is inherently limited in this industry. Throw in free home delivery, and you've got to become the Superman of productivity to make a profit. Throw out free home delivery, and what was a limited market to start with (many people like to squeeze the tomatoes; others can't be bothered to plan out their purchases in advance) shrinks even more. When you add up the costs of building the Webvan infrastructure—easily $1 billion plus—it's hard to see how the numbers can add up. Now imagine that there are literally tens of thousands of competitors—call them supermarkets—that can easily add home delivery, that do not need to spend millions (let alone billions) to do so, that already have customers and market presence, that offer products of essentially equal quality to your own, and that are—surprise!—not really dinosaurs after all, and you have an idea that is getting less good with each passing minute.

Don't Leave Bad Enough Alone: Extending the Business Model

Something was not quite right, yet Webvan's strategy evolved in ways that added complexity to the original far-from-simple business model. This pattern was common to Internet start-ups during the Great Bubble as investors, entrepreneurs, and occasionally even savvy managers such as George Shaheen struggled to find something that could work. The problem was, while they kept drawing a new card to try to improve their hand, they were still saddled with a set of cards that couldn't add up to much no matter how many times they were rearranged.

Webvan was no different. As losses mounted, the company drew a new card four times. First, in year 2000 Webvan created a series of strategic alliances that featured products on Webvan's Web site from companies such as Clorox, Kimberly-Clark, Nabisco, and Gymboree. Other products, such as magazines and mass transit, and a "store within a store" concept with PETsMART.com followed. These alliances made sense if you consider that the company needed to find the right hook to bring in customers and keep them coming back, and these products were as good as any. But, you can't help but get the feeling that someone should have paid a little more attention to what customers wanted before spending $1 billion to build warehouses.

Second, Webvan explicitly moved to extend its model beyond the grocery business. Best captured as the holy grail of the "last mile," the company wanted to own customer delivery, period. The core idea was this: Because an Internet company eliminates the cost of building and maintaining stores, it can bridge the gap between physical store and home. This was a strategy no other major Internet company was targeting—not Amazon, not eBay, not Yahoo. The last mile meant Webvan would bring virtually whatever a customer needed right to her door.

Third, in June 2000 Webvan announced the acquisition of its primary online competitor, HomeGrocer.com, for $1.2 billion. Eliminating a competitor can be a good thing (although paying big retention bonuses and keeping employees with identical jobs on the payroll make it less of a good thing). What buying a competitor doesn't do, however, is make it easier to build and successfully run distribution centers; in fact, it makes it harder because of integration challenges. For example, HomeGrocer Web sites were converted over to Webvan, uniting both businesses under the Webvan brand name. Unsurprisingly, such changes are seldom seamless. Orders dropped from seven hundred to three hundred a day in the first place this was tried—San Diego—as customers struggled with technological difficulties and an unfamiliar Web site. The cost of the deal was high. In the damning words of one former Webvan manager, "We bought them out, we killed their stock, we killed their company, and then we killed ourselves."[21]

While all this was happening, Webvan decided to expand delivery to customers beyond a sixty-mile radius. In principle, this would allow each distribution center to cover a wider delivery range, considerably extending their potential market reach. In practice, however, this meant adding spokes to a hub-and-spoke distribution system by creating stations where trucks could transfer goods to local delivery vans, which would then serve nearby metropolitan areas. The fact that we're even talking about something called "hub-and-spoke" to deliver groceries is cause for concern. We're talking about g-r-o-c-e-r-i-e-s. Is it really necessary to create a complex system that requires you to buy $100,000 trucks and pay drivers $30 hour to deliver groceries when a kid working at the corner supermarket can do the whole thing for so much less?[22]

The Inevitable Comes

George Shaheen resigned as CEO of Webvan on April 13, 2001. The stock price was hovering around fifty cents, and the company was in danger of being delisted from NASDAQ. Webvan lost money every single quarter of its short life. In departing, Shaheen said, "I am convinced . . . that Webvan has a solid business model, which over time will alter retailing and the way people shop."[23] Webvan filed for Chapter 11 on July 13, 2001.

Barnes & Noble Chairman Leonard Riggio gave us a good epitaph for Webvan, when he said, "I think it was hubris of the times. Instead of really testing the concept in one city and really perfecting it in one city, they were going to be first movers and they were going to take over the whole world before anyone could move so they basically raised $2, 3 billion dollars, too much too soon, and they never really got the concept down and they were overextended from day one. One day you will see some very, very good practitioners of online grocery and upscale shopping. No question about it, but it wasn't Webvan."[24]

Why Is New Venture Creation So Difficult . . . and What Can You Do About It?

The stories of General Magic, Iridium, Samsung Motors, and Webvan are unique in their own ways, yet there are remarkable consistencies in what went wrong, what special challenges emerged, and what lessons to take away from four failures in four seemingly different industries.

The Principal–Principal Problem

In the age of Enron, WorldCom, Global Crossing, Rite Aid, and Adelphia, the spotlight has shone like never before on managerial integrity and corporate control. But the problem of corporate governance is not a new one; no less than Adam Smith (writing in *The Wealth of Nations*) pointed out the dangers of separating ownership and control in modern corporations. Hired hands—let's call them CEOs—have incentives that are different from stockholders, whose interests run more to return on investment and shareholder value than individual pay and prestige. This so-called principal–agent problem can occur when managers (the agents) act more in their own self-interest than that of shareholders (the principal). But in all four companies profiled in this chapter—and many others we've studied—the gap between ownership and control was minimal. Rather than being a formula for reducing value-destroying initiatives and strategies, having owners be managers can cause all kinds of bad things to happen. Rather than a principal–agent problem, we've got a principal–principal problem.

Let's consider some of the evidence. In interviews with Korean managers, all unanimously agreed that Samsung had blindly entered into the automobile business.[25] They also pointed out that the company had a number of alternative investment opportunities that were less risky and could have provided a higher degree of synergy with existing business units. They claimed that the majority of the Group's employees, including many managers, opposed the idea because it was believed that going into the overcrowded auto market without any existing competency in producing and selling cars was too risky.

Regardless, Lee's leadership was so strong that executives and managers at Samsung were unwilling to challenge his decision. One executive recalled, "All of the board members were opposed to Samsung's expansion into the motor business, but none of them went against Lee's will at official meetings."[26] Another added, "What could they do? Samsung is virtually owned and managed by Lee and nobody could have stopped it."[27] One of the Samsung managers interviewed described Lee's leadership within the organization as "absolute power." Though few deny that his strong, charismatic leadership contributed greatly to Samsung's previous successes, it is clear that in this case, that strength became a liability.

What makes the Samsung case so interesting is that the primary shareholder is also the primary manager, a combination that is supposed to ensure superior decision making and value maximization. Samsung's decision to enter the motor business, however, turns the classic agency theory on its head. The decision to enter the new business was made and executed by the principal, even though it jeopardized the future of Samsung. Being the largest stockholder of the company and deeply involved in running it, Lee wielded extreme power that enabled him to quickly dismiss organizational resistance and bypass conventional protocol in decision making.

There seems to be a break point beyond which the healthy alignment of managerial interests with shareholders enters a different realm.[28] Attention to value creation often lags when CEO/owners call all the shots. In a world of checks and balances, when there is no real countervailing force to a CEO, individual preferences can dominate. Think about all the Internet companies that burned through their funding in record time (Value America, Boo.com, World Online International, countless others); these companies were all closely held.

Even established companies can fall victim to the same phenomenon. When Robert Haas took over as CEO of Levi Strauss in 1984, one of the first things he did was take the company through a leveraged buyout. Nevertheless, this owner–manager (his family controlled the company) proceeded to undertake a series of value-destroying initiatives that left Levi's in dire straits.

The Schwinn Bicycle Company made it to the fourth generation until a combination of narrow-minded decisions by CEO Ed Schwinn brought it to ruin (and bankruptcy). Here's how one competitor described the situation: "With Eddie Schwinn's huge ego, the company was run into the ground. He started outsourcing in China, and while the quality was poor, Schwinn eventually ended up teaching them how to make bikes, and at the same time allowed Giant [the Chinese supplier] to become a formidable competitor to Schwinn."[29]

Our perspective is so skewed from seeing too many CEOs become major stockholders that we've even looked favorably upon CEOs buying *more* stock.[30] Sometimes the ache for stock becomes so intense that CEOs have to borrow extensively to get their fix. That the CEO's employer actually ends up guaranteeing loans used by the stock addict to feed his habit is seldom remarked upon . . . until it's too late. John J. Rigas, whose family controlled cable operator Adelphia Communications for years, borrowed (along with other family members) more than $3 billion to buy company stock. Bernie Ebbers, the founder of World-Com, had loans greater than $400 million for the same purpose. Sam Waksal, the founder of ImClone who pleaded guilty to a variety of insider trading charges, borrowed money from his company to quickly buy stock while ImClone was negotiating with Bristol-Myers Squibb on a major investment in ImClone. Stephen Hilbert, who built Conseco into an insurance giant before being removed when the company collapsed following the particularly ill-conceived acquisition of Green Tree Financial Company, had the same story. It's hardly incidental that all four companies have been in, or near, Chapter 11 in the past few years.

What About the Board of Directors?

The principal–principal problem is just as much about the board of directors as it is about CEOs. Indeed, a core value of the corporate governance crowd is that members of the board of directors should have a significant investment in the company to ensure their vigilance. Interestingly enough, it was precisely this situation that was at the root of the failure of once high-flying General Magic.

Apple retained a minority stake, and General Magic quickly added such blue-chip investors—many of which had seats on the board—as Sony, Motorola, AT&T, Matsushita, Northern Telecom, NTT, Cable & Wireless, Sanyo, and Philips. Most of these companies had been losers in the personal computer wars, and they saw General Magic as the company that could create the software to drive their PDA hardware plans.

The "partner"-controlled board, however, meant that General Magic had to manage around countless rivalries and different and sometimes conflicting partner goals. Former General Counsel Mike Stern put it this way: "They constrained and enabled . . . and they did both at the same time."[31] CEO Marc Porat told us, "The . . . problem was the different agendas of fifteen partners, large manufacturers, and telecommunication giants. To manage the complexity, we formed the 'Founding Partners Council.' There should have been someone running the company while I was running the alliance."[32] A board of directors that should have been ideal according to traditional views of corporate governance was too involved, often in counterproductive ways. Primarily due to its commitments to partners, General Magic didn't begin development of an Internet-enabled product until mid-1996, more than two years after management recognized the dangers and potential of the Internet for a company making communication software.

Partnerships and alliances in and of themselves are not bad things for a start-up. If managed correctly, they could contribute to success. Finding partners with deep pockets eases fundraising burdens and opens new markets, but collecting such a wide array of corporate sponsors (especially those that compete head to head) in disparate industries can easily lead to disaster. That's the real problem here. How could General Magic jump into the Internet when its partners' strategies were all about building proprietary technology and dominating industry standards? Ironically, the *raison d'etre* for spinning out General Magic from Apple was to enable partnerships with leading hardware companies that might not have played ball if the company were a subsidiary of Apple. The unintended consequences of what seem like well–thought-out strategies— here, adding partners that can help to establish your new software—is a theme that we will return to often throughout this book.

General Magic was not alone. Iridium's ability to market its phones was constrained by the unwillingness of partners in numerous countries—many with seats on the board—to roll out service in their regions. Surely few boards can operate with twenty-eight members, most representing different constituencies holding different goals.[33] That all but one board member was a member of the Iridium consortium similarly speaks volumes about the vigilance of the board in fulfilling its oversight function. Actually, this type of board, consisting as it does of representatives of investors, is not as rare as you might think in high-technology start-ups. Companies such as Excite At Home and Net2Phone, among others, have all had multiple investors, typically represented on the board, and not always agreeing on strategic direction. The idea that highly motivated investors sitting on corporate boards will keep management in line is really a Faustian bargain. Classic corporate governance says such "partners" are exactly what you want because of their vigilance, but when their interests compete with your own, all bets are off.

The Dangers of Scale

In recent years a sizable number of major new ventures have depended on scale for success. Innumerable Internet start-ups, especially so-called "e-tailers," have spent vociferously to establish new brand names to capture share. Sometimes, like at Webvan, the business model called for massive expenditures on infrastructure. Many telecom start-ups adopted a similar strategy—build it, and build it, and they will come. These companies are all about scale—only when the build-out has been completed will customers benefit from the service offered. Here's the bargain such high–fixed-costs firms make: Break-even is very high, but once it's reached, the marginal profit of each subsequent sale is also very high. This was true at Iridium, this was true at Webvan, and this was true at other telecom players such as Global Crossing Teligent, Winstar, and ICG Communications (all bankrupt). It's also true for present-day developers of 3G cellular telephony. With these economics, there are several fundamental truths:

You can't win without enormous capital. Why did Amazon.com survive as long as it did while piling up hundreds of millions of dollars in losses? Answer: Because it could. Amazon raised $8 million from venture capitalists Kleiner Perkins and $54 million in its 1997 IPO, but the big one came in January of 1999 with its successful $1.25 billion bond offering. Probably the best thing that Amazon did was raise huge sums of money relatively early and relatively often. When the Internet bubble burst, Amazon was still sitting with much of the proceeds from its bond offering in the bank to fund its continuing very-high–cost rollout. Other purveyors of Internet glory—who were probably not burning through their money piles any less quickly than Amazon—simply didn't have enough chips to stay in the game. In some ways, we can look at Amazon and say they did have a first-mover advantage—not in creating an e-store before anyone else, but in drilling more and deeper holes in search of big-time dollars that enabled them to keep playing when the holes ran dry for everyone else. If Webvan, Iridium, and the others had had unlimited funds, they would still be with us today.[34]

Even with enormous capital, you might not win. When build-out costs are in the billions and customer demand is lagging far behind, businesses die. To say that eventually enough customers will come on board to justify the enterprise is to place a project's implicit cost of capital near zero. Telecom start-ups, Iridium, Webvan, and even Samsung's auto venture were all doomed from the start because getting and using money costs money. No business survives without customers, and when they don't come to play—maybe because online grocery shopping requires customers to change their buying habits, which takes a long time, or because customers have better alternatives, such as traditional cell phones—the clock keeps ticking down anyway. It is tempting to say that once the infrastructure is in place, these businesses could have been profitable, but money is not free, and we shouldn't forget that.

Look for entry barriers. If they're not there, run. Scale businesses are very expensive. If all that investment doesn't get you some good old-fashioned barriers to entry, head for the hills. This is the story of telecom. Sexy technology plays with tremendous growth prospects (broadband, wireless, data, 3G—all "unlimited" in potential) would make someone fabulous profits if . . . no one else had the same idea. But the combination of pizzazz and upside attracted other aggressive entrepreneurs who also saw the opportunity for enormous wealth creation (for themselves and their companies), *and there was nothing to stop them.* It didn't take long for reality to kick in, and it wasn't pretty. There just weren't enough customers to cover the infrastructure costs of too many similar telecom networks.

For Webvan, the competitors were always there—call them supermarkets—and they found that adding home delivery from the neighborhood grocery store (if they weren't already offering that service) was not particularly complicated. Webvan—and eToys, Pets.com, Socks.com, CDNow.com, and others—learned a similar story: Counting on your competitors to be slow and stupid for a long time is a heck of a way to build a business model.

In longtime–horizon businesses, think real options. Pearl S. Buck wrote in *What America Means to Me* that "Every great mistake has a halfway moment, a split second when it can be recalled and perhaps remedied."[35] This is particularly true for ventures with long concept-to-development times. These projects may seem like good investments during initial concept development; but by the time the actual product or service comes to market, both the competitive landscape and the company's ability to provide the service or product have often changed significantly. One approach to this problem is to evaluate these ventures as real options.

Iridium is a textbook example of a project that would have benefited from this type of thinking. The Iridium venture consisted of two stages. During stage one (1987–96), Motorola developed the technology behind Iridium. During stage two (1996–99), Motorola built and launched the satellites—and the majority of Iridium's costs occurred during this part of the project. By that time much more was known. Not only had growth in traditional cellular networks drastically eroded Iridium's target market, but Iridium's own technology was never able to overcome key design, cost, and operational problems. Put simply, it was apparent that Iridium didn't have a viable business plan. Why didn't it pull the plug? Recall the "fantasy of Motorola"—Chairmen Robert Galvin and later his son Christopher Galvin continued to support Iridium, looking to it as an example of Motorola's technological might.[36] That such psychological processes can take over is another reason to create "exit ramps" that correspond to critical milestones in a long-term project.

This is exactly what Boeing did late in 2002 when it cancelled the Sonic Cruiser after the much-admired aircraft garnered rave reviews from the press and even some customers, but not a single order. For such a strong engineering company as Boeing, locked in a battle with Airbus, this could not have been easy, yet it was the right call and saved billions of dollars in additional expenditures in a post-September 11 high-risk environment. One equity analyst quoted in a *Fortune* article said, "If Boeing built this thing, it would have become its Vietnam."[37]

Management Matters, a Lot

New ventures, like older ventures, depend on management; we know that. What we don't know is just how much. The principal–principal problem has been a disaster for many companies precisely because of the considerable discretion CEOs have in making new ventures work. More established companies develop systems to start taking over what may have been issues for the executive suite in earlier days. The bench strength of management ripens with experience. Yet two critical issues seem to keep coming up in the new ventures we studied that place management not as the solution, but as the problem: the remarkable tendency for CEOs and executives of new ventures to believe that they are absolutely right, and the tendency to overestimate the quality of managerial talent by relying on track record, especially in situations that differ markedly from the present new venture.

The hype index. General Magic was supposed to develop a palm-sized computer that would act as a beeper, FAX machine, cellular phone, email, appointment book, and note taker and serve as an easy-to-use link with thousands of databases offering information ranging from restaurant menus to financial data. The company set out to wire a pre-Internet, unwired world. This would be a monumental task for any company, let alone a start-up, yet General Magic's management and partners promised consumers and investors nothing short of a computing and telecommunications revolution. It promised technology that the world didn't yet know it needed using technology that didn't yet exist. All this raises the question, is aggressive promotion of a new venture a survival-enhancing strategy? Take a look at our "hype index":

- CEO George Shaheen: "[Webvan will] set the rules for the largest consumer sector in the economy."[38]
- General Magic lead developer Andy Hertzfeld: Personal digital assistants "will be widely available in 1994 . . . and be remembered as a historic shift."[39]
- General Magic general counsel Mike Stern: "The feeling was that 'we will create the market and people will come.' "[40]
- Samsung CEO Lee Kun Hee: "We are launching Samsung Motors for the sake of the nation."[41]

While executives who hype their businesses may be staking out territory in the marketplace or promoting the company to important stakeholders, they may also be sending an inadvertent signal about their own vulnerability. When you start believing your own hype (something venture capitalists call "sucking your exhaust"), real problems can happen. So many of the most hyped Internet start-ups, for example, barely ended up as footnotes in business history. From Value America's claim that it was "the Wal-Mart of the Internet" to eCoverage.com's boast that established insurance companies could not compete, hype doesn't seem to buy you much—unless you want to wake up competitors and encourage your own people to become complacent.

Dream teams. How many times have we seen executives with terrific track records stumble? Why do we continue to be surprised when this happens? General Magic put together an all-star team; Webvan was founded by Louis Borders and led by George Shaheen; Iridium's CEO was a big-time success at Motorola. Many Internet start-ups were prone to the dream team logic as well. CEOs should come with the same disclaimer as mutual funds: *Past success is no guarantee of future success.*

There is a natural tendency to attribute the success of a company to its leaders. Certainly one of the reasons why many Internet CEOs were heralded as celebrities early on was that they were personally credited with the success of those new ventures (judged only by stock price during the bubble, of course). This is the classic "attribution error"—well known to psychologists, unfathomable to modern compensation committees—and it holds an important lesson for new ventures. Celebrity CEOs and dream teams are no replacement for the basics of business: a logical business model, attention to real customers, development of valued capabilities, and effective competitive strategy. There are no guarantees in business, but we can safely say that CEOs and management teams that aggressively focus on these core issues will be a better bet than those that don't—regardless of how many times they've been on the cover of *BusinessWeek.*

Things to Remember When Embarking on a New Venture

- General Magic was almost in the business of collecting licenses with partners for its not-yet-developed software. Partnerships can be a valuable element in building credibility, but go in with open eyes. The motives of your partners are not going to necessarily be the same as your own goals.

- Boards of directors need to think very carefully about CEO incentives, especially the unintended consequences of stock options and stock grants. CEO and managerial stock ownership is good up to a point; too much ownership and individual preferences can begin to take precedence over what is best for the company.

- New ventures with long time horizons are not one-time investments. Before the venture even gets underway, build in specific guideposts where the entire project is evaluated. Make subsequent investments contingent on meeting predetermined metrics at each guidepost. Such exit ramps will help you keep sunk costs sunk.

- If you have a good idea, it's not impossible for someone else to have the same good idea. More importantly, even after you've established your new venture, competitors may emerge (from the shadows, as the supermarkets did to Webvan; or from a new place, as Palm, Sun, and the Internet did to General Magic). If you can't create entry barriers to protect your established business, expect to struggle.

- The balance of supply and demand is a dynamic process. What looked good for one telecom start-up began to look a lot less good when a dozen others joined the party. If new competitors push supply over demand—even if that demand had you drooling—you're going to lose. That is the lesson that the telecom bubble teaches us.

- Be conservative and rigorous in segmenting the market, but segment it you must. It's not enough to know that there are potential customers for your product or service; you also need to know everything about them. Iridium and Webvan both postulated large market opportunities that never materialized because they were insufficiently rigorous in asking the tough questions on who is likely to value (and be willing to pay for) what they were offering.

- Don't fall in love with your product or service; that's your customers' job. Webvan became so enamored with the presumed uniqueness and elegance of its last-mile strategy that it underestimated how difficult it was to build a market, especially when established supermarkets started offering comparable service. Similarly, it was Motorola engineers and their techtosterone culture that provided the fuel for Iridium, not customer demand. Kun-Hee Lee at Samsung and the development team at General Magic were also true believers; only their customers weren't.

- Expect the unexpected. Samsung believed that the government would bail it out of the auto venture; the government didn't. General Magic believed that Apple would rely on its Telescript software for the Apple Newton; Apple didn't. Iridium really believed that its telecommunication partners around the world considered Iridium a priority for development; they didn't.
- The scorecard for new ventures is not determined by how stellar the resumes of the management team are. Don't lose sight of what counts: strategy, capabilities, customers, and competitive advantage.

CHAPTER 3

Innovation and Change

Choosing Not to Cope

What do a company that appears in almost everyone's list of America's most innovative firms, a *Fortune* magazine "Most Admired Company," and a winner of the Malcolm Baldrige quality award have in common? They each had seemingly inexplicable innovation and change breakdowns that cost hundreds of millions of dollars. In this chapter we profile three all-stars—Johnson & Johnson, Rubbermaid ("Most Admired" in 1993; number 2 in five of the previous six years[1]) and Motorola (Baldrige award winner in 1988)—not because of something they did but because of something they didn't. The world was changing for each of these companies, and they knew it. Yet in each case—as in some other companies that will make cameo appearances in this chapter—they failed to respond until it was too late. Surprisingly, what we found again and again were managers who were fully aware of the competitive challenges and changing customer demands they were facing, yet chose not to act.

In some ways it will look like these are "irrational" companies with "irrational" senior managers, but they're not. The traps these companies and managers fell into are the same ones many other companies deal with all the time. How do you take advantage of the best of your culture and history without getting bogged down in the past? How should corporate managers at the very top provide the right structure and incentives to divisional managers, and then get out of the way so divisional managers can do their jobs? Why do corporate leaders often seem to miss major changes in their marketplaces? These are the tough challenges at the heart of being an open-minded organization, and the subject of this chapter.

Johnson & Johnson in the Stent Business

Here's a superstar company that created a revolutionary innovation. Market share passed *90 percent!* But customers were very demanding, and competitors were very aggressive. Both . . . were virtually ignored. Just two years later market share had fallen to around 8 percent. Sound like a fable to make a point? Could this really have happened? It sure did.

As one of the largest and most diverse health care companies in the world, with some 160 units in fifty-eight countries ranging in size from $100,000 in annual sales to more than $1 billion, Johnson & Johnson is an innovative powerhouse. It has grown by identifying promising new businesses, spinning them out as semi-autonomous companies, and then letting managerial expertise and the J&J brand name take over. More and more over the years, J&J has turned to acquisitions to find small firms capable of developing innovative new products into major franchises, and the stent business was no different. In 1987, J&J bought the patents for the so-called Palmaz-Schatz stent—a tiny stainless steel tube that's crimped on a miniature balloon and threaded into the heart's arteries in an angioplasty procedure. When the balloon is inflated to deploy the stent at a blockage site, a scaffold resembling a ballpoint-pen spring is created that helps keep the vessels open after the balloon is withdrawn.

How big a deal was this? Angioplasty was already established as the less costly alternative to heart bypass surgery by 1987. The stent was seen as a revolutionary product that significantly reduced restenosis, the recurring blockage of coronary arteries, giving cardiologists the tool they required to manage their patients' needs without bringing in cardiac surgeons. Seven years after J&J bought the Palmaz-Schatz stent, it was approved by the FDA. And then things really got interesting.

Seldom has a medical device so tiny had such a giant impact on medical care as the half-inch–long coronary stent has had. In its "rookie year" alone—1995—the stent was implanted in more than one hundred thousand U.S. patients.[2] Later that year J&J Interventional Systems (or JJIS, as the stent business was then called) bought Cordis Corp, a $500 million maker of high-pressure balloons used in angioplasty. The acquisition of Cordis was widely acclaimed to be a master stroke to broaden J&J's cardiology line.

With Cordis, J&J was now able to offer a complete angioplasty surgery package, bundling its stent and Cordis's requisite balloons and catheters to become the comprehensive one-vendor medical supplier that hospitals preferred. The combined company had sales in excess of $1.5 billion in 1996, with forecasted growth of 18 percent annually. Still, the price was steep—J&J paid $109 per share for Cordis, nearly twenty-three times the projected 1996 earnings, representing $1.9 billion in J&J stock, by far J&J's largest acquisition at the time. This was also J&J's first ever hostile takeover (although the companies officially reached an "agreement" to merge in the very end).

J&J was in nirvana. Through much of 1997 the company was fat and happy. Market share actually closed in on 95 percent, but, even better, gross margins were around 80 percent. The success of the stent business was trumpeted in J&J annual reports, and no wonder. This one business, only two years after product introduction, accounted for 9–10 percent of J&J's total net income in 1996 ($300 million, or $0.23 a share).[3]

What Could Go Wrong? (Part I)

At first, the signs were muted. J&J's stent brought a significant improvement to traditional angioplasty, but its design was far from perfect. Its width and rigidity made it difficult to use, considering the heart's fine and highly curved arteries. It also had limited visibility in X-ray pictures, which made it more difficult to guide the stent to the site of the blockage. In addition, the Palmaz-Schatz stent came in only one length, forcing doctors to frequently use two or more stents to treat long obstructions.

Leading cardiologists were starting to complain, but J&J wasn't listening. It dominated the market, had a virtual monopoly on a product that its customers desperately wanted, and seemed to have patents to protect that position.

But cardiologists—not a group renowned for their modesty—expect to work closely with manufacturers to improve medical devices. The last thing they want is to go to conferences in other countries and find colleagues using clearly superior equipment . . . but that's what happened.

Making matters worse, at $1,600 per stent, in addition to ignoring customer feedback, cardiologists accused J&J of price gouging, J&J offered no discounts and paid little heed to the intense pressure on other customers—hospitals—to control health care costs.

What Could Go Wrong? (Part II)

Remember the master stroke that was Cordis? Cordis was an entrepreneurial and customer-oriented company that brought more to the merged company than its market-leading angioplasty products—it was experienced with catheterization-lab technologies and in dealing with cardiologists. Cordis's "core teams" were widely known for their adeptness at rapid product development by integrating marketing, R&D, and manufacturing operations around specific business lines. Consequently, cardiologists expected that by matching J&J's deep pockets with Cordis's speed to market, the combined company would quickly provide the desired next-generation products that would overcome the technical shortcomings of the original Palmaz-Schatz stent.

The synergy between Johnson & Johnson and Cordis, however, never developed. J&J did two things after the acquisition. First, it proceeded very slowly in integrating the two businesses. And second, the little integration it did was all wrong. Those core teams that Cordis brought to the combined company were disbanded; the concerns of key managers and researchers were ignored; the entrepreneurial culture of Cordis was disregarded. Complicating matters was the resistance of Cordis people. One senior manager at J&J put it this way: "We got dependent on people who didn't care if they were there or not. All the people who really didn't want to stay bailed out. Of the people in the top sixty-four positions at the time of the merger, only a few are left."[4]

The new Cordis, previously known for its rapid product development, failed to come to market with a significantly new product until almost two years after the acquisition. J&J lost valuable time, resources, and opportunity in a slow and unfocused integration process.

What Goes Around Comes Around

The trouble was Europe. The European market differed from the U.S. market in two respects. First, it was smaller (about one-third the size), and, second, new products were generally approved faster, resulting in a more competitive market with lower-priced products and reduced profit margins. These differences made Europe a proving ground for subsequent changes in the U.S. And in Europe, J&J's coronary stent position eroded slowly and steadily as new competitors with improved stent designs reached the market there more than one year earlier than the U.S. market.

Leading U.S. cardiologists, ripe with envy for the superior technologies available in Europe, took an active role in urging the FDA to expedite approval of these improved stents for the U.S. market. Top cardiologists show little brand loyalty; rather, they are often known as high-tech junkies who thrive on implementing the newest technology. Guidant had just that technology, producing a stent that offered considerable improvements over J&J's product: greater stent flexibility, superior catheters, and a highly attentive and assertive sales force. The effect was sudden and complete. In October 1997, the FDA cleared Guidant's multilink stent—just twelve days after clinical trial data were in and the company filed its application. Forty-five days later Guidant had captured 70 percent of the market.[5] J&J's stent sales, meanwhile, went into free fall, plummeting to 8 percent by the end of 1998.

Making Sense of the Story

It all boils down to this: Why didn't J&J create a second-generation stent? It had the market, it had the resources, and it knew that customers were demanding a new and improved stent—so why didn't the company do it? The simple analysis is that it had a patent, so why bother? There is something to this, of course, and J&J managers kept telling us how strong they thought the patents were.[6] But we also heard Robert Croce, group chairman of J&J and worldwide chairman of the Cordis Franchise, say, "There is no question in my mind that we should have had a second-generation stent, but we didn't."[7] Another senior manager said, "There was perhaps too much comfort in the Palmaz patents."[8] Running a business in a way that drives customers crazy, damages a culture built on innovation, and upsets regulators cannot possibly be a good thing. Pushing short-term profits at the expense of long-term reputation and market position cannot be a good thing. We know it, and J&J knew it, so why did it happen?

There are three explanations: (1) live by merger, die by merger, (2) corporate arrogance and complacency, and (3) not understanding customers and competitors.

Live by merger, die by merger. J&J has a reputation as an innovative powerhouse, yet much of that innovation has been bought, not created in-
house. For example, growth in its medical sector businesses actually
came from acquisitions three times as often as it did from internal development. What's more, these acquired units were less likely to develop
new product lines over time.[9] Why? Because products, knowledge, and
capabilities tend to co-evolve; buying an innovation solves an immediate
problem but it also increases your vulnerability to new competitors that
can innovate more quickly than you can.

In addition, it may well be that internal innovative capability atro-
phies after an acquisition. After J&J bought the stent technology from
Palmaz, the company was on its own. Senior executive Stanton Rowe
told us that J&J "didn't have the capability in-house to do iterative development of the stent because Palmaz was the real stent designer" and
once he sold the technology, "it was out of his hands."[10] So, within JJIS,
there was an expectation that J&J Corporate would go out and buy another company to acquire next-generation technology, paralyzing in-
house innovation effort and creating a self-fulfilling prophecy. The
Cordis deal didn't help, both because it was further evidence that J&J
was thinking acquisition and because it bogged JJIS down with a cumbersome integration that alienated management and scientific talent.[11]
Even competitors saw the problem. Guidant CEO Ronald Dollens told
us, "Where are the horses to regenerate the product? After the merger,
people are ready to cash out and don't retain that competitive edge."[12]

Moving to an A&D (acquisition-and-development) philosophy is not a
bad idea if you are aware of the inherent limitations to this approach. After all, Cisco became a big-time player buying smaller companies with
innovative products. As long as there is a commitment to continue buying new product ideas from inventors and entrepreneurial companies,
this approach can work. But don't assume that old acquisitions are automatically going to generate new ideas.

Corporate arrogance and complacency. JJIS is the first of three stories in
this chapter where previously successful companies seemingly go out of
their way to thumb their noses at customers. While J&J's arrogance
comes through loud and clear in conversations with cardiologists, there
was also a more subtle problem at work—complacency. Dr. Topol of the

Cleveland Clinic described it as "a backlash related to an arrogance and remarkable complacency. . . . When we tried to ask them about volume discounting from the price of stents, we got a ridiculous response."[13]

The stent was a blockbuster product. It "took off so fast the company did nothing but spend their energies trying to make it. They were making stents that within forty-eight hours were implanted in patients. They could hardly keep up."[14] It's not hard to see how complacency creeps in, especially when things are going well. With time, J&J has recognized these mistakes. Former CEO Ralph Larsen acknowledged, "We stumbled on this one. . . . This isn't the most glowing example of our success,"[15] and Robert Croce told us, "You've got to . . . innovate and stay ahead of the game and never get complacent."[16]

Not understanding customers and competitors. J&J didn't understand its customers. A former senior manager at JJIS interviewed fully five years after Guidant entered the market told us with some exasperation, "There was no clinical outcomes reason for cardiologists to change. They would not get a better patient outcome with the change to a new stent."[17] And the customer? One cardiologist said, "One could say that the day the [original J&J] stent was released in '94 they were already obsolete."[18]

The threat of entry into the U.S. market by a competitor stent was significant, yet JJIS didn't see it. Guidant was a particularly potent adversary—an aggressive innovator and savvy marketer with a solid reputation. The notion that customers and competitors should be taken seriously is not a particularly difficult one to understand, yet companies we studied fell into this trap again and again. We will return to this problem in Chapter 7.

One More Chance: J&J in the Stent Business Today

Over the next twelve months or so, we will be able to observe just how well J&J learned its lessons from the stent debacle of the mid-1990s. In 2003 J&J introduced a drug-eluting stent to the market, this one coated with a drug shown in clinical trials to reduce restenosis. Because of the deterioration in innovative capability within Cordis dating back to the mid-1990s, the development of the new stent has been a long process that depended on additional acquisitions as well as a buildup in internal capability. The new drug-eluting stent is not an improvement over existing stents, but really another breakthrough that Dr. Topol predicts "will become the new standard because the technology essentially transcends any noncoated stent today."[19]

Analysts are predicting that J&J's share of the stent business will move up from the mid-20 percent range to close to 80 percent within months.[20] Is J&J ready? Here's what one senior executive told us: "I think we've gone to school on what went wrong with the Palmaz-Schatz stent. The one thing you can be sure of is that we are extremely conscious of the notion that we didn't do everything right the last time around."[21]

In the end, JJIS is an instructive story. Smart people, smart company, fully aware of the expectations of customers . . . but stumbling none the less. In Part II of this book, we'll unravel the underlying reasons why companies as successful as J&J do things that make us want to bang our heads against the wall. For now, let's keep in mind the key insight that emerges from the rubble. While traditional analysis says that monopolists should exploit their dominant position, the truth is that few monopoly positions are sustainable. Strategy is really a multiperiod game. This game was won in the first round by Johnson & Johnson, but squandered by its own devices in the next. The game continues today and will continue tomorrow. Companies that forget this basic lesson should hope for a rain-out.

Now we move from high-tech medical devices to everyday rubber-based products. In this case it's not a new innovation that changes the game, but a new game that changes innovation.

What Happened to Rubbermaid?

You invent a red rubber dustpan when the world only knows a metal one. During the Great Depression it sells for three times the price of the old one. Over time, your company becomes a product development machine, with countless new products brought to market every year. You grow by expanding both distribution (from department stores to supermarkets, discount stores, and grocery stores) and product breadth (through internal innovation and external acquisitions of such companies as Little Tikes and Seco Industries). This diversification—accelerated under CEO Stanley Gault—fuels consistent and dramatic growth during the 1980s. Sales more than triple from $350 million in 1981 to $1.45 billion in 1989. This story of product innovation without limits made a small Midwestern company into one of America's best-known brand names, Rubbermaid.

Rubbermaid's trademark and core competence—product innovation—was at the root of the company's success. Innovation and speed of roll-out gave Rubbermaid a monopoly in many product categories, allowing it to firmly establish its products before competitors could even copy the designs. By the late 1980s Rubbermaid produced over 365 products per year, a track record that was testimony to a fine-tuned product development process that enabled Rubbermaid to quickly bring new ideas to market. The core of that process—intense consumer contact, little market testing, and cross-functional teams—created a killer combination of speed and innovation.

Cross-functional teams from marketing, manufacturing, R&D, and finance gained expertise and speed by specializing in a specific product line. They developed product improvement ideas by interacting with consumers and observing how they used the products in their homes or businesses. If you were making commercial kitchen products, you spent weeks at McDonald's learning what products were needed and how they were used. As a result of its R&D teams being so close to products and consumers, Rubbermaid believed that minimal market testing was needed prior to the launch of a new product. This dramatically reduced the time to market as well as the likelihood of having competitors quickly come out with copycat versions. In effect, Rubbermaid's focus on speed and innovation gave it a virtual monopoly in many product categories, boosting margins and its power with retailers.

From Innovation and Speed to Logistics and Cost

But consumer expectations were increasing as the "shop-till-you-drop" 1980s gave way to the "more-for-less" 1990s. People were seeking out "a good value" and retailers were responding with strategies such as "everyday low prices." Rubbermaid—now under new CEO Wolfgang Schmitt after company legend Gault retired at age 65—continued what it knew best, even winning *Fortune* magazine's coveted "America's Most Admired Company" distinction in 1993 in large part due to its impressive reputation for product innovation. But product innovation expertise was no longer enough.

The 1990s brought a shift in power from manufacturers to retailers as consolidation took hold. Powerful retailers such as Wal-Mart—which accounted for 14 percent of Rubbermaid's total sales—were demanding, and getting, lower prices, higher service levels, and just-in-time delivery. At the same time, Rubbermaid's bargain-priced competitors were making substantial strides in product quality and moving more quickly to replicate the company's new, innovative products, giving retailers a real alternative to Rubbermaid.

The Meltdown

How does a company go from "Most Admired" in *Fortune*'s annual survey to number one hundred three years later? The answer—in the case of Rubbermaid—was a desensitized leader who missed the most telling signs of change in the industry, and an organization so wedded to the past that it had become slow, unresponsive, and stagnant. The storyline is clear. For years the organization had been infused at all levels with a *raison d'etre*—to meet consumer needs with new products and continuous improvement in product design. With this single-minded devotion to product innovation, Rubbermaid lived for decades in a cushy world of premium prices, ineffective competition, and malleable customers. Suddenly (actually it was more of a decade-long change) the strategy collapsed as newly powerful customers, the retailers, demanded better prices and services that energized competitors were more than happy to provide. That which made the company successful was no longer valued in the same way; rather, the rules of the game shifted to highlighting areas where the company had little competence. Here's why things fell apart: high prices combined with neglected manufacturing and distribution.

High prices. Rubbermaid was the industry's high-cost producer. Passing price increases to retailers had been standard practice for the industry leader. But eventually reliability and low prices became more valuable to retailers than product innovation.

Unfortunately, Rubbermaid was slow to catch on to this market shift. Wal-Mart and other big discounters pushed for lower wholesale prices, but when resin prices soared in 1995, the company passed those costs along month after month. The big discounters retaliated by giving the best shelf space to Rubbermaid's rivals and warned, "You will kill your business if you don't do something about your prices."[22] With little talent in cutting costs in-house, Rubbermaid looked to shift responsibility elsewhere. Suppliers were prodded to knock down their own prices, alienating some of the best, low-cost vendors in the process. CEO Schmitt, convinced that Rubbermaid still had bargaining power, pressured managers to "focus on making sure the customer understood the necessity of these price increases. In the past we have always had a good history of implementing price increases."[23]

As Rubbermaid struggled with internal strife, competitors streamlined manufacturing processes and kept prices low. With Rubbermaid's attempts to browbeat customers into accepting higher prices ineffective, margins began to erode. Not unrelatedly, retailers awakened to the quality of competitors' products and expanded the shelf space they allocated to these firms as a result. With less differentiation in quality or features, the basis of competition turned to price, which Rubbermaid was not prepared for. The days of selling a "laundry basket for [even] $7 if there's one that looks as good for half the price" were over.[24]

Neglected manufacturing and distribution. After years of product proliferation, Rubbermaid's production and distribution systems became a morass of complexity and inefficiency. Warehouse space "looked like spaghetti with lines going all over and multiple handling of products and pallets."[25] Cost savings across business unit were nonexistent, with even support functions such as purchasing and payroll decentralized; information systems varied across every division.

Delivery and fulfillment were equally inept. On-time deliveries were as low as 75–80 percent, disrupting customers' just-in-time inventory management systems. The company paid a steep price for such inefficiency. Wal-Mart, for instance, frustrated with late and incomplete deliveries, cleared many of Rubbermaid's Little Tike's toys from its shelves, giving the space to Fisher Price. Another executive at a major retail customer said, "They've been such lousy shippers. Not on time, terrible fill rates, and their products cost too much. They show you a new product line and then tell you they can ship only a third of what you want."[26] To pacify retailers, Rubbermaid's salespeople eventually offered deep price discounts, a practice that further eroded margins.

The end of the road for Rubbermaid wasn't much further. As often happens, when crash programs are put in place to make up for years of inaction, even more problems develop. At Rubbermaid, the heavy hand of CEO Schmitt coupled with the intense pressure to right the ship contributed to a mass exodus of managers in nearly all of Rubbermaid's businesses in the latter part of the 1990s. By 1998 the former "number 1" had been so weakened that Newell Corp., an experienced acquirer of companies in need of turnaround, acquired Rubbermaid.

Here's one insider's eulogy:

> We were really rigid. When retailers would ask for a different color, we would say, "No, you get it in blue or you get it in white." While the retailers of yesterday would say OK because it was Rubbermaid, the retailers of today say, "No, I want it in bright yellow," and they go to a competitor and give them the business. And when a customer like Wal-Mart or Target gives a competitor business, all of a sudden the competitor gets very big, very quickly. We probably put five or six competitors into business because of our lack of flexibility with customers.[27]

One of the more remarkable findings from our research is how often great companies stumble. Yes, there were plenty of companies such as Value America and General Magic that had their fifteen minutes of fame and then more or less disappeared, but so many of the blundering businesses we studied were (and some continue to be) stand-up companies. If J&J can't get its hands around innovation in medical devices, and Rubbermaid can't respond to fundamental changes in how its customers operated and what they wanted, we all have reason to worry. The next story is just as troubling. Motorola, with a history of innovation, finds itself a loser in a business it virtually created.

Motorola and the Cell Phone Business

The story begins in 1928, when the Galvin Manufacturing Corporation was founded by brothers Paul and Joseph Galvin. Two years later the company launched the first practical and affordable car radio under the brand name Motorola, which blended *motor* and *victrola*. From this start, Motorola developed a series of innovations ranging from the first hand-held two-way radio for the U.S. Army (the "Walkie-Talkie" of World War II) to the first television to sell for under $200 (in 1948). In the 1950s Motorola became involved in the American space program, sup-plying equipment to virtually every mission. The company launched the world's first pager, which became an instant hit in hospitals. By the 1970s Motorola had developed microprocessors (becoming the primary supplier to Apple) and was solidifying its reputation as a world leader in tech-nology. Then came cell phones.

The American Samurai: Cellular Telephony Dominance

Cellular telephony was developed at Bell Labs in the 1970s, but it wasn't until companies such as Motorola built their own capabilities that the business took off. Using acquisitions of small communications compa-nies and its own expertise, Motorola's first cellular system, the Dyna-TAC, began commercial operation in 1983. The first cellular phones were ex-pensive and bulky analog devices that appealed to businesspeople and professionals who depended on the ability to make and receive calls when a phone line was not at hand. Starting from this market, Motorola went on to dominate the cell phone business.

Internally, the company executed with precision. Motorola adopted TQM (Total Quality Management) at a time when U.S. manufacturing was declining relative to the Japanese, while the company's emphasis on employee empowerment earned the admiration of analysts and competi-tors alike. These efforts culminated in 1988 when Motorola won the first Malcolm Baldrige National Quality Award, given by the U.S. Con-gress to recognize and inspire the pursuit of quality in American busi-ness. By 1990 Motorola's revenues surpassed $10 billion and the company controlled 45 percent of the world cellular phone market as well as 85 percent of the world's pager market. As the global market for cell phones expanded, Motorola continued to aggressively pursue the busi-ness. As former CEO Robert Galvin said, "We were the unbridled leader in analog devices around the world."[28] From 1992 to 1995, Motorola seemed to prove that even a huge company, if managed correctly, could rack up impressive growth, as revenues grew an average of 27 percent to

$27 billion in 1995, while net income surged 58 percent a year over the same period, to $1.8 billion.

The Shift: Digital Mobile Telephony Comes to Town

In 1994, as Motorola claimed 60 percent of the U.S. cellular market, an alternative technology to analog began catching the eye of wireless carriers. The new technology was digital mobile telephony, which would first be available through a so-called PCS (Personal communications system). Analog technology transmitted calls via sound waves. Signals were subject to interference, calls were frequently dropped, and it was easy for interlopers to eavesdrop. PCS, on the other hand, translated calls into digital signals—interference could be programmed out, while security codes could be encrypted. The one advantage analog had over digital was likely to be a short-lived one—because analog had been around for some time, area coverage was much more extensive than it was for PCS.

The powerful underlying economics of digital technology provided a means to support true mass-market subscriber populations for the first time. As a rule of thumb, digital networks could accommodate around ten times more subscribers than their analog counterparts for a given chunk of radio spectrum, due to the easy-to-manipulate (and "compress") characteristics of digital technology. In essence, digital technology would spread fixed costs over a broader user base. It was this attribute of cellular that made it so attractive to service providers—digital could cut costs, creating opportunities to greatly expand the number of users by cutting price while still making a reasonable profit.

For gear suppliers such as Motorola, these changes also meant dealing with a new consumer profile with which it had limited experience. Unlike Motorola's typical analog customers, such as businesspeople, digital consumers would be price-sensitive and less functionally and more aesthetically demanding. The writing was on the wall for analog.

The Reaction: "Forty-Three Million Analog Customers Can't Be Wrong"[29]

Motorola being the leader in the cell phone business and the major American player (Nokia being a Finnish company; Ericsson, Swedish), it was natural that U.S. wireless carriers would look to Motorola as they made their move to digital. Consider what one major telephone carrier customer had to say:

> We're telling them, "We need digital, we need digital, we need digital." They come out with analog Star-TAC. They were thumbing their nose at us. The sales folks—they knew. But everyone knew. We went to Shaumburg [Motorola's head office in Illinois] in 1993, 1994, but they didn't do anything. They told us we didn't know what we were talking about. Even in 1996, after they missed the first wave of digital, we told them we needed a dual-band, dual-mode phone, that this was all we would be selling. These were not friendly conversations. But Motorola didn't do it; instead we launched with Ericsson, then Nokia."[30]

Without a digital phone to offer telephone carriers, Motorola pushed hard to move its analog phones, creating considerable resentment from some customers. In one instance, Motorola even tried to promote its analog phones by offering incentives to AT&T Wireless salespeople working at AT&T telephone shops. As one former executive at McCaw Cellular (AT&T Wireless) recalled, "Motorola hit on this crazy idea that they'd offer incentives to our own sales force to promote analog. They were bold and brazen—in one instance they had to be physically removed from our property."[31]

Of course, it wasn't just customers who were telling Motorola they wanted digital; competitors were also doing so, though in a different way. You see, while Motorola didn't introduce a digital cell phone for years, the company held several digital patents that it licensed to competitors such as Nokia and Ericsson. The royalties Motorola earned provided clear evidence of the increasing popularity of digital and acted as an early warning signal on the direction of the market. Yet even with such incontrovertible data on market trends and customer needs, Motorola chose to rely on internal forecasting models that predicted carriers would be better off with analog phones than digital.[32]

So, Motorola had the capability to make digital cell phones and had extensive data to indicate the market was demanding digital. It could have competed from the start, if not won the digital cell phone wars, but chose not to. Hence, we come face to face with "irrational" behavior in organizations.

It turns out that people and organizations conspire to sometimes produce "irrational" behavior, as they sometimes do "brilliant" behavior. At Motorola, cell phone division managers—who had tremendous autonomy because of the company's decentralized structure and because they were responsible for the "forty-three million" analog franchise—believed that what consumers really wanted were better, sleeker analog phones. One phone carrier executive heard this reaction to his request for Motorola to supply digital phones: "Remember the old phones in WWII—carried on backs. That is what your digital phone will look like. It can't be done."[33] Instead, Motorola focused attention on Star-TAC, a design as small as a cigarette pack, but still an analog phone. Such "smaller and cuter phones" were technological marvels, but they were not digital. Robert Galvin put it this way: "When one or the other thinks we're so damned smart we got the answer . . . that's arrogance."[34]

The Organization Strikes Out

Some of the leadership in the business at that time was focused too much on the short-term profits and they weren't spending enough for the future.
— Gary Tooker, former CEO, Motorola, interviewed on July 5, 2001

Former CEO Tooker may be correct, but there's more to the story. For years, the company followed a highly decentralized management system, with significant delegation of responsibility to the operating businesses. While such autonomy often breeds focus and attention to detail, at Motorola it also created "a company of warring tribes" that was exacerbated by strong division-based incentives. This played out in two dysfunctional ways. First, the "warring tribes" mentality disrupted coordination across divisions, so Motorola lost considerable time when it decided to develop the chips necessary for digital cellular in-house instead of outsourcing.[35]

Second, like many decentralized organizations, Motorola relied on division-based incentives to motivate divisional managers. Yet each division also had to cover its own costs of investment. The net effect may well have been that "Decision makers' thinking [in the cell phone division] was colored by the up-front costs they would have entailed by shifting from analog to digital."[36] Motorola's compensation system created a short-term disincentive to take on the costs of the transition to digital cell phones.

In the end, the Motorola story brings us back to leadership. When an organization is unwilling—yet perfectly capable—of coping with change and satisfying clear and persistent customer needs, there has been a breakdown in leadership. And this breakdown doesn't stop with those immediately responsible for the decision to stonewall customers demanding digital cell phones, but extends to the very top of the organization where ultimate responsibility for strategy, structure, and culture surely rests. To some extent Robert Galvin acknowledges this: "We were all lulled into a situation of digital coming at the pace it did. We plain just made a bum decision."[37] Yet cultural insularity and nominal divisional oversight have been part of the Motorola system for years and were allowed to propagate.

In the fast-moving cell phone business, by the time Motorola finally launched its own digital phone in 1997, the competition was far ahead. The hit to market share was dramatic. Motorola's U.S. share peaked at 60 percent in 1994 only to dip to 34 percent in early 1998, while Nokia's share went from 11 to 34 percent during the same time period.[38] In June 1998 Motorola announced layoffs of 20,000 people as it looked to cut costs in response to depressed profitability. So began a long series of layoffs, restructuring, and restrategizing that plagued the company for years.[39] At some point Motorola should come back—talent, technology, and time heal many wounds[40]—but the price tag for this lesson in innovation and change will amount to hundreds and hundreds of millions of dollars. Let's hope the lesson takes—for this company's sake and yours.

The Death of Innovation and Change: Organizational Rigidities in Action

Three stories about innovation and change. Three failures. Why is it so difficult for companies to respond to, let alone anticipate, changes in their competitive environments? All three of these companies lived in worlds where customer needs were dramatically changing, yet they refused, or were unable, to respond. Is the lesson as simple as this: Stay close to your customers? All three of these companies underestimated the ability of competitors to come to market with world-class products that their customers would prefer to their own. Is the lesson as straightforward as this: Pay close attention to your competition? All three companies let technology run away from them. Is the lesson as striking as this: Don't lose sight of technological developments in your marketplace?

The answer to all these questions is no. Lessons on customers, competitors, and technology are of obvious importance, but if we stop there we run the risk of focusing on symptoms—critical though they may be—without getting to the underlying causes of breakdowns in innovation and change, which are not unrelated to other executive blunders we've seen during our research. In this chapter we focus on the organizational rigidities that are behind the mistakes we've seen Johnson & Johnson, Rubbermaid, Motorola, and others make in dealing with changing competitive conditions.

In each of the three companies we just profiled, organizations were unable to respond effectively to an external challenge. At Motorola the rigidity came from a decentralized organizational structure and compensation system; at J&J it was the organizational focus on patent protection and the logic of monopoly; at Rubbermaid the organization was simply designed to do one thing very, very well, and could not adjust to a new reality. At the heart of such rigidity are several organizational attributes that are at once both fundamental to how companies operate, and the source of potentially deep dysfunctions.

History Counts!

If you really want to understand a company, you need to understand its history. One of the most common flaws in how we think about organizations—whether we are analysts, consultants, investors, or managers—is to disregard the past in trying to make sense of the present. Why did Motorola miss digital? One of the biggest dilemmas in-house was deciding what type of digital to back. There was CDMA, TDMA, and GSM—all different standards with no certainty as to which one would win out in the U.S. market, so Motorola waited. Years earlier the company had found itself backing the nonstandard Apple in the personal computer business (Motorola made the microchips), and it's likely there was concern about making the same mistake twice. So the company waited, until Nokia and Ericsson pushed it to the side even in the U.S. market.

Culture is also a major component of history, and Motorola is known as an engineering-driven company. Those who know the company well liken its mind-set to an "internal think tank"; focus on the market and on customers is secondary. The other distinguishing characteristic of Motorola's culture is its insularity. One knowledgeable observer alludes to a "fortress mentality, cut off from reality, in-bred, with tremendous self-confidence, and a lack of concern with the outside world."[41] If this cultural profile is accurate, it is not hard to imagine how senior managers might resist strategies that customers were demanding, or how arrogant attitudes might emerge in dealing with customers.

You'd think that learning would occur over time, and of course it does in some organizations. But at others, such as Motorola, the culture is so strong that there is tremendous persistence in how systems operate and people behave, even from decade to decade. Whether it is Motorola's history of being an innovative leader pushed aside by more market-savvy followers (think car radios, televisions, and . . . digital cell phones) or its tendency to put technology above customers, the results can be powerful. One former CEO lamented to us, "Every time we stumble significantly, it is because we have been so successful in one generation of the technology that we don't focus on replacing ourselves with the next technology quick enough."[42]

A culture as strong and successful as Motorola's is resistant to new ways of thinking. In its essence, that is the challenge of innovation, whether it is creating new cell phones, new stents, or new ways to deal with powerful customers. All organizations have an installed base of ideas that define the managerial mind-set, and this installed base is very difficult to overcome. This is what made it so difficult for the cell phone division at Motorola to accept digital phones as the rightful, and immediate, replacement for analog phones, and this is also what made it so difficult for Motorola's top management to break out of their insular technology-over-customers mind-set. In both cases, what was lost was that "healthy spirit of discontent"[43] that helped to define Motorola's innovative capability for years. What appears to be "irrational" behavior is often only too rational when the underlying dynamics of organizations and people are considered side-by-side.

Reveling in Inertia

Senior executives create playbooks to guide managerial action, and sometimes as much as the world changes they stubbornly hold on to those playbooks. Rather than respond to their challenges and mistakes, rather than actively learn from the problems of their competitors, they continue unimpeded in their quest for certainty, stability, and conformity.

Historian Barbara Tuchman, the author of *The March of Folly,* coined a perfect term to describe the behavior of executives at the companies profiled in this chapter: *Wooden-headedness,* which refers to the practice of relying on "preconceived fixed notions while ignoring or rejecting any contrary signs." Just as Tuchman describes such examples of wooden-headedness as the refusal of the French in 1914 to alter preparations for an invasion of Germany through the Rhine in spite of evidence that this plan left the French particularly vulnerable to an impending German march through Belgium and the lightly guarded French coastal provinces,[44] we wonder why historically innovative companies refuse to introduce second-generation products in spite of pleas from customers for precisely such products.

Inertia pervades all sorts of organizations, shutting down opportunities to adapt and change in accordance with new demands. If you get the feeling that your company seems like it's sometimes stuck in the mud, you're not alone. Consider the management of U.S. Navy ships. There is one can opener in the galley, and when it breaks down cooks use knives to open cans; personnel trained as aviation-electronics specialists count how many sailors prefer pork chops over hamburgers to help decide order sizes; sailors trained in offset printing must study books with obsolete information to get promoted (and the Navy doesn't even use offset printing anymore); there are no incentives to be efficient and labor is seen as a free good. Plans to reduce personnel and to use people more effectively are in place with target dates of implementation as long as twenty years later![45] Even the mundane can get bogged down in inertia.

Corporate Kills

Where is value created in an organization? If you ask that question to one hundred general managers of business units, you will get the same answer one hundred times—at the business unit where competition in product markets takes place. This is where you win or lose in the stent business and the cell phone business. But what happens at the corporate level, that part of the company where the CEO, CFO, and other most senior executives live? In companies that run more than one business (the vast majority of large companies would qualify), corporate is responsible for such activities as setting the core principles that govern how the company and its managers and employees should conduct themselves, hiring and firing business managers, reviewing the work of business managers, approving budgets and strategies, and allocating resources, among others. Nowhere in this "To Do" list does it say that executives should install dangerous incentives, abrogate responsibility for oversight, or micromanage business managers, yet these are precisely the pitfalls that create organizational rigidities.

The irony is that corporate can kill by being too hands-on or too hands-off. Think about decentralized structures, which provide autonomy and focus to business units and have been heralded by managers and management thinkers alike. Why should centralized top executives constrain managers that are competing at the product-market level from making the decisions they believe are correct? It's hard to argue with this logic, except that without any check on business unit managers, there is no organization. At Motorola, the cell phone division was never reined in by the CEO, so it continued to ignore the digital market.

Johnson & Johnson offers a different perspective. Again, we ask, "Why didn't J&J create a second-generation stent?" JJIS insiders say that one reason is that they expected J&J corporate to acquire the next-generation stent via acquisition. When it didn't, and Guidant and others introduced competing products, market share fell apart. J&J never expected the stent business to take off the way it did, and as a result corporate executives weren't prepared to make the additional investments needed to keep the franchise on top. The J&J story seen in this way is a story of resource allocation gone bad and Corporate J&J, far from being an innocent bystander, was an active perpetrator of the meltdown.

It need not be this way. For example, despite the challenges Microsoft has faced with antitrust rulings and keeping growth on track for a company that is so dependent on Windows-based software in the age of the Internet, the company has pushed next-generation innovation. If J&J

had a virtual monopoly in stents, Microsoft has been just as powerful in PC operating systems. Yet under CEO Steve Ballmer Microsoft is aggressively seeking a leading position in what it calls "next-generation Windows services." The contrast to J&J could not be clearer.

It's remarkable how often Corporate got in the way of innovation and change in the companies we studied. How could Rubbermaid move closer to what Wal-Mart and other customers were demanding when the CEO was pushing senior managers to pass along price increases? And the pressure from Corporate to "make your numbers" was so intense at Enron that according to one former manager, "People would come in with their [earnings] numbers whether we really did [achieve them] or not." Remarkably, Ken Lay apparently accepted the inflated reports without challenge.[46]

Which brings us back to Motorola. Where were the most senior Motorola executives in the digital conversion years? We interviewed three of the company's CEOs, and while there was some acknowledgment of personal responsibility for the cell phone disaster, we heard a lot more about arrogance and about incentives. Yet who is responsible for designing the incentive plan for top divisional managers? The untold story at Motorola may well be how corporate management let down the company.

Theory 2 Debunked

In Chapter 1 we offered up a theory about change, asserting that in many of the companies we studied, key decision makers knew that their world was changing, yet chose not to respond in a timely fashion— sometimes not at all. This turns out to be one of the most remarkable findings of our research and one of the most damning. Executive after executive, when faced with severe challenge, chose not to cope.

Let's go back to Rubbermaid. While few leaders would want to find themselves running an organization that is unable to deal with changing conditions because its core competencies have become less valuable over time, that's exactly what Rubbermaid did. It left itself vulnerable to customers and competitors for years, making little headway in meeting these challenges. But the mistake at Rubbermaid is not only that the company was *unable* to respond, it was also *unwilling* to adapt to the new environment. It was almost as if time stood still for Rubbermaid, that the changes of the 1990s never took place, and that the company was still living in the near-monopoly world it had enjoyed a decade earlier.

Innovation is not a "thing" that just happens. It's a natural outgrowth of a culture of open-mindedness, and a CEO who is not a central player in that game will find the innovation challenge much more difficult. It's one part "walking the talk" to make sure that all are clear on the importance of innovation, and one part real action—in dozens of different ways—that engenders and promotes an innovative culture. As one-time Pepsi CEO Andrall Pearson put it, "Innovative companies are led by innovative leaders."[47]

When organizations are unable to adapt to changing circumstances, it's bad enough. But when this inability is coupled with unwillingness at the very top to cope with this change, leadership is effectively dissolved. Consider Schwinn Bicycle Company. Readers of a certain generation will have the fondest of memories about this company. Schwinn's bikes were the best, and the Schwinn brand name was not only tops in the bicycle industry, but a standout in America. The market leading position spilled over to how it conducted business, as we heard from long-time competitor Tony Huffman of Huffy Bicycle Company: "Schwinn was the only nationally distributed brand. The Schwinns used to hold court at trade shows, and all the little manufacturers used to gather around. It was even true for the wives, who almost held court by the pool."[48]

Into this idyllic setting came three related developments that Schwinn couldn't cope with. First, mountain bikes and other models became popular while Schwinn watched. Second, previously loyal dealers began to open up their stores to other companies as Schwinn models fell behind the competition. And third, in an attempt to cut costs, Schwinn moved more and more of its manufacturing off-shore, creating powerful Chinese competitors in the process. Schwinn executives knew all this (indeed, they were the architects of each of these moves and nonmoves), yet they were unable to respond. Whether it was CEO Ed Schwinn refusing to hear of these problems, or company engineers telling mountain bike entrepreneur Gary Fisher, "We know bikes. You guys are all amateurs. We know better than anybody,"[49] or Schwinn marketing executives declaring, "We don't have competition; we're Schwinn"[50]—well, you get the picture. The failure of Schwinn was premeditated; the company did it to itself. In common with companies such as Motorola, J&J, Rubbermaid, General Magic, and many others, the roots of an organization's demise can often be traced to this same underlying leadership dynamic—choosing not to cope in the face of compelling evidence of its necessity. What the underlying dynamics are that put leaders and executives in this situation, and what you can do about it, will be a primary focus of Part II.

Things to Remember About Innovation and Change

- People do things for many reasons, only some of which are readily apparent to them. By highlighting the importance of history and culture, we take a step back to examine what is there but seldom discussed internally. It should be standard practice for executives to acknowledge the implicit biases that, often unwittingly, come with a company's history and culture.
- Ask questions. Not just any questions, but questions that can tap into potentially important changes that can significantly affect our organizations. For example, the rise of digital technology is relevant not only for Motorola but for companies in such industries as media, computers, photography, education, medical instruments, consumer electronics, and many others. How might such "sectorwide" changes affect your business?
- The effective management of risk seems like a lost art. Assessing the risk of managerial initiatives can raise questions while there is still time to make real-time adjustments. For example, Dell Computer is always asking what could go wrong and considering ways to mitigate the downside.
- Motorola's fall in the cell phone business spawned this idea from Robert Galvin: Each executive should keep an "anticipation registry" that records his or her insights on how the market is changing, and what he or she is doing about it. While not all ideas will be good ones, the practice of keeping score (particularly if tied to compensation) can be an important discipline.
- Never forget that even in the most decentralized companies, there is a critical role for corporate management to play. One of the riskiest decisions a company can make is to abdicate total responsibility to divisional managers without any oversight. One need not challenge the

basic value of decentralization, such as autonomy, focus, and entre-preneurship, to advocate some degree of parental supervision.

- This latter point highlights the relevance of "checks and balances" in corporate systems. Some control of independent divisions is required, but heavy-handed meddling by Corporate is counterproductive. How Corporate can add value to divisional management should be the leading agenda item at the very top of organizations. The choice is stark—if Corporate cannot provide such pluses as special expertise, a powerful brand name, cost savings, management development, and new business opportunities, then why should Corporate exist?

- When there are advantages to coordination across business units, re-inforce these pluses with team-based goals and incentives. Don't ex-pect your own warring tribes to go out of their way to cooperate when old-line division-based incentives predominate.

- If you really want to see innovation and change flourish at your company, you must both motivate awareness and facilitate action. Managers will pay attention when such behavior is rewarded via com-pensation and promotions, and reinforced through company culture. Enabling managers to pull the trigger, however, requires you to accept a degree of experimentation and the attendant failures that involves. We will return to this idea later; at this point let's not forget that while it is important to encourage responsibility for innovation and change throughout the organization, every leader must set the tone and ex-ample for others to follow.

CHAPTER 4

Mergers and Acquisitions

The Search for Synergy, the Quest for Integration

W hat accounts for hundreds of billions of dollars each year, is standard business practice throughout the globe, yet fails anywhere from 50 to 75 percent of the time? If you answered mergers and acquisitions(M&As), you win . . . or lose, if you're in the game. Here are the stats: In a study by Salomon Smith Barney of U.S. companies acquired between 1997 and 1999, the stock price of acquirers trailed the S&P 500-stock index by fourteen percentage points, and their peer group by four points, after the deals were announced.[1] PricewaterhouseCoopers LLP researched M&As completed between 1994 and 1997 and found that the average acquirer's stock was 3.7 percent lower than its industry peer group one year after the deal.[2] A study by A.T. Kearney of 115 global mergers in the mid-1990s found that total return to shareholders relative to peer industry groups was negative for 58 percent of the deals examined.[3] Summarizing dozens of academic studies up to the 1980s (and the conclusion still holds today), finance professors Michael Jensen and Richard Ruback[4] gave this ringing endorsement to M&As: "At best, bidding-firm shareholders do not lose."

With such an unconvincing track record, why do companies continue to go down this path? A study by KPMG International of seven hundred of the biggest deals between 1996 and 1998 sheds some light.[5] The consultants found that 83 percent of the M&As they analyzed did not boost shareholder value, and 53 percent actually reduced shareholder value. The most fascinating part of this study, however, came from the interviews KPMG did with executives from 107 of these companies. When asked if their deals were successful, 82 percent answered yes, perhaps reflecting that less than half actually conducted any postacquisition review. Here's a classic case of the "don't ask, don't tell" rule—better not to study in depth what really happened in case it doesn't look so good.

Just as revealing, the KPMG study is a rather stark illustration of the classic "we're different" rule: Just because most companies fail in the M&A game doesn't mean that we won't beat the odds. To some extent this rule must be in operation for every acquisition, since the general outline of the statistics is well known to most managers. Why execute the deal if you don't think your situation, or talent, is better? One senior manager at a large pharmaceutical company told us, "There's this feeling at the top that we can take any business and just improve it, based on egotism. They believe we can just go in and tell these companies what to do."[6]

Of course, all deals don't fail.[7] There are clearly many successful mergers—IBM's acquisition of Lotus and Eaton's acquisition of Westinghouse's distribution and controls business, for example. It is in the contrast between failure and success that the most important lessons lie. For example, in the A.T. Kearney study, the bottom quartile of M&A performers returned negative 41 percent relative to their industry index while the top quartile reported an average of 25 percent return to shareholders relative to peers. What accounts for these differences? What are the mistakes that occur repeatedly that we can learn from?

We'll now study three companies that failed at the M&A game. Quaker Oats, in its infamous acquisition of the Snapple Beverage Company, is a textbook example of what can go wrong when a big company buys a smaller one. The second acquisition was even more unsuccessful, if judged by total losses and write-offs, and adds the complication of a cross-border arrangement: Sony's 1989 acquisition of Columbia Pictures. And third, the story of Saatchi & Saatchi is offered as a classic example of hubris in action, raising questions that resonate in mergers and acquisitions, and strategic leadership, every day.

When Quaker Met Snapple: Love at First Sight

The Quaker Oats Company was one of the oldest food companies in America, founded in 1891. If you ate oatmeal, you knew Quaker. If you drank Gatorade, you knew Quaker—well, you probably didn't, even though it was Quaker under CEO William D. Smithburg that found a diamond in the rough of the Stokely-Van Camp acquisition in 1983 and turned it into the powerhouse of sports drinks. Remarkably, Quaker and Smithburg became better known for another beverage product, though not in the way the company or CEO would have preferred. The 1994 acquisition of Snapple by Quaker hit a nerve. It became front-page business news almost from the start—and lingered there until Snapple was sold to the Triarc Company for $300 million, some $1.4 billion less than what Quaker paid. What went wrong? How did the company that hit a home run with Gatorade fall so dramatically flat in such an apparently similar business? To find the answers we went back to the principals— a founder of Snapple, key distributors, the former CEO of Triarc who engineered the turnaround, company insiders, and Smithburg himself. Here's what happened.

The Rise of the Snapple Beverage Corporation

We made the first ready-to-drink tea that didn't taste like battery acid.
—Arnold Greenberg, cofounder, Snapple, *Company Histories,* 1993

Snapple, formerly known as Unadulterated Food Products, Inc., when it began in 1972, was created by two window-washing brothers-in-law (Leonard Marsh and Hyman Golden) and a health food store owner (Arnold Greenberg). The New York City natives began distributing fruit juices, all-natural sodas and seltzers, and fruit drinks to local health stores by 1986, emphasizing a wholesome image through its slogan, "Made from the best stuff on earth." The partners entered the developing iced tea market the next year with a brewed, high-quality, "new age" ready-to-drink (RTD) tea, which would prove to be a pivotal early move.

After a leveraged buyout, the now-renamed "Snapple" went public in 1993. Wanting to propel the brand to national distribution, Snapple emphasized a "regular people" theme via employee Wendy Kaufman, who quickly became the "face" of Snapple on TV with her friendly "Greetings from Snapple!" salute and her penchant for answering fan mail on the air. Snapple also enlisted the support of offbeat personalities, including radio stars Howard Stern and Rush Limbaugh, to create an individualist image that wooed a cultlike following. The popular company was regarded as innovative, pioneering the hot package process for teas, which would later become the category standard, and developing novel glass-front vending machines and coolers to display its unique wide-mouth bottles.

The secret ingredient to Snapple's success was its extensive and dependable network of independent copackers and distributors, who prepared, bottled, warehoused, and sold its products. Snapple cultivated the distributors, and it paid off. As one distributor described it, "They sent people here to work with us, help sell the product alongside the salesmen. They spent a lot of time and energy at the retail level—the small guy—because they knew that's where the root of their business was."[8] The combination of innovative product, ingenious marketing, and hyperloyal and effective distributors catapulted Snapple into a money-making machine in the early 1990s.

Trouble Begins to Brew

Two years after the LBO, the market turned. As is often the case, warning signs were clear for all to see. By the end of 1994 the RTD tea market growth rate was beginning to slow down, for the first time breaking out of the 50–100 percent range. The RTD tea products joint ventures created by Coca-Cola (with Nestlé) and PepsiCo (with Lipton) were quickly becoming major forces in the segment. New entrants, such as Arizona Iced Teas, Nantucket Nectars, and Mystic, started carving away at Snapple's market-leading position through various niche strategies and innovations as well. Finally, the cooler-than-expected summer and fall of 1994 created serious inventory problems for Snapple. The company's stock price reflected these difficulties, having fallen 50 percent from its year-earlier highs.

Into this quagmire leaped Quaker. On December 6, 1994, Quaker bought Snapple for $1.7 billion, representing a premium of 28.6 times earnings and 330 percent of revenues. Not long afterwards, to help pay down the resulting debt, Quaker divested a number of businesses that had historically provided a steady stream of earnings and global reach. Selling off its pet food and candy businesses, however, brought further troubles as hefty capital gains taxes on those sales were incurred. It quickly became clear that Quaker's investment in Snapple was going to be an uphill battle.

Quaker's Mistake: Snapple Was Not Gatorade

It is human nature to want to return to the site of your greatest victories and relive the experience all over again. This is nowhere more true than for CEOs of large, complex businesses—people who remember clearly the accolades for a past success and, even more importantly, the personal satisfaction that came with that success.

Yet it is by looking to the past that many companies stumble, particularly when they believe that the lessons of the past will apply equally well to the present. The past for Quaker was the highly successful expansion of the Gatorade brand after 1983. Quaker CEO William Smithburg rightly saw this as his greatest triumph:

> Our people built Gatorade from a small $90 million business in 1983 to over $2 billion today and it still delivers double-digit growth and better than an 80 percent share despite Coke and Pepsi entering the market in the early 90s. They couldn't beat us, so one of them had to buy the company to get Gatorade.[9]

Could Snapple provide the opportunity for a repeat? There seems little doubt that Quaker management saw Snapple as a high-potential brand, like Gatorade a decade earlier, and believed that the same marketing expertise that made Gatorade explode into a megabrand could be applied to Snapple. The beverage division president said things such as, "We have an excellent sales and marketing team here at Gatorade. We believe we do know how to build brands, we do know how to advance businesses. And our expectation is that we will do the same as we take Snapple as well as Gatorade to the next level."[10] Equally important was the dominant belief that Quaker would be able to "exploit the synergies."[11] What they didn't see is all that was different. Snapple was an "image" drink, while Gatorade was a "fluid replacement product"; Snapple's success to that point was based on "quirky" marketing that created a "cult" drink, while Gatorade was aggressively segmented and promoted in a more traditional fashion; Snapple relied on entrepreneurial distributors, while Gatorade used a warehouse system. As former Triarc CEO Michael Weinstein told us, "Quaker believed the Gatorade model could be applied to Snapple, but this just scared the system. Smithburg never got it."[12]

Remember the Secret Ingredient?

With these insights, the rest of the story is like a movie where you've figured out who'll get killed at the end, but you're still not sure how. At Quaker, the key players were the distributors. Quaker created a new beverage division consisting of both Gatorade and Snapple and planned to create a hybrid distribution system whereby Snapple distributors would have the right to deliver cold, single-serve Gatorade via its Direct Store Delivery system if they turned over part of their unrefrigerated Snapple business to Gatorade's warehouse distribution system. The trade fell flat for two reasons. First, some old-line Snapple distributors didn't trust Quaker, in part because one of Quaker's first moves after acquiring Snapple was to try to renegotiate contracts that were in-perpetuity. Needless to say, that didn't work. Second, trading Snapples for Gatorades was bad for business. Distributors told Quaker that Snapple's "$4-per-case margins are roughly double what they could make on Gatorade"[13] and also significantly outperformed the $1–$2 margin in soft drinks; "We just saw loss. We saw business going away that was not going to be offset by something else. We were not willing to give up that right that we built over the years."[14]

With distributors unwilling to play ball, the "exploit the synergies" strategy fell apart. Compounding the problem were the "unexpected" surprises that always turn up after a deal—manufacturing was much slower than anticipated, outdated Snapple cans were stuck in inventory, and the exodus of salespeople (another blow to relationships with distributors who had depended on them at times) and management (including two of the three founders) ensued. It took Quaker until May 1996, almost a year and a half, to make the distribution system workable and introduce a new marketing campaign. By this time, however, competition in RTD teas and fruit drinks had been intensifying so strongly since 1994 that it was virtually impossible for Quaker to win back lost market share.

Endgame

Finally, with the sale of Snapple to Triarc in 1997, the experiment was over. Snapple was not Gatorade, and thinking that it was so turned out to be a billion-dollar mistake.[15] When Quaker tried to "Gatorize"

Snapple, it effectively disregarded Snapple's "tribal" knowledge—about customers, about distribution channels, and about product promotion—in favor of its own set of beliefs on how to sell a bottled drink, eviscerating the very thing it had acquired. Some of that tacit knowledge was embodied in Leonard Marsh, the only one of the three Snapple co-founders who stayed on with Quaker. Yet, as Marsh put it, "I was the executive vice president in charge of nothing."[16] What more can we say?

Sony Goes Hollywood

Quick. What is the best-known company in Japan? Few Japanese companies rival Sony in prestige and influence, yet even the great ones stumble. And stumble Sony did in the 1989 acquisition of Columbia Pictures from then owner Coca-Cola.

The Early Years: The Betamax Lesson

Masaru Ibuka and Akio Morita founded Tokyo Tsushin Kogyo (Tokyo Telecommunications Engineering Company) in 1946 with a mission to be "a clever company that would make new high technology products in ingenious ways."[17] With the development of the transistor, the cassette tape, and the pocket-sized radio by 1957, the company renamed itself Sony, from the Latin word *sonus* meaning "sound." In 1967, Sony formed a joint venture with CBS Records to manufacture and sell records in Japan. By 1975, with the launch of the Betamax home videocassette recorder, Sony was in the big leagues.

The Betamax was a watershed for Sony. Here was a breakthrough product—offering consumers the opportunity to record and play their favorite TV shows or watch movies whenever they wanted. Yet within two years a new videocassette recorder (VCR) made by archrival Matsushita using the VHS standard became the product of choice for consumers. Why? Sony, working from a playbook that Apple would pick up just a few years later, was more protective of its Betamax format and less aggressive in aligning other electronics firms in its camp than was Matsushita. When VHS started to take hold, motion picture studios began to release a larger number of their library titles in that format than in Betamax, relegating Betamax to also-ran status despite some technological advantages.[18] "We didn't put enough effort into making a family. The other side, coming later, made a family," Morita later said, referring to the fact that Matsushita had aggressively licensed its technology and created an electronics-industrywide effort to unseat Betamax.[19]

Enter Software: CBS Records and Columbia Pictures

In the late 1970s we began to recognize the need to take Sony beyond hardware. Through our experience with Betamax, we discovered that the compelling motivation for the purchase of hardware is software.

—Mickey Schulhof, former president, Sony USA, *Fortune*, September 9, 1991

As we saw in Chapter 3, history counts. If you want to understand a company's strategy, you need to understand its history. And at Sony, the history lesson was clear. First came CBS Records, which Sony bought in 1988 for $2 billion. Convinced that its record library had helped to guarantee the success of the compact disc, Sony looked to CBS Records to provide the software necessary to ensure the success of its new digital audio tape.

Not long after the CBS Records deal was finalized, Sony acquired Columbia Pictures and its two production units—Columbia and Tri-Star—as well as a library that included such classics as *Lawrence of Arabia* and contemporary titles *Tootsie* and *Ghostbusters*. Also under the Columbia umbrella was a syndicated television operation that included hits such as *Married . . . with Children* and *Wheel of Fortune*. What didn't come with the deal, however, was a CEO. Outgoing Columbia boss Victor Kaufman told Sony that he would not stay on to run Columbia after the merger. Sony had its candidate for a studio; now it needed a management team.

The Rain Men: Guber-Peters Entertainment Company

Sony North America chief Mickey Schulhof, charged with recruiting a studio chief for Columbia Pictures, settled on Peter Guber and Jon Peters, who ran the Guber-Peters Entertainment Company. Guber had credits for *The Way We Were* and *The Deep*, and was, well, very California. When we spoke to Guber about his track record, he told us, "I first tap into my intuitive because I believe every business decision is a creative decision. My intuitive really is the cartel . . . of all my intellect, my experience, my observations, and my collective unconscious and I tap into it because that's a place I have no fear. . . . I focus on my macro-goal or macro-opportunity before I go to bed to feed my unconscious."[20]

Peters made a name for himself coproducing *A Star Is Born* with then-girlfriend Barbra Streisand. In May 1980, Guber and Peters joined forces and secured credits on many successful projects including *Flash-dance* and *The Color Purple*. Hollywood insiders, however, were critical of the team, especially of Peters' notorious temper.[21] Steven Spielberg reportedly would not let the two on the set of *The Color Purple*. Despite having his picture taken with the duo for the Oscar *Rain Man* won, ex-Columbia boss Frank Price claimed, "They were never around while it was being made."[22] Nonetheless, there was no question that Guber and Peters had hands-on involvement in the highest-grossing picture in Warner Bros. history, *Batman*.

The recent success of the Guber-Peters Entertainment Company (GPEC), along with Guber's polished demeanor, was enough to convince Sony that it had found a suitable management team for its studio—even though Guber and Peters had just signed a five-year contract with Warner Bros. This meant that to get the dynamic duo, Sony would have to purchase their production company, which it did for $200 million, nearly 40 percent above its market value. Guber and Peters split a cool $80 million from the sale of their stock and, as studio chiefs, would receive a salary of $2.7 million, a share of any increase in the studio's market value, and a $50 million bonus pool (to be parceled out at their discretion) at the end of five years.

Columbia Pictures was sold to Sony for $3.4 billion, which along with assumed debt, brought the total cost to nearly $5 billion (a 70 percent premium). Then, when Warner Bros. chief Steve Ross refused to let Guber and Peters out of their contract at the eleventh hour, Sony ended up conceding to Warner (1) the portion of its Burbank lot controlled by Columbia in exchange for Warner's old MGM lot in less desirable Culver City, (2) a 50 percent equity stake in Sony's lucrative Columbia House mail-order music club, and (3) the rights to distribute Columbia's library over its cable networks. The settlement terms were "deemed so disadvantageous to Sony that for weeks afterward they are the talk of the lunch crowd at Le Dome, where they are referred to as 'Pearl Harbor

Revenged.' "[23] The total value of the settlement was estimated to be over $500 million.

Guber and Peters Take Over

Sony's total acquisition bill for Columbia Pictures reached nearly $6 billion when Guber and Peters took control.[24] Almost immediately, the two embarked on a lavish spending spree. The old MGM lot received in the Warner ransom went through an extensive renovation costing almost $1 billion. Offices were decorated with antique desks and chairs costing up to $26,000 each. In one famous instance, Jon Peters approved a $250,000 decorating budget for a producer, something he would not comment on when asked in an interview.[25]

Over the next two years, spending on production, management, and television also ballooned. Overhead increased by 50 percent to $300 million by 1991, some $60 million greater than at other major studios, and its $700 million production budget was nearly twice that of its competitors. The average Sony motion picture cost $40 million versus the industry average of $28 million. The excessive overhead and production costs pinched the company in 1991 as the industry saw year-over-year box-office sales slump 25 percent in the worst take in twenty years. Management was also unstable, as a succession of studio chiefs came and went, invariably with very generous severance packages. Even Peters (with $50 million and funding for a new production company) left. The executive turnover at Columbia caught the eye of the media and prompted *Spy* magazine to write, "The hottest sport in Hollywood is Sony Lotto—a get-rich-quick scheme in which the lucky player is fired by the studio in exchange for a fortune."[26]

Despite the spending and turmoil, Guber argued that $2 billion of Sony's money brought a happy result—Sony was number one at the box office in 1991.[27] In truth, Sony's ranking in the early 1990s was largely the result of distribution agreements with two small production companies: Castle Rock and Carolco. (Carolco's *Terminator 2* alone was responsible for one-half of Sony's box-office take in 1991.) Even in Sony's best year, 1992, its $400 million operating income was entirely eroded by interest and goodwill charges. With the Japanese recession, a slump in hardware sales, and a rising yen against the dollar, Sony executives in Tokyo started to put pressure on the studio to improve its results.

Fade to Black

Sony decided to pull out all the stops for its most anticipated film of 1993, Arnold Schwarzenegger's *The Last Action Hero.* The $90 million movie was to be the showpiece for every type of "synergy" that existed between hardware and software: a Sony movie filmed using Sony HDTV equipment; Sony products prominently featured; a soundtrack released through Sony Music; and a premiere in Sony Theaters equipped with Sony's proprietary SDDS surround sound. Everything was in place except for one thing: One of the most expensive motion pictures ever made was a box-office bomb. A string of less publicized but expensive losers followed, paralyzing the studio. By autumn 1994, Guber had gone nearly six months without approving a script for production. All together, seventeen of the twenty-six movies Sony released in 1994 lost money, bringing the filmmaking loss that year to $150 million.

That was enough for Sony. On September 29, 1994, Guber "resigned," but not without extracting one last "macro-opportunity"—a $275 million production package that included an annual salary estimated at between $5 and $10 million. Sony Picture's market share, after climbing significantly in 1991–92, had returned to where it was in 1989, but the financial damage was yet to be revealed. The Guber–Peters era finally ended in November 1994, as Sony announced a $3.2 billion write-off related to Columbia Pictures that wiped out nearly 25 percent of Sony's shareholders' equity. Not long after, Sony USA President Mickey Schulhof would be ousted as Sony set out to rebuild its motion picture operations. When asked what he might have done differently, Schulhof said, "Perhaps they should have changed the management."[28]

Epilogue

What can we learn from Sony's acquisition of Columbia Pictures? Yes, they sunk a tremendous amount of money into the movie studio, and yes they did abdicate management and even oversight to two Hollywood insiders that ended up costing them even more money. But consider the logic behind the deal. Remember that Sony—then as now—is first and foremost a hardware company, yet it believed that the establishment of a new hardware technology required the availability of related software demanded by the marketplace. This logic was a direct outgrowth of

Sony's experience with the Betamax video recorder and the compact disc. Recall that the popularity among consumers for VHS hardware spurred movie studios to produce in that format, and Betamax died. CD players, on the other hand, took off because Philips (which owned Poly-Gram Records) and Sony (through CBS Records) pushed the product aggressively to customers in Japan, Europe, and the United States.

While software is clearly an important driver in hardware success, there's another dynamic at work that, while recognized by some at Sony, never really took hold in its strategic calculations. That other factor, acknowledged by former Sony Chairman Akio Morita, was the importance of "building a family." With the Betamax, Morita firmly believed that a stronger "family" was needed after Matsushita built a more extensive alliance that undercut Sony's lead and made the need for Betamax obsolete. In this analysis, the availability of format-specific software was a consequence of the successful alliances created by Matsushita—VHS video recorders dominated the hardware market, so what else would software makers produce?

What's particularly interesting here is that the acquisition of Columbia Pictures could only make sense if we accept the "software" logic and not the "family" logic, because Columbia Pictures could never on its own have the market power to dictate market acceptance of Sony hardware products. Controlling a movie studio was seen as the solution to the old "Betamax" problem and as the lever to promote Sony's new HDTV and eight-mm video formats. Unfortunately, the lessons from the past were incomplete and misleading—software availability was a consequence, not a cause, of market power.[29]

Sometimes it's the strategic logic that is off, but other times merger problems are driven by dynamics of a much more personal nature. Our next story demonstrates just how powerful such leadership dynamics can be.

The Saga of the Saatchi Brothers

COME TO THE EDGE.
It's too high.
COME TO THE EDGE!
We might fly.

COME TO THE EDGE!!!
And they came.
And he pushed.
And they flew.[30]

From tiny London agency to largest advertising machine in the world in just sixteen years. From designing ads to offering advice on everything from employee compensation to jury selection, from real estate strategies to computer systems. From poor Iraqi immigrants to Tory party insiders, Maurice and Charles Saatchi rewrote the rules and in the process created a great company, yet one that was brought down in classic Greek tragedy style—by their own failings.

Take No Prisoners

They were aggressive from the start. Refusing to join the British Advertising Association, which promoted "ethical" standards and thus prohibited members from soliciting the competition's clients, Maurice Saatchi openly cold-called prospective clients while Charles leaked news of their newly won accounts to the trade journals. Even as small start-up, they didn't think twice about offering to buy other London agencies, regardless of size and price.

Who were these brothers who knew no limits? Charles has been described as "a dynamic, entrepreneurial force," "brilliant," and a "creative genius."[31] He began his advertising career at eighteen, when he went to work for a small London agency as an office assistant. Later, he joined London's then most innovative ad agency, Collett Dickenson Pearce, where he quickly built a creative reputation for himself, leaving soon afterward to start his own ad firm. Maurice was the dealmaker and managerial force in the partnership. Earning a degree in sociology from the London School of Economics, he went into business development for a London-based trade magazine. The brothers joined forces in 1970 to form Saatchi & Saatchi with nine employees in a small Soho office. Charles was responsible for creative work; Maurice handled sales, financial controls, and long-term strategy.

Together, they turned out to be skilled at hiring talented people and creating innovative ads. In 1975, the agency produced a famous ad for the British Health Education Council regarding public awareness of birth control featuring a "pregnant" man with an anxious look on his face and the caption "Would you be more careful if it were *you* who got pregnant?" Saatchi & Saatchi was soon earning numerous awards for creativity in advertising, which in turn helped attract the most innovative professionals. Add in the brothers' desire to pay the highest salaries in the industry and a reputation for creative freedom, and you have managers and staff years later recalling old poems that served as a call to arms, a "magical feeling for everyone,"[32] and that "people would do anything for them."[33] We even heard the following perhaps apocryphal story: The company wanted to rehire a talented person who had gone to another agency, and at the end of the negotiations to rejoin Saatchi & Saatchi, she said, "OK, I'll come back, but I want a car . . . a red one." When she shows up at work there is a red car, a red Ferrari.[34]

The Saatchi & Saatchi Vision: To Be "Number One"

What does it mean to be "number one"? For Saatchi & Saatchi, being number one was a code word for being on top of the world, beating everyone, and making sure that everyone knew you had won. To be number one was to be bigger, better, more powerful, and more dominant than anyone else. It took a few years, but the brothers made the vision come true, at least in advertising. After nibbling on a few UK-based agencies in the 1970s, they took a big step up in 1982 with the acquisition of old and well-established Compton Advertising. This was the one that opened the floodgates, with Saatchi & Saatchi subsequently buying agencies throughout Europe and the U.S.

By 1986 Saatchi & Saatchi had become established as the foremost agency for global advertising and had gobbled up several of the largest agencies, including the $450 million deal for Ted Bates, catapulting the company to the top spot in the world. So focused were the brothers on making acquisitions, however, that concerns for integration and even price became secondary. For example, one merger brought the accounts of two industry rivals under one roof, a clear violation of standard conflict-of-interest norms that cost Saatchi & Saatchi the Colgate-Palmolive account.

Imagine a company that makes global acquisitions of professional service firms without meeting the principals, without apparent interest in how the acquired firm would fit into the structure and operations of the parent, and with only minimal concern for price. That was Saatchi &

Saatchi in its heyday. Just as importantly, Saatchi & Saatchi was unable to transfer its core competence—a tremendous culture of winning and an ingenuity for advertising—to the agencies it acquired, perhaps because what the Saatchi brothers had created was too powerful, too cult-like, to easily take hold elsewhere. The bottom line for Saatchi & Saatchi: "The acquisition strategy was pretty mindless."[35]

Despite all these cracks showing, the brothers had made it, and made it big. A ten-year buying binge made Saatchi & Saatchi the largest ad agency in the world, with $7.5 billion in annual billings and a work force of eighteen thousand employees in five hundred offices in sixty-five countries. It had spent over $1 billion to acquire thirty-seven companies and, in 1987, became the first company in the world to be listed on three major stock exchanges: London, New York, and Tokyo.

A Classic Story of Hubris

What do you do when your vision is to be "number one"? The brothers never said, "number one in advertising," just "number one." So, in the mid-1980s Saatchi & Saatchi accelerated its acquisition pace, this time in consulting and communications firms. Starting with compensation consultants Hay Group, it went on to spend hundreds of millions of pounds on twelve consulting businesses. Then, in 1987 as a sort of *pièce de résistance*, Saatchi & Saatchi made a bid for troubled Midland Bank PLC. Though the deal was rebuffed, the company made clear that Midland was not even its first attempt at entering the international money world.[36] One analyst sighed, "I can't even pretend to see any synergies there," and the market slapped Saatchi's stock down 8.2 percent.[37]

Now, one may well ask at this point, what was the point? Why consulting, and why banking? Said Maurice Saatchi, "We are not shy about the fact that we would like to achieve market leadership in each sector."[38] Perhaps it was true that "Their greatest desire in the world was to be talked about,"[39] but it was apparent that their vision had no bounds. Hence, it was a simple matter for Saatchi & Saatchi to move from buying every advertising agency it could to seeking acquisitions in consulting and banking, businesses for which the Saatchis possessed neither competence nor passion.

Even more than for Peter Guber and Jon Peters at Sony Pictures, success for the Saatchi brothers unearthed deep-seated fault lines they were unable to keep under control. It became more important to inter-act with the elite of British society, to hobnob at the very top political circles, than to run a mere advertising agency, even one that was the biggest in the world. Even an aspiration of becoming the world's largest professional services company was somehow unfulfilling, for, as Maurice used to say, "It's not enough to succeed, others must fail."[40]

As with Quaker and Sony, it's impossible to understand mergers and acquisitions, or even corporate strategy, without understanding leader-ship and the people who make up organizational life. The shadow the Saatchi brothers cast across the company was not only long but also deep, and cut both ways. In interviews with people who were part of the old Saatchi & Saatchi, the same themes of "nothing is impossible," "peo-ple would do anything for the agency," and "the brothers were creative geniuses, brilliant, dynamic, and entrepreneurial" kept emerging.[41]

The shadow grew longer as the firm became more successful, and the Saatchi brothers changed. Now people were saying, "They did not have to play by the rules," "The decision to be number one overwhelmed everything else," "They did not understand how to operate the com-pany," and even "These [people] are lunatics."[42] As the focus on growth and nothing but growth took off, fundamental mistakes in mergers and acquisitions followed. With leaders at the top pushing to be number one, and incentives created for senior executives to make deals, the firm made one acquisition after another, yet never developed a competency in M&As. Not only were there breakdowns in strategic logic—witness the consulting and financial industry merger effort devoid of realistic synergies—but fundamental mistakes in due diligence and integration plagued the firm. It is a story of vision without restraint, driven by in-tense ambition and striving ego, and a cautionary tale for other CEOs possessed by boundless competitive instincts and overwrought vision.

The Bill Comes Due for the Saatchi Brothers

In June 1989 Saatchi & Saatchi announced that the consulting division was up for sale. It was official—the megagrowth strategy had been a fail-ure. Making matters worse, the recession beginning in mid-1989 and rolling over into the early 1990s hit Saatchi & Saatchi especially hard. Earnings fell, debt increased, and the stock lost 98 percent of its value by 1989. The brothers brought in turnaround expert Robert Louis-Dreyfus and managed to hang on for five more years as the company suffered through endless cost cutting and the disposal of twelve subsidiaries. The creative spark somehow got lost during the dark days as well, so perhaps it was almost a relief when a shareholder revolt finally forced the resignation of Charles and Maurice Saatchi in December 1994 from the firm they had created some twenty-four years earlier.

The Return of the Saatchis

Are there second acts for defeated generals? Can CEOs learn from their mistakes? The remarkable resurgence of the brothers, especially Maurice Saatchi, must surely be one of the most unexpected comebacks in recent business history. Less than one year after leaving their namesake firm, the brothers created M&C Saatchi, quickly poaching clients such as British Airways, Qantas, and the Tory party from their former firm. The old creative touch came back. In 1996 M&C took home Agency of the Year honors from the International Advertising Festival in Cannes.[43]

Seven years later, the Saatchi brothers find themselves sitting among the advertising world's elite once again. M&C Saatchi currently has twelve offices on four continents with about 550 employees generating more than $600 million in billings.[44] The eighth largest advertising agency in the world—it's only three spots below the old Saatchi & Saatchi— M&C continues to win advertising industry awards, including the prestigious Agency of the Year award from *Campaign* magazine in 2000. Maurice, who now runs the company (Charles has been in and out of active duty at the agency for some time), also found an international media services partner in the French firm Publicis, headed by CEO Maurice Levy.

Meanwhile, while the old Saatchi & Saatchi agency did recover somewhat, it remained a second-tier player for several years, slowed by numerous organizational changes designed to make sense of the hodgepodge of agencies under the corporate umbrella. In June 2000, however, the French advertising group Publicis (already partnered with M&C Saatchi) purchased Saatchi & Saatchi. The deal created the world's fifth largest advertising agency and, perhaps more interestingly, presents the possibility that Levy will eventually reunite Saatchi & Saatchi with M&C Saatchi.

In an interview in *The Independent* in England, Maurice looked back on what went wrong:

> We (at M&C Saatchi) don't have those linear ambitions [that the old Saatchi & Saatchi had]. We don't want to be top of a league table or bigger than anybody else. I now have an ability to appreciate what a wonderful place this is and not be distracted by a constant desire to move on to the next thing. I was afflicted by that . . . insecurity and paranoia. The catalogue of errors and mistakes would fill the British Library. Hubris? That would be about right, yes.[45]

Strategy Mistakes in Mergers and Acquisitions: From Synergy to Hubris

Studying the case histories of failed acquisitions opens up a window to a process often more muddy than clear. Quaker (or, rather, Smithburg et al.) made a mistake; Snapple lost three-quarters of its value under Quaker. Sony (Schulhof, then Guber and Peters) made mistakes; Sony took a $3.2 billion write-off from its acquisition of Columbia Pictures. And the Saatchi brothers, brilliant in the business of advertising but bereft of logic and intuition in the business of acquisitions, made mistakes; S&S almost went bankrupt after its acquisition spree. Examining these executive mistakes can give us tremendous insight on making mergers and acquisitions work.

Why Is It So Difficult to Realize Synergies and Create Value?

Jean-Marie Messier used to run a water utility in France. That's before he got into the entertainment business by snapping up companies such as Seagram (bringing Universal Studios and Universal Music), pay-TV group Canal Plus, mobile phone group Cegetel, USA Networks, Houghton Mifflin, and an assortment of phone companies, software developers, and other multimedia properties. The master plan: combining entertainment content and wireless distribution to create a powerful vertically integrated multimedia giant. Unfortunately, the vision was grander than reality, and Vivendi Universal could never generate the synergies behind the deal. The price tag—billions of dollars in shareholder value destroyed, and Messier's job.

Synergies 101. Synergies—a combination of assets that create more value when together than separate—come from cost savings or revenue enhancements. From Boeing using McDonnell's underutilized lines and tool-making capacity when those companies merged in 1997 to Eaton's consolidation of plants and products following its acquisition of Westinghouse's Distribution and Controls business in 1994, cost synergies are often essential to the strategic logic of a deal.

Executives sometimes try to wring out revenue enhancements in an acquisition by combining complementary assets. For example, when Unilever acquired Ben & Jerry's Ice Cream, it brought a worldwide distribution network, expanding the markets open to Ben & Jerry's. Sony predicated its acquisition of Columbia Pictures on the notion that software could increase hardware sales, and Quaker expected that it could transfer its marketing expertise to Snapple to boost its revenues. While virtually all acquisitions are predicated on realizing cost or revenue synergies, making that happen is quite another matter.

All synergies are not created equally. The first lesson you must remember about synergies is that they are almost always much more difficult to realize than they appear. The more significant the synergy potential, the more momentous the challenge. When synergy potential is modest, as it might be if two companies share few activities or customers, achieving these benefits will be relatively straightforward. For example, combining treasury and legal services isn't difficult, though its yield is limited. As synergy potential becomes progressively more encompassing, the complexity of reaching the pot of gold increases. Vivendi could never figure out how to make money by combining the impressive assets it collected; content and distribution sound like they could go together, but how? Vivendi never could get past that challenge.

Time counts. As basic as the notion of present value is, executives sometimes seem to forget that cost savings materializing three years after an acquisition are not the same as an immediate savings. Synergies that are difficult to attain, and hence will take longer to realize, are not worth as much as those that are more immediate. When promises made at the time a deal is penned turn out to be considerably less robust over time, the market tends to extract a price, something AOL Time Warner learned when the $1 billion boost to cash flow pledged by then CEO Gerald Levin never materialized.

Synergies are not free. Making synergies happen is not without cost— downsizing expenses, time spent on coordination and interaction to realize synergies, additional training and relocation costs, and higher overhead during integration. These are not the only costs associated with mergers, but are the ones most directly related to achieving synergies. As a rule of thumb, synergy realization costs often come in at two to three times the value of annual synergy benefits.

Negative synergies. Sony's acquisition of Columbia Pictures was expected to yield synergies, yet it didn't. Why? The hardware and software sides of the business had different motives and cultures; why should one compromise for the other? For example, despite having a huge catalog of titles, Sony was unsuccessful in making its digital audio tape (DAT) and minidisc formats stick in the U.S. This failure was due in part to the fact that Sony's software division was afraid of the potential for piracy that digital recording technology presented. Coordination problems between the hardware and software sides of Sony were exacerbated by fundamental differences in pay, perceived work ethic, and even location (hardware was in Japan and software was in New York). Even in 1998, Sony Music Entertainment resisted Sony Electronics' desire to manufacture portable MP3 playback devices. This hesitation allowed new competitors to emerge both in the MP3 playback device market and in the digital content market.

How Do You Know if an Acquisition Is Wise?

Let's start with this first principle: Acquisitions should only take place when they advance the overall strategy of the company in compelling ways. CEOs must be able to convincingly say, "By making this deal we will improve our competitive position in the marketplace."

The second test is whether the combination of assets will create more value than it destroys. Richard Parsons, CEO of AOL Time Warner, had this thought front and center when he said during a crisis in 2002, "The whole should be—and will be, under this management team—greater than the sum of its parts."[46]

Given that negative synergies are common, how will an acquisition overcome its drawbacks to generate positive benefits for your company? In essence, passing the value creation test requires the realization of cost saving and revenue enhancements in excess of all the costs involved in the deal. Key questions to ask are, how will you as a corporate parent generate the expected synergy benefits, and in what ways might you destroy value? And how can you minimize those costs? The value creation test provides a rationale for demerging as much as it does for merging. For example, Palm was spun out of 3Com in 2000 after it became clear that 3Com was stifling Palm's growth opportunities. (An independent Palm could use stock options to lure engineers, which it could not do as a unit of 3Com.) In addition, the two companies were actually in different businesses—Palm in hand-held computers and 3Com in networking equipment—providing little in the way of synergies. With little value creation and some value destruction, the spin-off made sense.

Is your acquisition justified? There should be absolute clarity within the organization on the purpose of the acquisition and why it's important. Not only will you motivate people, but an acquisition justification can serve as a beacon to point the way during the problems, complexity, and confusion that inevitably occur during integration.

Is your core competency in M&A? Successful companies develop critical core competencies that drive their competitive strategy. In a similar vein, successful M&A companies must develop core competencies that make them superior acquirers, something that is difficult to do when each acquisition is considered a unique event. The experience people gain from participation in one deal should be captured, disseminated to others, and built upon with subsequent deals, as Cisco, GE, Eaton, and other great acquirers do.

Is your M&A strategy tailored to your organization? The appropriate strategy for any company is one that is tailored to its own capabilities, people, and overall competitive strategy. What is needed in another company is not necessarily the same as in yours. For example, while Conseco was very successful in buying smaller insurers and folding them into its system—eliminating duplication and overhead while streamlining back-office processes—its 1998 acquisition of Green Tree was different. A company in a complementary, but not identical, business, Green Tree sold mortgages to the same low-income customers that Conseco targeted for insurance products, forcing Conseco to master cross-selling rather than ruthless efficiency, which it could not do.

What Are the Keys to Due Diligence?

The Snapple deal is a classic example of failed due diligence. The hybrid distribution system rejected by the independent distributors was the key to the deal, yet Quaker never realized that the distributors held all the cards—their contracts with Snapple gave them ironclad in-perpetuity rights to the product—or how different the old-line Quaker company was to the entrepreneurial distributors. As one top Snapple distributor said, "[Quaker] just didn't know our business."[47] Smithburg acknowledges the problem: "I am not critical of the distributors. Our error was not understanding them or their business and culture as well as we should have."[48]

Was Quaker blinded by the Snapple opportunity and its own self-confidence as a brand builder? Former Triarc CEO Michael Weinstein, who spearheaded the Snapple turnaround after buying the company from Quaker, put it this way: "Quaker believed three guys from Brooklyn stumbled onto this thing that became a great success. Bringing on board some smart guys would make it all work better. Quaker just didn't understand the entrepreneurial nature of the business."[49] Three years after selling Snapple to Triarc, Smithburg recognized the flaws in due diligence. "There was so much excitement about bringing in a new brand, a brand with legs. We should have had a couple of people arguing the 'no side' of the evaluation."[50]

Almost everyone understands due diligence. It's all about making sure you don't buy a lemon. When savvy dealmakers such as HFS's Henry Silverman can get blindsided by fraudulent accounting practices at merger partner CUC International, leading to a $2.8 billion shareholder settlement, it's a reminder that we all need to pay attention to the warning signs. When the Australian insurance company AMP acquired GIO in 1998, it did so just days after GIO announced unexpected losses in its reinsurance business. Within a year these losses totaled over one billion Australian dollars (around U.S. $600 million). In Mattel's ill-fated $3.5

billion acquisition in 1999 of the Learning Company, critical reports pointed out numerous warning signs. Yet Mattel paid a hefty 4.5 times sales for the company. While CEO exuberance over the impending deals may have had something to do with these acquisitions going forward in spite of loud warning signs, there are some important principles of due diligence that must be considered.

Details. Due diligence is all about the details, and they are often there for the taking. Along with massive publicly available data on public and many private companies, there is nothing to keep a prospective acquirer from conducting its own data collection. How many people work at a target's factory? Count the cars in the parking lot. What do a target's office buildings look like inside? Blueprints are usually available from local zoning offices. How solid is a target's finances? Look at the red flags, such as cutbacks in new project investments, reductions in advertising and other discretionary expenditures, and open jobs not being filled. How good are a target's products and services? Buy them, use them, reverse engineer them. What do suppliers, competitors, distributors, and customers say about a target's business? Ask them. People are often more than happy to share what they know—just be a good listener.

Driving too fast. Speed was the mantra of the new economy, but its extension into M&A due diligence wasn't successful. When Cisco acquired the fiber-optics maker Cerent for $7.2 billion in 1999, negotiations reportedly took only 2½ hours over three days. But this speed masks months of pre-activity, something that might fool novice acquirers into thinking, If Cisco doesn't need to spend much time doing its acquisitions, why should we? In fact, Cisco had owned 9 percent of Cerent since 1998, giving it a window to the company and its R&D. Cisco CEO John Chambers knew Cerent CEO Carl Russo well. Cisco understood the marketplace extremely well, making the strategic logic for the deal clear. Cisco had an experienced integration machine for high-tech mergers that enabled it to move quickly and effectively after the deal closed. Cisco was able to move very fast when it came time to make a deal only because of the connections that had been forged ahead of time. Most deals take time—lots of time.

Get information from the trenches. You have a choice: Develop your own information sources, or depend on investment bankers to identify acquisition candidates. So, you can talk to suppliers, customers, even competitors. You can rely on division managers in the competitive trenches. Ask whom they have noticed that has an interesting product or service that fits well with current offerings, that has great managerial talent, and so on. Or, you can wait for the "books" that make their rounds on Wall Street with one express purpose—to entice you to buy assets that are currently for sale at the highest price possible. It's your call.

Many pharma and high-tech companies (including Merck, Intel, and Cisco) acquire minority stakes in dozens of start-ups, providing early information on potential. Since most of these companies are private and often small, they can easily fall under the radar screen of even effective intelligence-gathering companies. Such investments or alliances represent real options that can be cashed in if and when the related market opportunity gains critical mass. In addition, companies that have made successful acquisitions in the past build reputations that can draw potential sellers into its orbit. Reputation is critical because potential buyers are likely to talk to CEOs of previously acquired companies to discover exactly what happened. Make sure that they have a good story to tell.

Integration: Death by One Thousand Mistakes

"Merger fails because of integration breakdowns" How often have we heard that? It seems no one is immune. Even the 1997 merger of the Stephen Covey empire (*The 7 Habits of Highly Effective People*) with time-management guru Hyrum Smith to form Franklin Covey fell into many of the classic traps: separate headquarters for the two parts of the company; differences in how people were treated; an "us versus them" mentality in which both sides kept doing what they had always done while new structures were tested. The result was classic negative synergies, with overhead costs increasing from 35 percent of sales a year before the merger to 40 percent the following year.

Consider how Quaker, Sony, and Saatchi & Saatchi dealt with integration. Quaker was undone by one integration problem after another, some of which could have been foreseen with better due diligence; Sony's integration was subject to the twin troubles of culture and coordination; Saatchi & Saatchi assiduously ignored integration whenever it could. Our research indicates that merger integration mistakes occur because companies don't know what to do once the deal is done, because of cultural disruptions, and because of unintended vulnerabilities opened up by the deal itself.

What to Do When the Deal Is Done

Keep track of time. The longer the deal takes, the more you risk losing the payoff from the synergies you've tapped. Luckily, acquisitions come with built-in opportunities to take advantage of time. Take, for example, the period of time from acquisition announcement to closing, which can range anywhere from a few weeks to even years (when antitrust issues cloud a deal's closure). This is the time to begin the transition and generate a detailed integration plan, like Eaton did in the acquisition of Westinghouse's Distribution and Controls business in 1994 during the lag before antitrust approval came. Its planning included detailed assessments of each plant, product category, and product style—thousands in all—so they were prepared to move quickly toward consolidation and rationalization when the deal officially closed.

Designate a deal champion. Acquisition champions take personal responsibility for integrating an acquisition and are given the authority to match. They are often managers who first saw the acquisition opportunity—and, hence, are naturally energized by the deal and what it means for the company. In fact, at Cisco, if a business unit general manager expresses interest in a company as a potential acquisition, he or she must be willing to become the de facto champion of the acquisition and subsequently assume responsibility for the successful integration and ongoing performance of the target company.

Script the first fifteen plays. Like legendary former San Francisco 49er coach Bill Walsh, laying out the first integration moves in advance opens up more management time and "thinking space" to deal with the issues and problems that could not have been anticipated in advance. Among the most important of these plays is inevitably the first payroll. There is no better way to signal to employees of the acquired company that you don't care about them than to mess up their first paycheck.

Empower integration teams. Appoint a small team of dedicated integration specialists to serve as the catalyst around which a "virtual team" of functional specialists forms (finance, human resources, engineering services, manufacturing and information services). While much of the work of these teams will fall into the postacquisition time period, their quick organization and empowerment reduces uncertainty within the acquired organization.

Start preparing for the unexpected. If there is one certainty about integration, it is that the unexpected will occur. While the designation of champions, scripted plays, and integration teams provide structure and a game plan, we should not fool ourselves into believing that this is an entirely controllable process. To help fight the inevitable fires that break out, it sure helps to have talent in reserve, as Eaton does with its "navy seals" teams ready to move to unplanned trouble spots to put out fires.

Break Through Cultural Roadblocks

When Daimler-Benz and Chrysler announced their $36 billion merger in May 1998, many critics hailed the move as visionary and bold for its potential to rewrite the rules of the global auto industry. Chrysler would bring its small-car expertise to Germany, which was struggling with its SmartCar at the time. Mercedes engineers would reenergize Chrysler's line, learn more about the minivan business, and improve overall Chrysler car quality. Together, the companies could take out excess capacity from the industry and still become a major global player to rival GM, Ford, and Toyota. It has taken years, however, to get close to this initial vision, in large part due to the wide range of cultural barriers plaguing acquisition integration. Consider some of the differences:

Compensation and benefits. Chrysler executives earned two to four times more than their counterparts at Daimler, but kept personal expenses under tight wraps; Daimler executives would spend extravagantly (particularly when they traveled), leading to endless arguments about $500 suites and flying on the *Concorde.*

Management style. Jürgen Schrempp (Daimler's CEO) was aggressive, passionate, dynamic, focused, and extroverted, while Robert Eaton (Chrysler's CEO) was sensitive, restrained, and relatively self-effacing.

Hierarchy: Daimler executives had teams of aides that prepared detailed position papers on all decisions, while Chrysler managers depended on their own information networks.

Financial management. The Germans focused on annual earnings more than quarterly, often looking to end the year with a bang. The Americans managed analysts and their expectations constantly, assiduously avoiding any surprises.

Cultural roadblocks such as these are insidious because they help to create other, related, integration "neuroses" that only magnify the problem. Here are a few examples of such neuroses we observed in other mergers:

"I will kill you rather than join you." Hospital mergers, which are typically driven by the need to cut costs to deal with intense competition, pressure from managed care, and cuts in Medicare reimbursements, often bypass real integration of operations because of the huge power physicians yield in the system. The problems encountered by one merger that tried such integration—Boston's Beth Israel and Deaconess Hospitals—are a case in point. For example, a merger of the anesthesiology departments took eighteen months, with the Deaconess anesthesiologists actually choosing to resign rather than compromise on such issues as work schedules, compensation, and administration of the department.[51]

"Buy, but don't touch." Foreign acquirers—particularly in very big deals—tend to be remarkably "hands-off" in integration. Whether driven by fear of political fallout and bad press, or a reflection of a perceived lack of understanding of the foreign business practices, several companies have displayed an almost cavalier approach to integration. For five years following Japan-based Bridgestone's acquisition of Firestone, Bridgestone left senior Firestone management in place in spite of their poor track record. By 1992 total losses were $1 billion, finally forcing Bridgestone to bring in its own people and attack the problem, spending some $1.5 billion to upgrade and expand Firestone's operations. Unfortunately, the bottom line on this acquisition has continued to spiral downward for years, first with major labor unrest that made front-page headlines and even

involved President Clinton in 1995 and, more recently, the massive tire recall related to Ford Explorer accidents.

"We're not really that different." Sometimes the neurosis takes the opposite tack, when apparently small differences in culture and management style are not perceived at all, as was the case when Pharmacia (Sweden) and Upjohn (U.S.) merged in 1995. Although Sweden and the United States resemble each other in many respects, small differences in habits and norms can make a big difference. For example, while vacations during the month of July in Sweden are commonplace, Upjohn executives were unaware of this ritual and scheduled a series of meetings during the month that angered their Swedish counterparts. In addition, the Americans managed with a directive, detail-oriented style that did not mesh well with the Swedish penchant for open discussion and consensus. The merger took years to right itself, as misleading assumptions on cultural similarity fueled endless friction between the companies.

"We don't need to change." Most people tend to prefer stability to change. It may be no surprise, then, that classic denial has found a place in acquisition lore. For example, there is the old story about engineers at McDonnell Aircraft whittling down their pencils to remove the "Douglas" name after the companies merged to form McDonnell Douglas. Even senior managers may find it easier to support the status quo than adapt. When asked whether Daimler's German executives had failed to understand Chrysler's culture or the nature of its American business, CEO Jürgen Schrempp referred to Chrysler as a "division" and irritably brushed off further questions about culture. "Our management style is to give divisional leadership the maximum freedom," he said. "That has always been our management style and was also our management style in the case of Chrysler. That is my answer to that one."[52]

Beware of Critical Stakeholder Vulnerabilities

The business of integrating acquisitions is a messy, complex, and time-consuming affair. It is so time-consuming, in fact, that mergers can create critical stakeholder vulnerabilities when managers are so consumed by integration that they start to neglect customers and employees.

Customers. Following a merger you have to pay special attention to your customers or you will lose them to competitors. When Compaq acquired Digital Equipment in 1998, CEO Michael Dell of Dell Computer said, "I gotta believe these guys have just handed us a huge gift."[53] While Dell had many things going for it, it did pull even in market share with Compaq during the immediate postacquisition integration period. It's not surprising that Dell said much the same thing when H-P and Compaq merged in 2002. When Wells Fargo and Bank of America went on acquisition sprees a few years back, small savings and loan banks in California took out major ads in local newspapers promising to provide the personal service that was conspicuously missing from the big banks distracted by mergers.

Special efforts are required to avoid losing customers after a deal. To protect themselves, Eaton appoints both integration managers and operating managers to help ensure that attention does not get diverted away from customers during integration activities. Customer satisfaction should be carefully, and regularly, monitored throughout the integration process, and senior executives must make sure to visit major customers as early as possible to describe why the merger is happening and what it means to those customers.

Employees. There is a real risk that some of your most valuable people will see the merger as an opportunity to go elsewhere. With everything else going on following a merger, it's not hard for a company to take its eye off the ball and neglect key people. People retention problems in professional service firms are legion. When Bank of America (formerly Nations Bank) acquired the small investment banking firm Montgomery Securities in 1997 for $1.3 billion, it didn't take long for management clashes to lead to the massive departure of some one hundred Montgomery employees (to a firm started by former Montgomery chairman Tom Weisel). Remember, during an acquisition, the primary question on the lips of managers and employees of the acquired company is "What happens to me?" Your response is the lens through which they will evaluate their personal decision to stay or to leave, to fight and disrupt or to accommodate and adjust.

Pride Goeth Before a . . .

We cannot leave the topic of acquisitions without raising the issue of CEO hubris and emotion. Consider the acquisition of Columbia Pictures by Sony. In discussing M&A pricing, former CEO Akio Morita said, "I can always recover money. I can't recover people or companies and in the long-term scheme of things it doesn't matter whether we pay a little more or a little less." While talent and companies are clearly important, at some point this type of logic goes over the line. Peter Guber on the Sony acquisition of Columbia Pictures, remarked, "There is an emotional momentum to a deal. Once it kicks in, nothing can stop the deal from happening."[54] Does this sound familiar?

In a fascinating study on CEO hubris, professors Mathew Hayward and Donald Hambrick investigated whether hubris was related to the price paid by the CEO's company in an acquisition. Tapping such indicators of hubris as media praise for the CEO and CEO compensation relative to the number-two executive, they found that the higher the CEO hubris, the more money it spent. For example, on average each additional highly favorable press account of the CEO translated to an almost 5 percent increase in premium paid.[55] That's right, glowing press reports puffed up CEOs to believe that they could pay more because they were good enough to make it back and then some. Unfortunately, the smart executives at Quaker, Sony, and Saatchi & Saatchi found out that making mergers and acquisitions work is a lot tougher than they thought.

Things to Remember About Mergers and Acquisitions

- Just as board members at companies such as Enron and Tyco have taken the heat for standing by while accounting scandals ran amuck, they must be held responsible for acquisitions that defy logic. Saatchi & Saatchi buying Midlands Banks? It just isn't meant to be.
- Synergies are elusive. Pre-acquisition analysis must realistically evaluate potential synergies, paying particular attention to the possibility of negative synergies, the rush of time, and the cost involved.
- We wouldn't buy a car or a house without carefully studying just what it is we are buying. Why should buying companies be any different?

More ships have been wrecked by inept due diligence—think Quaker—than almost any other aspect of deal making.

- The hard work really starts when the deal is done. Effective integration may not be easy, but absentee management or wanton disregard for those affected by the merger won't help. Sony and Saatchi & Saatchi paid little attention to the aftermath of their business deals, and paid a price.

- Acquisition isn't a "one-off" exercise. The best acquirers have managed to remember what they've learned from each deal and use that knowledge as a weapon for growth.

- Build managerial continuity. Just as there is tribal knowledge within organizations that needs to be revealed and transferred during acquisitions, managers involved in integration are valuable resources. Harnessing their expertise means developing a cadre of people whose primary responsibility becomes M&As; with each subsequent involvement in a deal the knowledge base of such people expands, making the company a formidable contender.

- Don't forget to celebrate successes. The work behind integration is very hard, and often very frustrating. Look for small wins early on, and give the team a chance to celebrate those wins.

CHAPTER 5

Strategy Gone Bad:
Doing the Wrong Thing

Why Strategists Misread Competitors and
Select "Irrational" Strategies

Whaat is strategy? Countless books, MBA programs, executive education initiatives, and consultants are available to answer this question in excruciating detail. But let's cut to the chase. Strategy is what a company does, or doesn't do, to fulfill its vision in a competitive marketplace. Dell's strategy is to deliver directly to customers a built-to-order personal computer (and more recently other computer-related products). The strategy at Southwest Airlines is to provide world-class customer satisfaction to flyers who value high-frequency, low-cost flights.

There are three things you should know about strategy.

- To have a solid strategy, you must know the "who, what, and how" of your company. Who are you selling to? (People who value easy customization and speedy delivery at Dell; customers who value low prices at Southwest) What are you selling? (Dell—reliable computer products; Southwest—convenient travel) How are you selling it? (By focusing on logistics and execution at Dell; customer service and speed of airplane turnaround at Southwest)
- Strategy is just as much about what you decide not to do as it is what you do. If you try to do everything, then you don't really have much of a strategy. Dell doesn't sell branded products via resellers: Southwest doesn't offer first-class cabins. This is one of the toughest things for executives to grasp. Sometimes you have to say no.
- Not all strategies are created equal. Strategies should be based on real internal competence that customers value enough to pay for and that competitors cannot easily replicate. H-P knows how to make per-

sonal computers, but it loses against Dell because it can't easily switch from its reliance on channels and resellers to a direct-to-customer model (resellers tend to get upset when you try to bypass them and go directly to end users). Many established airlines have been unable to weather the post–September 11 storm precisely because their standard operating procedures make it so difficult to take on attributes of the Southwest business model.

Yes, we know strategy can be complicated, much more complicated than this, but there's real value in focusing on these basic principles, especially when much of what passes for strategy is just an elaboration of these ideas. What's more, these principles will go a long way in helping us to understand what went wrong in the companies profiled in this chapter. Of course, we've been talking about strategy throughout the book, without labeling it as such. Strategy helps to explain why some new ventures work and many others don't; strategy is the reason why innovation and change are so critical; mergers and acquisitions are designed to advance a company's strategy. In this chapter, strategy is our primary focus, both because it helps to consolidate many of the themes in Part I and because it is the perfect segue into Part II (where we channel Indiana Jones and dig deep down to reveal the broad behavioral patterns that lead to executive failure). And as always, while the companies we unveil come from many different worlds—varying by industry, time, and location—the commonalities stand out to provide powerful lessons for executives and investors alike.

Wang Laboratories—Greek Tragedy?

The classic Greek tragedies often involved a deep-seated defect in the protagonist that led to his eventual downfall. Tragically, this "self-inflicted wound"—whether hubris, arrogance, or a need for power and control—was often an accompaniment to genius. In the classic tradition, some of these very characteristics that enable greatness are also responsible for eventual failure, a theme that at its most basic level explains the story of An Wang and Wang Labs.

An Wang was an exceptional man—an inventor and innovator, a true business creator. He came to America with little money, earned a doctorate in applied physics in 1948 from Harvard University, and went on to invent the magnetic pulse memory core, a technology that would be essential in computers for the next two decades. He was the first to develop and realize the potential of the calculator market, and Wang was personally responsible for numerous patents and product ideas. This quest for breakthrough technologies was not only his driving force, but it was also embedded in the culture of the company he created—Wang Labs—which grew to become a $2 billion powerhouse.

The early years of the company were prophetic. Wang Labs was intertwined with IBM right from the start. The design for Wang's magnetic pulse memory core was sold to IBM in 1956, but not before four years of arduous negotiations. It did not go unnoticed that this deal closed just weeks before Wang was awarded a patent on this technology; years later, he would suggest that IBM had challenged his patent claim as a means of closing the sale.[1]

By the late 1950s, Wang had several additional inventions under his belt, but his business prowess was still catching up to his technical prowess. When Wang patented a phototypesetting device that increased the productivity of newspaper printing, he bungled the licensing agreement and lost exclusive manufacturing rights. In need of additional capital, Wang grudgingly sold 25 percent of the company to a machine tools company for $150,000. Wang later wrote that he regretted giving up so much control for such a small price.[2]

The next two decades were good years for Wang. The introduction of the LOCI electronic scientific calculator in 1965 literally began the desk calculator market, which Wang dominated for the next five years. Riding the wave, Wang Labs went public under much fanfare in July 1967, with Dr. Wang personally retaining control of over 50 percent of the company. The Wang 2200 minicomputer and the cutting-edge 1200 BASIC word processing machine debuted in 1973, but it wasn't until the company introduced a cathode ray tube–based word processing minicomputer in 1976 that Wang had his next big hit. By 1978 Wang Labs was ranked as the thirty-second largest computer provider, and was cocky enough to launch an aggressive television advertising campaign aimed directly against number-one IBM. An Wang brazenly proclaimed that his company would replace IBM as the dominant computer company in the world by the mid-1990s. As one former manager told us, "He had two suits, both gray, and in the breast pocket he always kept a little chart showing how Wang Labs would one day surpass IBM. This at a time when sales at Wang were around $3 billion and IBM was at $47 billion."

Arrogance + Hatred + Disrespect for Your Competitor = Disaster

The story of the word processor and the IBM PC highlights the dangers of strategic breakdowns as well as anything. Rather than see the word processor as a product, An Wang fell head-over-heels in love with it. While an innovative company must truly be in love with the process of creating new products, as we saw in Chapter 2 loving the actual product is much more dangerous. So when, as the story goes, son Fred points out that IBM's PC is a real threat to the word processor, An Wang says, "The PC is the stupidest thing I ever heard of." Then, akin to Apple's resistance to licensing its technology, not only was Wang slow to market with a PC, but when the company did enter the market it chose to use its own non-IBM compatible proprietary system. With one part arrogance bred on past success, and one part attempted defiance of the emerging IBM hegemony in PCs, An Wang's blind hatred of IBM created an unwinnable strategy. Ever since he had sold his rights to the magnetic pulse memory core, he had felt cheated and exploited by the giant computer company—and he would be damned if he would let that happen again.

To Understand Strategy, Study the Strategists

The story of An Wang and the PC—almost a fable—provides a window into the closed world of Wang. Right from the beginning, An Wang had served concurrently as president, CEO, and director of research, creating a "benevolent dictatorship" where he retained ultimate control over every facet of the company. In a touching story told to us by his son Fred, An's desire for control even extended to the IPO process:

> At night he'd read an Agatha Christie mystery before falling asleep. He'd usually read a page or two before he would just fall off and the book would just plop off to the floor. During the summer of 1967, just before the company went public, he had gotten hold of some handbook on taking companies public—one of these coffee-table-

size books—and he'd take that to bed at night, read a couple of pages, and then you'd hear the book fall because when that thing fell, the whole house shuddered. He basically read through that during the course of the summer and was able to question and direct the investment bankers who helped us with the IPO. He knew more about some of the things than they did just by having spent the time reading through materials.[3]

Where did this pre-occupation with control come from? While there were almost certainly psychodynamic attributes that contributed to An Wang's actions, the main reason is that An Wang always regretted giving up too much control when the company first went public. He may well have felt that he was bullied and taken advantage of by IBM. And he lost control of exclusive manufacturing rights because of a slipshod licensing agreement. Much of what happened subsequently to Wang can be seen as his attempt to avoid the mistakes of the past, but each solution turned out to be more toxic than the problem it was meant to cure. These three events—all centered on the theme of loss of control—drove Wang to make decisions that destroyed his company.

Two decisions were most critical. By the early 1980s, Wang Labs was too big for him to manage alone. The first person Wang elevated to president—an experienced executive with strong credentials—lasted only three years as it became apparent that An intended to promote his son, Fred, to that position. When Fred did take over, however, many people wondered whether he was the right man for the job.[4]

While continuing a line of family members as CEO is hardly unique to Wang—Schwinn, Coors, and Barneys also place a high value on continuing the family traditions—for Dr. Wang his decision may well have been more about his legacy than about family. This was not a family-run company in the way that Schwinn, Coors, and Barneys were; rather, Fred's ascension to the throne was an affirmation of An Wang's professional and personal success. Even on his deathbed in 1990, An Wang scribbled a note, sealed with hospital tape, asking then CEO Richard Miller to keep the company's name intact no matter what the future should hold.[5]

With the market having shifted from word processors to PCs, and Wang's entry stalling, the company was in trouble. The sales force didn't want PCs—Wang was an also-ran in PCs—and besides, they made much more money on word processors. The only problem was that the word processor market continued to dip. Losses mounted, and their effect was concentrated because of a decision—the second one that doomed the company—An Wang had made during the years of growth. Unhappy that he had to give up so much of the company when he went public,[6] he subsequently refused to dilute his holdings to raise additional capital. With limited opportunities for equity, the only thing left is debt, and Wang had managed to accumulate over $1 billion of it, including $575 million in bank loans by 1989.[7] While the company struggled through several more years, by 1992 it was over. Wang Labs—for years one of the most innovative companies in the computer industry—filed for Chapter 11 bankruptcy protection.

Wang Labs died of self-inflicted wounds. That which made the company great—an obsessive desire by a benevolent and brilliant dictator to control every aspect of the company—led to its downfall. Wang Labs is a remarkable example of an entrepreneurial start-up that never matured. Driven to control as much of his personal environment as he could, and riding a wave of success that made him a very wealthy man, An Wang made a series of fundamental mistakes that eventually cost his company the longevity, and him personally the legacy, he so desperately wanted.

In the next two case histories the locus of influence was not only at the top but also in the middle, and in both companies the middle rises to do great harm. In addition, both are tales of seemingly irrational behavior by rational executives. It may come as a surprise, then, to learn that the first company is Japanese and sells milk and meat, while the second company is the pride of New England—the Boston Red Sox.

Snow Brand Milk Doesn't Learn from Its Mistakes

On March 1, 1955, nine elementary schools in the Tokyo area reported a major outbreak of food poisoning affecting over nineteen hundred people. Two days later, Tokyo officials announced that they had found staphylococcus in low-fat milk produced by a company called Snow Brand Milk. The company—founded in 1925 as a farmers' cooperative in Hokkaido, the northernmost island in Japan and a region known for agriculture and dairy production—was shocked when the contamination was traced to Snow Brand's Yagumo factory in Hokkaido, where a temporary blackout and problems with new equipment caused the problem.

Snow Brand's reaction was swift. CEO Mitsugi Sato immediately ordered a product recall and halted all sales. He took out advertising space in all the major newspapers to publish a public apology, and rushed off to the factory himself to investigate the matter. Consequently, responsibility for quality control and testing was consolidated in an independent division and multiple layers of quality testing were integrated into the production process. Sato also set out to instill quality into the culture of Snow Brand, distributing regular messages to all employees about the importance of quality and elevating it to a central position in the company's credo.[8] These efforts were successful, and Snow Brand went on to become one of the most trusted names in Japan. By 2000, the company was the largest producer of milk and dairy products in the country.

In Chapter 3 we profiled companies such as Motorola and Rubbermaid and described how influential a company's history can be on subsequent strategic actions. At Snow Brand, the story of the Tokyo food poisoning was kept alive for years. The importance of quality was reinforced via continued distribution of company literature to employees. Somewhere along the line, however, memory started to fade and the practice of sending out quality reminders was stopped. In addition, by the 1990s market conditions began to shift. Deregulation enabled supermarkets to become larger and more consolidated, shifting bargaining power from producer to retailer. Even well-known brands such as Snow Brand were pushed to lower prices as retailers filled shelves with their own private-label store brands. Seeking to meet profitability targets in this tough market, plant managers looked to cut costs wherever they could. Factory production was stepped up not only to keep up with demand but also to squeeze maximum capacity from existing facilities.

The pressure to cut costs came up against the traditional Japanese consumer preference for product freshness. Japanese food producers historically labeled perishables with the production date instead of the expiry date. Milk production followed what was known as a "D-1" schedule—milk was delivered one day after it was produced. Product testing took place while the milk was already on route to stores; even though the test required sixteen hours, if problems were discovered there was still time to recall the product. As pressure grew for product freshness, milk producers even began a "D-0" delivery schedule that brought the product to stores the same day it was produced. Critically, the D-0 schedule prohibited timely testing of product quality, increasing the risk of food poisoning. While the Ministry of Agriculture, Forestry, and Fisheries in Japan advised manufacturers not to deliver within the D-0 window, some companies, including Snow Brand, chose to continue the practice.[9] Now there was no margin for error.

Disaster Strikes

As the pressure increased, something had to give, and it was quality. The Osaka factory started producing one hundred thousand tons of milk, far above its sixty thousand-ton capacity. Production dates were disguised, milk that was returned from stores was reused in other products unbeknownst to customers, numerous breakdowns in cleanliness occurred (e.g., machine valves were not washed or sterilized properly), and operational records were falsified.

The public knew nothing of this . . . until June 27, 2000. That morning the customer service center for Western Japan received a complaint that milk produced by the Osaka factory was causing some people to become nauseous and sick. The first complaint was quickly followed by dozens more, but Osaka took no action. It didn't contact the head office in Tokyo, and D-0 deliveries continued for two more days.

The next day, June 28, the Osaka public health office received a report from a doctor concerning food poisoning apparently due to Snow Brand's low-fat milk. Public health officials quickly started investigating the Osaka factory, but the tainted milk continued to sit on store shelves. As it turned out, June 28 was also the day of Snow Brand Milk's shareholder meeting. The Osaka factory did not report anything to either the Western Japan branch office or corporate headquarters.

Snow Brand top management were finally informed that milk from the Osaka factory was causing food poisoning on the morning of June 29. Later that day, at 4 P.M., the City of Osaka announced that Snow Brand milk was responsible for an outbreak that had sickened more than two hundred people. Finally, at 9:45 P.M. that evening, some sixty hours after the first reports had come in, the president of the Western Japan branch of Snow Brand Milk held a press conference where he admitted that the company's products were responsible for the food poisoning. During this entire time, Snow Brand milk remained on shelves and in customers' refrigerators, exposing additional people to the tainted product.

By July 1, more than six thousand people had become sick, and consumers and the media were outraged that top executives in Tokyo had not even acknowledged the incident, let alone taken responsibility.[10] At a late-night press conference three days later, Snow Brand Milk President Tetsuro Ishikawa abruptly stopped answering questions and rushed to the elevator. Pursued by reporters who demanded that he continue the press conference, he angrily yelled out at them from the elevator, "I haven't slept!"

A reporter responded, "So what? We haven't slept either! Have you ever given thought to the poor children who are suffering in the hospital?"

Ishikawa had no response and quietly agreed to continue the press conference. Captured on camera, this scene was broadcast on national television over and over again, enraging not only consumers in Osaka, but consumers, distributors and even Snow Brand employees all over Japan. Two days later, Ishikawa announced his resignation.

The unsanitary and ill-conceived practices in the Osaka plant came to light in subsequent investigations. In all, thirteen thousand people became ill in this incident, the worst in Japan since World War II. Sales of Snow Brand milk declined 88 percent in July compared to the previous year. Market share dropped from almost 40 percent in June to less than 10 percent. The company swung from a net profit of 3.3 billion yen in fiscal 1999 to a loss of 51.6 billion yen in fiscal 2001.

Disaster Strikes . . . Again

Snow Brand Milk consisted of several subsidiaries besides the large milk business, one of which was Snow Brand Foods—a major Japanese producer of beef, chicken, and pork. In September 2001 the Japanese beef business was hit with bovine spongiform encephalopathy (mad cow disease). The Ministry of Agriculture, Forestry, and Fisheries reacted quickly to protect the beef industry and started a program the following month to buy back domestic beef that had to be destroyed for fear of contamination.

With rapidly declining sales, and the same pressure to meet targets the company had seen earlier with Snow Brand Milk, the temptation to cut corners reemerged. Here's the scam Snow Brand Foods came up with. Buying cheaper imported beef from Australia and labeling it as Japanese beef, Snow Brand Foods submitted the beef to the Ministry's program and pocketed the difference. Unfortunately for Snow Brand Foods, the government inspected one of the company's processing centers the following January and found 13.8 tons of mislabeled beef. Under pressure from the government and consumers, the company voluntarily stopped selling beef and processed beef three days later. Follow-up investigations revealed that the company not only had engaged in similar practices in other processing centers, but had also been disguising the origin of beef and pork for some time to enable higher selling prices.

It didn't take long for the hammer to come down. On February 1, 2002, the government brought charges of fraud and police raided headquarters and other offices to gather additional evidence. After the milk poisoning disaster only two years earlier, the company had depleted its goodwill and ended up closing down the entire Snow Brand Food subsidiary just three months later. Snow Brand Milk looked for ways to isolate the damage and spun out some business operations to joint ventures, including the manufacture and sale of powdered milk for babies. Nevertheless, the stock price sank to as low as 150 yen in May 2002 (from 600 yen a year earlier) before recovering slightly. Snow Brand Milk may yet survive, but the damage is done.

How Could This Happen?

In looking back, it was almost as if Snow Brand management was operating in a vacuum. Delivering milk on a D-0 schedule is about as risky a strategy as you can imagine in an industry where 100 percent safety and reliability is required. One mistake is one mistake too many. In contrast to other high-reliability organizations such as the military, nuclear power plants, and aircraft manufacturers, the lack of production controls seems extraordinary. At Snow Brand, there was a willful attempt to avoid and bypass controls that had historically been in place. Why?

There are three primary reasons. First, the pressure for results had built up to such an extent that plant managers were increasingly unable to extricate themselves from riskier, and over time unethical and illegal, actions. At what point does a drive for efficiency go over the line? How do managers in high-pressure environments know where to draw that line? This is probably why revelations of wrongdoing, or at least cutting corners, kept dribbling out from Enron, WorldCom, and Tyco long after the initial "scandal" story broke. For example, months after Tyco CEO Kozlowski resigned, we were still reading stories in *The Wall Street Journal* about how the company's ADT subsidiary accounted for cancelled security alarm contracts.[11] And for a while it seemed like the totality of WorldCom's accounting "mistakes" would increase week by week. When the culture is wrong, it permeates the entire organization and reaches so far down that it can take years to hear the other shoe drop.

Missing throughout the Snow Brand story is senior executive leadership—people who not only can raise the profitability stakes but can also set unimpeachable ethical standards and provide a guiding light to help meet those aggressive targets. In the absence of clear guidelines on what is appropriate and inappropriate, some people might push the envelope too far. Coupled with a tough competitive environment and intense pressure for results, others might join them. Snow Brand middle management was caught in a powerful centrifugal force from which they could not disentangle themselves.

Second, Snow Brand's was not a culture where it was OK to make or admit mistakes. This was a successful company, a star company really, and one that had built a reputation for excellence. When the milk poisoning hit, Osaka was shocked. But rather than acknowledge that something had gone very, very wrong, Osaka created the fiction that it could solve the problem itself. Its resistance to informing the head office about mass food poisoning speaks volumes about its confidence in containing the problem and its overwhelming fear of admitting that its milk was bad. The notion that the corporate office was preoccupied with the shareholder meeting was simply an excuse to avoid informing the bosses. But while Osaka tried to figure out how to deal with the disaster on its own, its products remained on grocery shelves and refrigerators, infecting additional people that need not have been hurt.

Finally, in the cases of both milk and beef, illegal practices and activities were going on for some time before they were discovered. In fact, they might still be going on if not for the milk poisoning or the government inspection of beef plants. These were not one-time transgressions but a steady pattern of inappropriate behavior. These practices could not have lasted if managers had doubted what they were doing. But it never occurred to Snow Brand management that they could get caught. This was a company with a stellar brand name and a terrific reputation among customers. They could do no wrong . . . so they did. The company's response to announcements of milk poisoning says a great deal. No admission of responsibility, no formal investigations, and a CEO who makes the ultimate public relations blunder by demonstrating a lack of compassion. Meanwhile, none of this sinks in with executives at Snow Brand Foods, who proceed to virtually repeat the disaster in the beef business just a few months later. It's not just that they didn't learn their lesson—they refused to learn their lesson.

This unwillingness to learn, even in the face of clear evidence to the contrary, may have reached its zenith with the Boston Red Sox. And in contrast to virtually every other case we investigated, many of the people we spoke to here—including the first black ballplayer for the Sox (Pumpsie Green) and Mrs. Jackie Robinson—refused to be quoted even after participating in extensive interviews. Why so sensitive? Because the story of why the Red Sox were so slow to break the major league baseball color barrier is really a story about racism, perhaps the ultimate example of irrational behavior.

The Boston Red Sox and the Integration of African-American Players

It matters not what branch of mankind the player sprang from with the fan, if he can deliver the goods. The Mick, the Sheeney, the Wop, the Dutch and the Chink, the Cuban, the Indian, the Jap, the so-called Anglo-Saxon—his nationality is never a matter of moment if he can pitch, or hit, or field. In organized baseball there had been no distinction raised—except tacit understanding that a player of Ethiopian descent is ineligible—the wisdom of which we will not discuss except to say by such rule some of the greatest players the game has ever known have been denied their opportunity.

—unsigned editorial, *Sporting News*, December 6, 1923

On July 21, 1959, Elijah "Pumpsie" Green appeared as a pinch runner for the Boston Red Sox at Chicago's Comiskey Park, thereby becoming the first African-American to appear in a Boston Red Sox uniform in a regular season game. This was a full twelve years after Jackie Robinson integrated baseball with the Brooklyn Dodgers. The Red Sox were the last team in the major leagues to integrate. In the late 1940s, the Red Sox were one of the dominant teams in the American League, averaging 94.6 wins from 1946 to 1950, winning one pennant and twice finishing one game back in the divisional standings. Beginning in 1951, however, the fortunes of the team rapidly deteriorated. From 1951 to 1959, the Red Sox would average only eighty wins, finishing an average of eighteen games behind the eventual American League winner.

While a variety of reasons may have played into this decline, one strong and deciding factor was the unwillingness of the Red Sox management to racially integrate the team. The questions this story raises go directly to the heart of leadership and the core of our thesis. Why did the Red Sox not bring on board an African-American until twelve years after the first major league team had done so? Why did team management choose not to address the shifting dynamics of the diversifying marketplace for player talent? And, remarkably, why did they adopt this posture in spite of the apparent costs to team performance and reputation?

History of Integration and the Rise of the Negro Leagues

Racism was ingrained in organized baseball from its very beginning. As early as 1867, the country's first organized league—the National Association of Base Ball Players—rejected the application of an African-American team for club status. Although sixty African-American athletes played in the majors before 1900, a "gentleman's agreement" among baseball's owners effectively segregated professional baseball with Moses Fleetwood Walker, a catcher for the Toledo Mudhens of the American Association serving as the last African-American to play major league baseball until Jackie Robinson.

As a result of this informal segregation, by the 1920s "Negro Leagues" began to operate as regular leagues, though they were severely limited in financing and organizational stability relative to the established major leagues. Most of the organized black teams survived by barnstorming across the country, sometimes playing several games a day. As James "Cool Papa" Bell, one of the Negro League stars of the 1930s and 1940s, later described it, "We would frequently play two or three games a day. We'd play a twilight game, ride forty miles, and play another game under the lights."[12] Despite the disorganized nature of the Negro Leagues, interest was strong with attendance peaking at over three million fans in

1942. It was the large number of African-Americans who served during WWII, however, that propelled calls for integration. Picketers outside Yankee Stadium proclaimed, "If we are able to stop bullets, why not balls?"[13] While several major league teams expressed interest in Negro League stars by 1942, it wasn't until after the death of baseball Commissioner Kenesaw Mountain Landis, a staunch opponent of integration, two years later that progress was made.

In 1945, Brooklyn Dodgers General Manager Branch Rickey, fed up with the high costs of player development, turned to the Negro Leagues in an attempt to find lower-priced talent. He stated to his traveling secretary, "Son, the greatest untapped reservoir of raw material in the history of our game is the black race. The Negro will make us winners for years to come. And for that I will happily bear being a bleeding heart, and a do-gooder, and all that humanitarian rot."[14] The result: In April 1947, Jackie Robinson exploded onto the field as the first black player in the major leagues, going on to become Most Valuable Player (MVP) in 1949, and beginning a stretch where 9 of the next 11 MVP awards would be won by African-Americans.

The Red Sox and Integration

One of the oldest teams in the American League, the team that would eventually become the Boston Red Sox was founded in 1901 and quickly became a dominant team, winning five World Series from 1903 to 1918. After it traded Babe Ruth following the 1919 season, the famous "Curse of the Bambino" relegated the Red Sox to second-division status for years. By 1946, however, the ball club was once again approaching the upper echelon of the American League, placing eight players on the All Star team and advancing to the World Series before losing to the St. Louis Cardinals in seven games. Over the next four years, the Red Sox established themselves as one of the top teams in the American League, with fans expecting the team to contend for the title each year.

Yet along with every other team in the majors, the Red Sox were tested by the Dodgers signing of Jackie Robinson. Back when discussions concerning integration first arose in the 1930s, the Red Sox organization displayed little interest. Racism, subtle and unsubtle, seemed to pervade the ball club. As David Halberstam writes in *Summer of '49*, "The top management of the Red Sox was mostly Irish, the most powerful group in Boston. They had established their own ethnic pecking order, which in essence regarded WASPs with respect and grudging admiration for being where they already were; Jews with both admiration and suspicion for being smart, perhaps a little too smart; and Italians by and large with disdain for being immigrants and Catholic and yet failing to be Irish. Blacks were well below the Italians."[15]

Ironically, the Red Sox had an opportunity to sign Robinson when he came to Fenway Park for a tryout with fellow Negro League players Sam Jethroe and Marvin Williams on April 16, 1945. The tryout, however, may well have had more to do with the desire of the Red Sox to placate integration proponent Isadore Muchnick, who, as a member of the Boston City Council, could veto the profitable practice of scheduling games on Sunday. One Red Sox scout in attendance commented that Robinson showed as much potential as any other player he had seen, but Red Sox management apparently decided that the players were not ready for the majors and that it would be difficult to assign them to the Red Sox AAA affiliate in racially hostile Louisville.[16]

Willie Mays was another one who got away. Mays, now generally acknowledged as one of the best all-around baseball players ever, was playing for a minor league team known as the Birmingham Black Barons in 1949. The Black Barons played in the same park as the Birmingham Barons, a Boston Red Sox farm team. George Digby, the local Red Sox scout, was impressed with Mays' exceptional talent and immediately called Red Sox General Manager Joe Cronin to tell him Mays was "the best-looking kid I've seen all year"; signing rights were available for $5,000. Cronin later sent another scout down to see Mays, who then reported that Mays was "not the Red Sox type." The ball club thus forfeited a golden opportunity to sign a future Hall-of-Famer.[17]

Although Pumpsie Green finally broke the Red Sox color barrier in 1959,[18] the organization did not make it easy. Signed in 1956, Green had advanced through the Red Sox system, integrating some teams along the way. As spring training began before the 1959 season, pressure was building on the Red Sox to keep Green on the major league roster. With Ozzie Virgil integrating the Detroit Tigers in June 1958, the Red Sox were the last major league team to put an African-American in uniform. Green had a great spring, leading the team in hitting and being voted spring training rookie of the year by Boston writers. The *Boston Globe* wrote,

"Pumpsie Green's performance this spring will earn him a spot on the Red Sox varsity." Nevertheless, Manager Mike Higgins sent Green back to the minor leagues at the end of camp, explaining that "Pumpsie Green is just not ready."[19]

The demotion sparked a firestorm of criticism. The local chapter of the NAACP deemed the move "outrageous" and launched protests. Angry fans carried signs outside Fenway Park declaring "We Want a Pennant, Not a White Team." The Massachusetts Commission against Discrimination also launched an investigation that ended when Red Sox General Manager Bucky Harris promised to integrate accommodations at the Sox spring training facilities in Scottsdale, Arizona, and try to end segregation on the team. Green would not be promoted back to the majors, however, until Higgins was fired and replaced with Billy Jurges later that summer.

Would the Red Sox Have Performed Better with African-American Players?

It's not news that racism was at the heart of the Boston Red Sox story during the era of integration. But was this racism responsible for the team's dismal won–lost record during this time? To answer this question we collected data on major league teams from 1947 to 1959 to assess the relationship between the presence of black players on major league rosters and team success.

First, we identified all African-American baseball players in the major leagues from 1947 (five players) to 1959 (seventy-five players) and their teams. Then, we statistically tested whether a team's won–lost record was influenced by the presence of black players on each team. Our findings: The number of black players relative to league averages was positively correlated with won–lost percentage. Further, thirteen of sixteen teams improved their records after adding black players and, in general, teams with more African-American ball players posted higher win percentages than teams with fewer black players.[20]

Dealing with "Irrational" Behavior: Why Didn't the Red Sox Integrate?

Our quantitative evidence is clear: Baseball teams that chose not to add African-American players to their rosters, or were slower to do so than their competitors, posted weaker won–lost records. Stated differently, organizations that adopted a segregationist strategy were following an irrational strategy, if we assume that it is irrational for baseball teams to adopt low-performance strategies. Why did this happen? Why did the Boston Red Sox act irrationally?

The short answer, of course, is that racism is irrational. But it still begs the question of why people in organizations choose to adopt value-destroying strategies. Here is a classic case of "wooden-headedness." If we could strip out the hate, it is in its own way not much different than other value-destroying, irrational strategies adopted by companies from Motorola to Wang Labs. In each case, there is a fundamental series of choices—sometimes by one person, often by many—that create disadvantage, competitive disadvantage, that can take years, if that, to recover from. Once Motorola fell behind in cell phones, the entire company entered a downward spiral that relegated the company to its own second-division status—an improbable (short-lived?) place for such a storied and successful company. Wang Labs never recovered, lived in a Chapter 11 wasteland for a decade, and then was sold off. And the Boston Red Sox decision to pass on Jackie Robinson, to pass on Willie Mays, to wait until twelve years after competitors began to shift strategies has arguably been the single worst decision in the history of the team.[21]

There were two related organizational pathologies in the Boston Red Sox that enabled irrational behavior to take hold. First, the leadership of owner Tom Yawkey lacked vigilance and logic, and second, the organizational system created to identify and evaluate baseball talent became subverted by individual biases.

Few believe that Tom Yawkey harbored strong racist beliefs, yet he led an organization where racist attitudes and actions met little resistance.[22] Surely the CEO is responsible for setting not just the moral compass of an organization, but its dominant logic as well. Like many CEOs, he relied on his organization to make things happen; yet the organization he was responsible for developing and leading consistently chose to avoid integration. Some have even said that once integration took hold, Yawkey pushed his scouting system to identify potential black ballplayers. In response, old-time scouts would often avoid black prospects, and when they did go to see someone play, they would typically rate the athlete poorly, effectively closing the book on each opportunity as it came up. As baseball historian Glenn Stout said in an interview with the *Boston Globe*'s Gordon Edes, "Yawkey would allegedly go to Red Sox scouts and say, 'How come we don't have any African-American players?' Their response would be, 'We can't find any,' and Yawkey's response to that would be, 'Well, if we can't find any, we can't find any.' "[23]

Beyond the stonewalling of the scouting system, Yawkey also tended to depend too heavily on a comfortable "old boys" network, as he routinely mixed his personal and professional lives by hiring friends to work for the Red Sox. The cronyism that developed became detrimental to the club, as management and hiring decisions were influenced by friends' feelings rather than objective, informed measures. It was this combination of weak leadership, and an organizational system that was only too happy to take advantage of these weaknesses to further their own prejudices, that held the Red Sox in place. Without a moral compass to break through the barriers, or a dominant logic to elevate organizational goals above personal ones, the Boston Red Sox organization chose to adopt an "irrational" strategy with severe, and detrimental, long-term consequences.

The world changed for the Boston Red Sox in the post–World War II years, and they were unable to change with it. This fact, however, misses one of the most important lessons that comes from studying this sorry chapter in sports history. The evidence points clearly to the culpability of the CEO and key management personnel; the Red Sox may be a complex organization with established routines and systems, but it was people, individual people, who chose not to adapt to the wave of integration in major league baseball. They chose not to cope, even in the face of declining team performance (and evidence that the performances of most teams that were quicker to integrate were actually better). While the irrationality of racism is readily apparent to most observers, in other organizations where choosing not to cope takes on less offensive but equally egregious forms—for example, maintenance of market share in the face of new technologies that can leapfrog established positions—managerial actions, or inactions, can have equally calamitous effects. And as with the Red Sox, the roots of such human error lie in the intersection between leadership and organization, and, hence, are present in every company.

Strategy Redux: A Search for the Lessons

When does strategy go wrong? As we have suggested, there are funda-mental fault lines that reside just beneath the surface of many compa-nies that can rise up to shatter strategic initiatives. Vulnerabilities from executive mind-set failures, delusional attitudes, organizational break-downs, and leadership pathologies can all derail strategy, but even before we get to the autopsy, mistakes in strategy can be boiled down to two things: a wrong idea and bad stewardship of that idea. An idea that is "wrong" is not just a bad idea, but an idea that is wrong-headed. It should never have come up in the first place, but it did, usually because of a fundamental misreading of the competitive landscape. In many ways, the idea is almost nonsensical and the stewards of that idea (who include not just CEOs but the managers who are charged with making the idea come to life) put themselves in an even worse place when they try to make the nonsense come true.

That's why Wang Labs is such a classic story of strategy gone bad. The idea that Wang could control every aspect of its existence while it developed a strategy that could destroy IBM was wrong-headed; it was not only unattainable, it also misdirected attention away from what the market and customers were demanding. The stewards of that idea—An Wang and his benevolent dictatorship—followed a logic of action that hindered rather than helped the company compete. Misreading what the customer wanted, relying on proprietary systems, and restricting eq-uity ownership all exacerbated the effects of a bad idea to the point that Wang's strategy just broke down. Companies such as Snow Brand, the Boston Red Sox, General Motors in the 1980s, Mattel, and Schwinn all experienced analogous breakdowns in strategy by relying on wrong-headed ideas and ineffective stewardship. Let's look at the lessons that emerge from stories such as these.

Misreading the Competitive Landscape

Wang Labs underestimated the power of the IBM PC and placed too much emphasis on the importance of proprietary systems (it was not alone in this mistake—see Apple Computer circa 1980). The Red Sox didn't see how efforts by other teams to integrate were improving the quality of those teams. And in a slightly different twist, Snow Brand

Milk didn't realize how competitive pressures to deliver D-0 freshness could undermine its entire business.

One of the most damaging examples of a company misreading competition and, hence, developing a strategy that should never have been adopted, was General Motors in the 1980s. Although the decline of GM is a familiar story, the extent to which the damage stems from this fundamental misreading of the competitive landscape hasn't been sufficiently appreciated.

There were two facts of life that GM faced in the 1980s. First, low-cost, high-quality Japanese imports were starting to gain a foothold in the U.S. market. And second, GM's labor relations were horrible. What to do? The questions GM CEO Roger Smith asked aren't hard to reconstruct. What was the biggest expense on GM's balance sheet? Workers. Who prevented increased operation speeds by threatening to strike? Workers. Who made the production line errors that resulted in defective cars? Workers. Who made life difficult for managers by refusing to do what they were told? Workers.

Roger Smith's solution was bold, brilliant in its simplicity, and, in retrospect, more than a little loony. He would solve all his problems at once by eliminating workers. The vision that inspired him was one of a factory running at high speed, day and night, with no need to pay wages, no complaints, no strikes, and no worker errors. What would make this possible? Robots. Roger Smith would eliminate GM's workers by replacing them with robots. That was how GM would win.

It wasn't completely crazy. Robotics had been improving rapidly and the Japanese were already using robots extensively. The idea of getting ahead of the Japanese, when it came to installing robots, sounded like a good one. Most of all, Roger Smith's vision of the factory of the future sounded to automobile executives like the Promised Land. They were desperately eager to have Smith lead them there.

The problem was that the automation strategy was predicated on a false assumption—that replacing people with machines could turn back the Japanese attack and return GM to dominance in the global auto industry. Rather than adopt the lean manufacturing techniques that still define the Toyota production system today, GM let a virtual obsession with robotics take over. By not understanding how people and machines could be effectively integrated, GM missed the essence of Toyota's low-cost production success. Former Ford President Phil Benton put it this way: Automation would not make the list of major problems facing the auto industry in the 1980s. Consistency of manufacture must come before automation. Toyota is not as automated as Nissan, for example, but is more successful. "Everything goes back to management. What you need to do is engineer the product to the skills of your work force."[24]

The Japanese also excelled at the other fundamental components of lean manufacturing, including just-in-time inventory, supply chain integration, and quality management. "[Automation] didn't save the company very much because GM still needed people," explained Charles McElyea, a factory automation engineer.[25] By simply using the technology without the prepared work force, "all you can do is to automate confusion."[26] Robert Lutz, someone who has witnessed firsthand many of the changes in the auto industry over the years as a senior executive at Ford, Chrysler, and most recently GM, gave this assessment:

> With these totally automated facilities you lose all flexibility, and they are extremely capital intensive. They were prisoners of the great North American manufacturing cost accounting system that says, as you eliminate labor, your costs go down. But what they forgot was they were getting rid of direct labor but replacing it with indirect labor and huge capital costs. These costs were high because the technicians and other people needed in an automated plant were much more expensive than the hourly laborer. You need to look at every worker. You look at his value-added time versus his wait time and you arrange the production flow in such a way that you maximize the value-added time of each worker and reduce the waiting time. You concentrate on the worker, not on the machinery. Use automation only where necessary.[27]

In the end, General Motors invested more than $45 billion in automation during the 1980s, a sum that would have been enough to purchase both Toyota and Nissan.[28] Research by Marvin Lieberman and Rajeev Dhawan of UCLA, who studied productivity trends in the auto industry from the mid-1960s to the 1990s, confirm the story: GM's plant productivity, which had lagged behind Toyota's for years, actually declined further from 1984 to 1991, a period that should have reflected the gains from GM's automation push.[29]

Blinded by the Light: True Believers in Trouble

We are driven by a natural desire to avoid uncertainty, so when we see certainty in direction and action—certainty in strategy—we're impressed. But certainty is not all it's made out to be. How many times have we seen executives and organizations fully ensconced in a world of their making . . . while the rest of the world goes off in another direction? The strategies of the companies outlined in this chapter all have this one attribute in common. They are true believers in trouble.

Wang, like some of the other founder-controlled companies profiled in Chapter 2, broached little opposition in his world. As long as his instincts and actions were on target—as they were in the early years of the company—everyone prospered. But as industry dynamics became more complicated, the Wang style no longer worked so well.

At GM, the problem of vigilance was twofold. On the one hand, Roger Smith was so powerful that few other independent voices could be heard. At the same time, however, the board of directors was ill suited to oversee the feasibility of major initiatives, such as the $45 billion push for robotics.

Snow Brand was so concerned about meeting its profitability targets that managers felt bound by no constraints. Cutting corners was acceptable, and senior management had little interaction with what was going on in the production plants. Even after the milk scandal was well established, Snow Brand's CEO let other executives take responsibility without stepping up himself.

Finally, the Boston Red Sox created an organization that clung to its racist tendencies while other teams were slowly adapting. What was missing was a clear signal from the top that such behavior was no longer acceptable or at least was going to be viewed as counterproductive. Without any real controls on how people could behave in their evaluation of African-American ballplayers, what transpired is not that surprising.

Each of these cases is a cautionary tale for all who seek a world of certainty. Just as we observed in earlier chapters, there is real danger in the status quo, and the risk is highest when true believers take over the organization. It is an argument for flexibility and open-mindedness, two of the core principles for effective strategy and leadership that we will return to in subsequent chapters.

The Mind of the Strategist

When we talk about strategy, it is clear that we must also talk about the strategists. Much of what passes for strategic analysis in companies is based on assessments of competitor attributes and actions as well as economic, demographic, and technological developments and internal strengths and weaknesses. How often do we also consider who the key strategists are? How often do we evaluate competitor moves by paying attention to who is sitting in the driver's seat? Despite these omissions, has any of us seen an organization that is devoid of people making or not making decisions? When strategists make choices, they do so on the basis of their experience, values, and personality, and the more you know about that the more you can understand why companies do what they do.

Combine this idea with an insight we brought up in Chapter 3—history counts too. The culture of a company, along with the strategists who pull the levers, are the two "soft spots" in strategic analysis that are leading indicators of action, or inaction. If you understand An Wang and his demons, then you know a lot about what Wang Labs is going to do. If you understand the history and culture of the Boston Red Sox, you are a little less surprised that they are the last major league team to integrate. Take a close look at your culture and your strategists—they provide a true reflection of your company's strategy.

Desperation Management

We observed a pattern of missed opportunities and escalating commitment in companies such as Iridium, General Magic, Motorola, and Saatchi & Saatchi. But we also saw something in many more companies than we would have anticipated before their ultimate fall—almost desperate actions to right the ship before it sinks. This happens most often when the markets turn against you with a vengeance for missed targets and erratic strategy. How else to explain Tyco's announcement in 2002 that it was giving up on the core strategy of growth that had driven its evolution into a once-successful conglomerate? The pressure was on, questions on accounting were coming up regularly, the economy was in recession, and Tyco's stock was plummeting. Not long afterward, when then CEO Dennis Kozlowski announced that the split-up was off, the press and the market were merciless. Call it desperation management—a late-inning attempt to hit a five-run homer off of Cy Young.

While markets and customers are often accessories to desperation management, it is leaders who pull the trigger. This was true at Tyco, and it was true at Bristol-Myers Squibb (BMS) when it acquired a stake in biotech ImClone in 2001. BMS CEO Peter Dolan took over a company that had let its drug pipeline collapse, and he was under great pressure to find the next blockbuster. He overlooked numerous warning signs—ImClone CEO Sam Waksal's troubling track record, plus questions of whether the FDA would actually approve ImClone's cancer drug Erbitux—to pay a premium price for ImClone.

Desperation management can lead companies to jump from one solution to another, never getting it right in the process. For example, Kmart shifted from diversification (Office Max, Sports Authority, etc.) to IT in an attempt to "out–Wal-Mart" Wal-Mart.

At WorldCom the old formula of debt and acquisitions couldn't make it any more once the telecom bubble burst. Perhaps it was the desire to avoid impending disaster that led some people in the company to book billions of dollars in regular expenses as capital expenditures, boosting earnings.

Finally, at Snow Brand managers in the Osaka plant who were desperate to find the cure ended up creating more damage by not informing authorities of what they had uncovered, leaving tainted milk on store shelves that ended up devastating the brand. What all of these examples have in common is a strategy made worse by falling so far behind that "hail Marys" were seen as the only way out. Two lessons are apparent: For CEOs, don't become so wed to a strategy that you ignore opportunities to adjust course, and for boards of directors, don't let the CEO go to bat in the bottom of the ninth when he has struck out every day for the past four months.

Sometimes It Just Spreads Too Far

In an age of CEO malfeasance and questionable ethics, the desire to rid oneself of all that is wrong in one fell swoop is overwhelming. The usual method is to fire the CEO, and boards have increasingly turned toward this rather coarse tactic to effect a turnaround. While the usual cast of characters appear as Exhibit A—Arthur Andersen LLP, Global Crossing,

Qwest Communications, Conseco, Enron, WorldCom, Tyco, Adelphia, Vivendi, Lernout & Hauspie, Kmart—in actuality a remarkably diverse and well-known set of companies have removed their CEOs in the past five years or so. They include Mattel, Snow Brand, McDonald's, Ford, Bristol-Myers Squibb, CMS Energy, Webvan, ImClone, Gap, Deutsche Telekom, AOL Time Warner, Bertelsmann, and Lucent Technologies, among others.

Whether or not a turnaround ensues after the scapegoat CEO is replaced is far from a foregone conclusion. In some instances, the damage to the organization is so deep, or the extent to which adherence to a flawed logic has spread so wide, that simply replacing the CEO isn't going to do the trick. We see this in major league sports, where the coach of a poorly performing team is sacked in an attempt to shake the players out of their downward spiral. The evidence on the success of this approach is not particularly inspiring,[30] yet the tactic persists because it is impractical to change the entire team. Still, there is considerable risk in relying on the CEO's replacement to fix a company's problems, particularly when those problems not only have spread throughout the organization but have actually been generated by people and the corporate culture they live in.

The Snow Brand story illustrates this trap perfectly. When the milk poisoning scandal hit, it was clear that the CEO was something less than an effective leader in a crisis management situation. His hapless performance in the July news conference made him the perfect scapegoat, but after he left the company did not change at all. Within months the beef business was caught in another scam. It's almost as if a cancer was detected in the organization, the CEO was removed to stop the cancer, but the cancer had spread throughout the managerial ranks.

Does this mean that you can never dismiss the CEO and expect a turnaround? Of course not. There are numerous instances where exactly this type of tough decision needs to be made by a board of directors. And after reading Chapter 9, few readers will think otherwise. However, the key takeaway point here is that sometimes firing the CEO, even if warranted, does not solve the problem, and we should be careful not to assume that it does. Without considering a bigger picture, which may involve cultural breakdowns that influenced and were influenced by a

CEO's tenure, critical stakeholders such as boards, investors, employees, and customers may be in for a big disappointment.

Moving Forward

Removing the CEO may be the right move, but there is no guarantee that such action will create the desired turnaround. This is the real danger in confronting companies with strategies that go wrong, and an important warning sign for us all. A deeper diagnosis into the underlying causes for strategies gone bad is needed—is it the CEO's bad idea, or does the organization itself bear some responsibility? What is the executive mind-set, and how accurately does it reflect the world? Are executives willing to question what is going right and what is going wrong? Are organizational systems and procedures constraining the company's ability to address its challenges? Answers to questions such as these require an even deeper analysis to uncover the true causes of failure. Hence, it's time to stop analyzing what goes wrong at each of the major organizational transitions and stages—be they new ventures, innovative challenges, mergers and acquisitions, or the creation of competitive strategy itself—and refocus our lens on the underlying causes of failure that cut across all types of transitions and stages.

As we shift our thinking and our analysis to the causes of failure, let's keep in mind not only the lessons learned on how to manage the transitions and stages of business, but also the questions that still remain with us. Why do fundamental execution errors continue to occur? Why do successful companies have so much trouble questioning their own actions? Why do organizations adopt systems and procedures that destroy rather than create value? Why are many leaders not just unable to cope with change, but also seemingly unwilling to deal with change? What are the clues that can warn us of potential trouble to come? Why do leaders and organizations find it so difficult to learn from their experience? And above all, how can we develop leaders and organizations that don't keep making these mistakes, that don't fall into the traps that exist in every organization, and that can rise up above the noise and confusion and chaos of everyday business to excel rather than fail? We'll find the answers in Part II.

Things to Remember About Strategy and Managing Competitive Threats

- Competition is nothing more than a group of people in another company who believe that they can offer something to customers that is superior to what you presently offer. Paying attention to what those competitors are doing for your customers is critical.
- There are many ways to assess your strategic position in a marketplace, but something as simple as the "who, what, how" framework can be powerful. Who are you selling to, what are you selling to them, and how are you selling it?
- To understand the strategy of a company, you need to understand the strategists. Without knowing about An Wang's history, could you really understand why his company made the decisions that it did?
- Do you view your competitors as worthy opponents? Beware of the overconfidence that can come with being a market leader. There are too many examples of industry leaders losing position to newcomers who weren't accorded adequate respect.
- Listen to all the sources of information you can find in deliberating on strategy, especially salespeople who are in daily contact with customers. Access to diverse sources of information is valuable to avoid becoming a company of true believers who disregard data that might tell another story.
- Executives who run into trouble tend to rely too much on their own personal preferences that are not backed up with sufficient supporting evidence. General Motors' robotics solution was based on assumptions that would not have been supported if debated openly.
- Pay special attention to struggling CEOs trying to turn around a desperate situation with one well-timed initiative or decision. Often the result will be even worse.
- Don't assume that managers left to implement a senior executive's strategy will actually do what was originally intended. As happened at the Boston Red Sox and Snow Brand Milk, their goals, motives, and methods can lead them badly astray. Leadership at the top is one of the best ways to establish common principles that managers can rely on in doing their jobs.

PART II

THE CAUSES OF FAILURE

While Part I focused on documenting a series of case histories to illustrate what could go wrong during critical business challenges, in Part II we identify the underlying causes of failure evident even across different types of corporate mistakes. As such, Part II offers a deeper analysis of the common patterns of behavior that executives in failing companies exhibited. The four destructive syndromes we discovered were breakdowns in how executives perceived reality for their companies, how people within an organization faced up to their reality, how information and control systems in organizations were mismanaged, and how organizational leaders adopted spectacularly unsuccessful habits. Each of the four chapters in Part II examines one of these underlying factors that account for failure to better understand just what is behind the stories we profiled in Part I, and that we continue to observe in our everyday lives.

The usual theories of failure simply don't explain the fiascoes we witnessed in Part I. The cause of failure is not that executives are unintelligent; you don't have to personally know executives such as An Wang, George Shaheen, Bary Bertiger, Marc Porat, Kun-Hee Lee, William Smithburg, Maurice and Charles Saatchi, Wolfgang Schmitt, and the rest to appreciate their intelligence. The causes of failure are not due to unforeseeable events; as we saw in Part I companies such as Schwinn, Motorola, J&J, Rubbermaid, Wang Labs, and the Boston Red Sox actually knew trouble was brewing but chose not to do much about it. The causes of failure are not any of the other simple explanations that question executive motivation, leadership ability, honesty, the ability to execute, or resource abundance. The real story is much more complex than any of these explanations, and much more fascinating.

CHAPTER 6

Brilliantly Fulfilling the Wrong Vision

How Executive Mind-set Failures Push Businesses
to the Brink . . . and Beyond

The Special Forces moved in with remarkable efficiency. Every phase of the operation had been planned in advance. The soldiers couldn't predict exactly how the opposition would respond, but the alternative scenarios had been thoroughly rehearsed. Each time an unexpected obstacle arose, the team knew how to handle it. Their high-tech communications system kept them in constant contact with each other. Their weaponry was devastating. By the time the operation was over, they had killed or captured everyone in the base they were attacking, suffering few casualties. There was only one problem: The base they had captured belonged to friendly forces. The Special Forces had neutralized the personnel they were there to support.

How did this happen? One suggestion was that the Special Forces had been dropped off at the wrong town. Another suggestion was that the target had been chosen by aerial reconnaissance with no one on the ground verifying the choice. Still another suggestion was that the base had been occupied earlier by enemy forces, but that the battle lines had recently changed.

Whatever the source of the error, the soldiers carried out the operation brilliantly. They were simply operating with a picture of reality that was seriously inaccurate.[1]

Most business failures are like that. In the scores of business failures we investigated for this book, there wasn't a single major breakdown that was due to a company carrying out operations badly. In every case, the real problem was that the company was carrying out the *wrong* operations.

Of course, once a business breakdown has gone far enough, regular operations will begin to break down as well. Many of the companies we studied eventually reached the point where they couldn't seem to do anything right. But the failure to execute operations effectively was a *symptom* of the breakdown, usually one that developed fairly late. It wasn't a *cause* of the breakdown. You can run yourself ragged dealing with execution errors—and of course they require your attention—but to protect yourself and your company, it's crucial that we understand and learn to avoid the more fundamental breakdowns that account for the Motorolas, Wangs, and Webvans profiled in this book.

The real causes of nearly every major business breakdown are the things that put a company on the wrong course and keep it there. There are usually several things that need to go wrong in a business before a full-scale crash is inevitable. But there is one blind spot that appears somewhere near the center of almost every major business disaster: a seriously inaccurate perception of reality among executives.

Where do these mistaken pictures of reality come from? To get a feel for executive mind-set failures and how they hurt a company, it's useful to look at some of the more common varieties. These examples often sound like cases of temporary insanity. But while shaking our heads in amazement, it's important to appreciate how easily an executive could fall into the same traps.

Strategic Misintent

One of the biggest ideas that came out of the 1990s strategy guru's handbook was the notion of strategic intent. The idea is straightforward enough. Focus on a clear, powerful goal that defines what victory would be for your company. Marshal all resources in that direction and never waver in your resolve. In principle, strategic intent is a powerful idea. In practice, well . . . people just seem to get in the way. What looks like a logical intent often breaks down when executives let themselves get caught up in "the one big idea" fallacy without regard to natural and practical limits to the logic. We saw three common patterns of strategic misintent in the companies we studied, each evoking a poignant metaphor: the search for the magic answer, the pursuit of the Holy Grail, and a fixation on the wrong scoreboard.

The Magic Answer

The most seductive of all strategic misintentions is "the magic answer." This is what managers have fallen for when they let all their decisions be guided by one principle they believe is the secret to success. Pursuing the magic answer leads managers to focus on one principle or one model to the exclusion of all others. It encourages one big bet that is often the wrong one.

Most magic answers attribute excessive importance to one single causal factor. They involve a plan or model that is partially valid, but is simply too incomplete to offer an accurate picture of what is going on or what is possible. Many of the failures discussed in this book are due to companies pursuing magic answers at the expense of other, more urgent priorities. The magic answer for General Motors under Roger Smith in the 1980s was robotics. This led GM to invest tens of billions of dollars in automation, despite the fact that its problems stemmed more from production processes than from labor issues. Sony believed that the magic answer for succeeding with new consumer electronic hardware was the availability of compatible software. This led the company to underestimate the importance of alliances with hardware manufacturers, so that its electronic products simply weren't compatible with enough other hardware.

Long-Term Capital Management (LTCM) offers the most spectacular example of all. The hedge fund had a magic answer so seductive that its bosses felt invulnerable, despite having accumulated the biggest liabilities in the history of world business. They were like gamblers convinced that they had the ultimate system for winning at the gaming tables. What made them so confident? They had a Theorem.

The Nobel Prize winners behind the company were said to have a mathematical proof that investing in certain pairs of securities would guarantee a profit. The basis of this proof was the idea that securities with the same ultimate payoff rate would have to converge in price over time. After all, on the day those securities matured, they would be worth the same amount. All LTCM had to do was bet on the higher-priced security going down at the same time that it bet on the lower-priced security going up. When the securities converged in value, LTCM would make money, regardless of whether things such as exchange rates had sent the real value of the securities up or down.[2] From a business stand-point, LTCM's option pricing formula seemed better than a perpetual motion machine because you didn't have to figure out how to harness the output. You just collected your profits, secure in the knowledge that mathematics had proved that the money would keep pouring in.

The warning bells should have gone off as soon as someone used the word *theorem* in connection with a business operation. A theorem is a proposition that is deductively true within the context of a hypothetical, abstract system. The fact that a theorem is "true" tells us nothing about whether the hypothetical system corresponds to something in the real world.

LTCM lost track of this distinction. This is because the option pric-ing model at the core of its operations actually corresponded closely to reality—but only in certain market contexts and under certain condi-tions. Most of all, LTCM's management assumed that securities would continue to be traded and that markets would keep on functioning. They ignored the many ways in which real-world markets could be dis-rupted by outside forces. In effect, they focused so narrowly on their magic answer that they forgot the many constraining assumptions that were necessary for their magic answer to work. When LTCM's picture of reality was ultimately punctured—by real-world events—as seriously inadequate, the effects were disastrous. Losses amounted to more than a billion dollars, with the hedge fund losing 92 percent of its capital.[3]

The Holy Grail

If some businesses head in the wrong direction by universally applying a magic answer, others head in the wrong direction by pursuing a "Holy Grail." A Holy Grail, in business terms, is a strategy that remains forever unattainable. Unlike a magic answer, which attributes excessive impor-tance to one single causal factor, a Holy Grail attributes overwhelming importance to a causal factor *that doesn't even exist.*

The most alluring Holy Grail in recent business history was the "first-mover advantage." Remember the rhetoric that spurred so much early Internet investment? "It's a land grab! A high-tech gold rush! Stake out your territory now!" The main thing that sent so many Internet knights charging pell-mell into the field was this vision of first-mover advantage. It seemed to be forever hovering in the air, just out of reach. It sent everyone stampeding first one way, then another. But it remained exasperatingly elusive. Why?

First-mover advantage, when it exists, comes from three sources. First, the first movers get ahead on the learning curve, leaving latecomers unable to match their expertise. Second, the first movers capture the most productive fixed assets, leaving latecomers to make do with the less productive ones. Third, they lock in potential customers and suppliers, making it expensive for those customers and suppliers to switch their business later.[4]

Internet entrepreneurs were quick to use the learning curve argument. "We've been doing it longer," boasted a senior manager at eToys, a couple of years into the Internet boom. "It takes a long time to get this business right. They can't catch us." But the "they" in this case was Toys"R"Us. Although new to the specific procedures of e-commerce, Toys"R"Us had spent years working its way up the learning curve of selling toys in large volumes at low costs to mass markets. In the bigger business game, it was eToys and the other dot-coms who were behind on the learning curve.[5]

The idea that dot-coms were capturing the most productive assets by moving in first was equally wrong. Internet "real estate" didn't have a limited number of "best locations." Cyberspace could be created as needed.

Finally, the idea of "locking in" customers and suppliers proved almost completely illusionary in this dot-com world. Customers buying from a dot-com weren't committing themselves to any particular system. Switching to a new seller was as easy and inexpensive as a few mouse clicks. Suppliers couldn't be locked in either. Few were willing to make concessions to a dot-com that might jeopardize their longer-established sales channels. It was no different on the supply side, with a seemingly endless array of B2B (business-to-business) start-ups coming online to offer . . . exactly the same service. Near the peak of the Internet boom in 2000, *BusinessWeek* estimated that there were between eight hundred and fourteen hundred business-to-business Internet marketplaces.[6] Doesn't sound like much of an advantage for the early movers, does it?

The whole subject of first-mover advantage should have drawn attention to the vulnerability of most Internet businesses. It was really the longer-established, conventional businesses that had first-mover advantage. To the extent that Internet business represented something truly new, it was a world where first-mover advantage either didn't exist or had to be achieved in entirely new ways. "The good news," said venture capitalist J. William Gurley, "is you can build a portal overnight; the bad news is so can everyone else."[7]

So why did so many clever people go stampeding after the Holy Grail of first-mover advantage in Internet business? It was partly the fear of being left behind, of not being part of the new business revolution. But it was partly the vision of the grail itself. The Holy Grails that people in business periodically pursue are remarkable—but they usually don't exist.

The Wrong Scoreboard

You can avoid the temptations of the magic answer and the Holy Grail and still pursue the wrong goal. This is what happens when a company employs "the wrong scoreboard." A wrong scoreboard is simply an inappropriate measurement of success. A company using the wrong scoreboard might have a fairly realistic idea of what it is trying to do in other respects, but it has chosen the wrong indicator to judge how well it is doing. Any time company executives put too much emphasis on a barometer that doesn't accurately reflect its true level of success, the company risks doing itself damage. When a company goes further, using the wrong scoreboard to the exclusion of all other measurements, it's heading for disaster.

The most common example of a wrong scoreboard is market share. In many contexts, of course, market share is an important indicator of how well a company is doing. But it doesn't measure the value a company is actually creating, nor the value it can capture. What's more, market share does not necessarily translate into profitability, since significant investments are typically needed to build share in the first place. Sony provided a good example of this after acquiring Columbia Pictures. In overseeing the film studio, it let market share take priority over every other aspect of the film production operation, including the level of expenditures employed to achieve market share. The result was that Columbia produced pictures that attracted massive audiences, but cost so much that they also suffered huge losses.

Sometimes a company will choose a more unusual kind of wrong scoreboard. After being celebrated for a specific strength, executives will begin paying too much attention to that strength. If there is some number that purports to measure that area of excellence, executives will start watching that number. This leads executives into using a scoreboard that, over time, will almost certainly turn out to be the wrong one.

In the case of Rubbermaid, the wrong scoreboard was the rate of new product introductions. During the years when it was one of the most admired companies in America, Rubbermaid was constantly praised for its extraordinary rate of innovation in products and designs. Journalists liked to call the company a "new product machine." Management gurus loved to cite the amazing number of new products Rubbermaid had introduced in each previous year. Gradually, the company itself adopted these kinds of descriptions in its public statements and annual reports. In assessing its own performance, Rubbermaid let the rate of new product innovations take priority over almost everything else.

Not only was this the wrong scoreboard, it encouraged Rubbermaid to add to the capabilities it already had in abundance, while further neglecting the capabilities it had never bothered to develop. Rushing new products so rapidly to market left little time for market research and no time for market testing. As a result, Rubbermaid grew more and more out of touch with what its customers wanted, which was often lower prices. Meanwhile, the strategy of always being the sole manufacturer of each new product meant that Rubbermaid had hardly any experience competing on costs. In fact, Rubbermaid was so focused on its rate of new product introductions, that it didn't even know where it stood on other scoreboards, such as cost per unit, compared to the competition. Is it OK to excel in only one core function? Sure, as long as it is excellence in that function that customers care about.

These stories of strategic misintent should give us all pause. Smart executives know that laying out a compelling future is important, even critical, but in their quest to design a persuasive and "stretch" target, many fall prey to the three fundamental traps we just covered. Hopefully we can all learn from the mistakes committed by the executives in this section, but even if we do, we're not out of the woods yet. Beyond strategic misintent is a phenomenon we saw so often during our research that we decided to highlight it in all its guises to help managers avoid making the same mistakes in their own organizations. The phenomenon: "negative transfer."

Negative Transfer: Good Intellect, Bad Place

How many times have we seen executives, consultants, and academics talk about "core competence," "knowledge management," and "learning organizations"? There is little question that over the past fifteen years many companies have concentrated their resources on a few core capabilities and (following the lead of winners such as Intel, Microsoft, Goldman Sachs, Merck, and GE) caught onto the tremendous upside in developing intellectual assets that command huge premiums in the marketplace.[8] Unfortunately, while there is a set of companies that have mastered this strategy, a remarkable number of the companies we studied have stumbled, often badly, in the same arena. Rather than suggest that the strategy is invalid, however, we believe our research shows just how many pitfalls exist on the way to the top—and the main culprit is negative transfer.

We identified four executive mindset failures that get to the heart of why strategies based on intellectual assets don't always work. In each case smart executives rely on flawed assumptions about what works and what doesn't—either for their own companies or for competitors—that provoke inappropriate strategic actions. As you read these next pages, think about how you view your own world—in business or elsewhere—and see if some of the assumptions you make about what works and what doesn't can stand up to scrutiny.

Yesterday's Answer

Yesterday's answer, where a business is concerned, is any picture of reality that once worked, but is no longer valid. The seductive thing about yesterday's answer is that it already seems to have withstood the test of practical application. People defending yesterday's answer will invariably point out how successful it has been. "You can't argue with success," they say implicitly, if not outright. But companies operating with yesterday's answer are assuming that a formula that worked in the past is still valid today. In a world of rapid change, this is often not the case.

Many of yesterday's answers are summed up in the statement, "We know what our customers want." Barneys, the New York clothing store, provides a particularly striking example. The Pressman brothers, who inherited the store, believed without question that they knew what their customers wanted—and what would make them willing to pay premium prices. It was exclusivity, and the best way to convey this aura was to invest heavily in the most luxurious store furnishings possible. The chronicler of Barneys' rise and fall, Joshua Levine, described this business concept as "Pressman's Law"—the idea that "whatever you spend on interior decoration, you will recoup through higher-priced garments."[9] It was this concept that led Barneys to prosper mightily throughout the 1960s and 1970s.

The problem was that by the mid-1980s times had changed. The expenditures necessary to create an atmosphere of luxury had risen enormously, especially in a large department store such as Barneys. Meanwhile, trendy designer boutiques were offering more exciting shopping experiences to the same customers, providing exclusivity that a big department store, no matter how lavishly appointed, could not. But the response of the Pressmans, to the extent that they were aware of the problem, was to spend even more on yesterday's answer, a type of negative transfer.

The most common of yesterday's answers are well-designed and well-made products that fulfill customers' needs from the past, but are no longer what customers want. Usually, the pride that a manufacturer takes in its product often prevents it from recognizing that its customers would increasingly prefer something else. Schwinn was offering this type of yesterday's answer when it continued to build traditional bikes, rather than mountain bikes, trail bikes, stunt bikes, and the other specialty bikes that people increasingly preferred. Motorola did the same when it continued to build fancy analog phones, rather than the digital variety its customers were clamoring for. The fact that such companies often have famous brands or are making regular improvements in their products only distracts them from the fact that they've lost touch with their customers' needs.

Even when companies *do*, in fact, know what their customers want, they can do terrible damage by employing yesterday's answer when it comes to supplying that want. This is often fairly obvious, at least in retrospect, when it comes to new technology. No one has demonstrated this better than the American steel companies that have continued to rely on giant mills after the introduction of minimills. Without huge subsidies in the form of tariffs, they had little hope of surviving. Relying on

146 ■ WHY SMART EXECUTIVES FAIL

yesterday's technology when the world has moved on is clearly a good prescription for business failure. But yesterday's answer can be *any* business practice that fails to meet customers' needs as well or at as low a cost as the newer practices.

The Boston Red Sox were guilty of relying on yesterday's answer when it came to satisfying their customers' wants. They didn't have any confusion about the fact that their fans wanted to see the team play brilliant baseball and win games. But the team's managers and owners thought they could meet that need without hiring any African-American athletes. For a dozen years, teams playing against the Red Sox increasingly drew on African-American players to help field more competitive teams, but the Boston Red Sox stuck with yesterday's answer, losing games, fans, and money.

An equally effective way to destroy a company is to employ yesterday's answer when it comes to negotiations. The most common mistake is to assume a company's bargaining power has remained the same, despite changing market conditions. Companies doing this will often tell themselves, "They need us so much, they'll have to keep doing it our way."

Britannica's experience in this area was an especially dramatic one because its senior executives destroyed most of the company's value simply by applying yesterday's answer in its negotiations with software providers. CD-ROMs, high-capacity hard drives, and the Internet made it possible to search and deliver the information in an encyclopedia much more cheaply and conveniently than before. Huge populations that could never have afforded a printed encyclopedia would be willing to pay a modest sum for an electronic version. Hence, Britannica possessed an asset of enormous value, but only if it was willing to accept a much smaller share of a much bigger volume of sales. Companies such as Microsoft that were interested in producing an electronic version of the famous encyclopedia understood this. But Britannica met them with yesterday's answer, assuming its best strategy was to capture the lion's share of a high-priced product. When negotiations broke down, Britannica produced its own CD-ROM version but at a price hardly anyone was willing to pay. Even today, years after CD-ROMs and Internet options became standards, Britannica is still struggling to market an electronic encyclopedia that can stand up against Microsoft's Encarta product and other competitors.

Executives who rely on yesterday's answer in their company's product designs are also frequently guilty of employing yesterday's answer in their negotiations. Schwinn, for example, believed that it had fierce customer loyalty and, because of this, thought that it controlled its suppliers such as Giant Bicycle and CBC. In fact, the relationship had flip-flopped to where it was Schwinn that was the dependent partner. By manufacturing a product that was closer to what Schwinn's customers wanted and at a lower price, Schwinn's suppliers were able to go around it and sell directly to Schwinn's market.

A Different Game

A company's perceptions of reality often become obsolete not because times have changed, but because it has moved into a new area where its version of reality is no longer valid. Often the company is already very successful in a market that doesn't allow much further room for expansion. In an attempt to leverage its core competencies, it will attempt to apply those competencies to another market that seems on the surface to be very similar. But it will miss the differences beneath the surface that require a different approach.

A company in this situation has begun playing "a different game," even though its executives haven't recognized the fact. Usually, executives simply assume that skills and formulas that worked before will keep on working in the new market or for the new product. "We're the experts at this," they assure anyone who questions the way they're handling things. For example, Toro went from building lawn mowers to manufacturing snow throwers, a natural extension of product directed toward potentially similar customers. Yet, the surface similarities—seasonal market, mid-range price, homeowner customers—masked a simple, yet critical, difference. Grass grows, but snow doesn't always fall! Then, despite one snowless winter, Toro continued to make snow throwers, only to be hit with another season without snow. As former Toro CEO David McLaughlin said, "We were blind to the risk."[10]

Companies can stumble into a different game when they move to or expand beyond a geographical area where things look much the same, but aren't. This is what happened to the Food Lion grocery chain, for example. As long as it stayed in the Southeastern U.S., its formula emphasizing low costs and low prices delivered what its customers wanted. But as soon as Food Lion moved into the Southwest, it ran into trouble. Even though everything looked much the same outwardly, Southwestern customers expected a variety of selection and a level of service that Food Lion didn't know how to provide.[11] Brilliant cost cutting in this different game was actually a formula for failure.

A company can find itself in a different game without moving into new territory in a geographic sense. This is what happened to Quaker, for example, when it expanded beyond Gatorade to take over the Snapple brand. The Gatorade model wouldn't work for Snapple, however, because Quaker executives never understood the differences in brand image and distribution. It was a different game.

A False Self-Image

Being wrong about your own competencies can be just as destructive as being wrong about what game you are playing. In fact, if a company has a "false self-image," any expansion or other change in activities tends to put it in the wrong game. The company will try to leverage its capabilities. But, having a false idea of what it is, the company will try to do something that it's not really good at, in a sense transferring intellect it doesn't even have! Meanwhile, the company will neglect or even squander its genuine strengths.

This regularly happens to companies that have had a great degree of success, but misunderstand the reason why. A company will set out to make shoes, for example, or manage advertising campaigns. Somewhere along the way it will carry out an activity connected with this task so well that it's catapulted to a new level of success. But the company's self-image will usually be based on what it set out to do, not on the particular thing it did that made it successful.

L.A. Gear is a perfect example. It made the mistake of thinking that it was a maker and seller of athletic shoes. "Wait a minute," you might say. "L.A. Gear *was* a maker and seller of athletic shoes." Well, yes, that's what it originally set out to be. But what catapulted it in five years from $11 million to $820 million in sales was actually an insight into girls' fashions. Entrepreneur Robert Greenberg noticed that his daughter's junior high school friends were wearing boys' hightop athletic shoes. In place of the canvas workout shoe he'd already been selling, Greenberg introduced girls' hightop basketball shoes with pink, turquoise, and silver trim. When these caught on, he added shoes with rhinestones, palm tree silhouettes, and other styling details. These were promoted with TV ads featuring sexy, athletic girls enjoying an idyllic Southern California lifestyle. Soon L.A. Gear was selling more athletic shoes than any other company except Nike and Reebok.[12]

The problem was that Robert Greenberg thought that L.A. Gear was good at making and selling athletic shoes, when what it was really good at was producing a girl's fashion accessory. This misconception led the company to expand from girls' fashion shoes into men's high-performance athletic shoes. The new type of product required different shoe technologies and different marketing strategies, directed at a different kind of customer. But L.A. Gear went after the new market with garish Michael Jackson buckle shoes and other ploys that would have been more appropriate for thirteen-year-old "Valley girls."[13] In the process, it completely undermined its cool image. The comic mishaps culminated in a televised basketball game in which the players' complimentary L.A. Gear shoes actually fell apart during the broadcast. What wasn't comic was the effect on sales, which fell by 80 percent, and on inventories of unsold shoes, which soon totaled twelve million pair. L.A. Gear's false self-image helped to drive the company into bankruptcy.

The Film Producer Error

Making the film producer error means failing to take sufficient account of the specific and often unique attributes that made a particular venture so successful. We call it "the film producer error" because no group of businesspeople commits this sort of error more spectacularly, more frequently, and more publicly than film and television producers. Each time there is a huge hit in movie theaters or on television, there will be dozens of expensive failures that have no reason for getting produced . . . except that they have some superficial quality in common with the hit. If a movie adapted from a superhero comic becomes a huge hit, there will be another dozen movies produced that have nothing to recommend them, except that they were adapted from superhero comics. If a television show featuring crime scene investigations hits big, there will be a string of lackluster follow-up series, pilots, and made-for-TV movies featuring crime scene investigations.

Pharmaceutical giants SmithKline Beecham and Eli Lilly made the film producer error when their rival Merck surprised them by acquiring a pharmacy benefit manager (PBM). This was new; it was not previously an element of either company's strategy. In fact, Eli Lilly's CFO said later, "We looked at Merck's move and said, 'What the hell is a PBM?' "[14] But both companies thought Merck must know what it was doing, and if Merck had a PBM, they figured that they each better have one too. So the following year, SmithKline Beecham bought one for $2.3 billion, and Eli Lilly bought one for $4 billion. The rationale for the purchases was that a pharmacy benefit manager would give them more control over downstream distribution. But this was an untested strategy, and it made more sense for Merck, which had made detailed plans for its acquisition, than it did for the other pharmaceutical giants. Within a few years, each of the copycat companies had sold its acquisition at a stiff discount, and even Merck was in the midst of spinning off its own PBM, Merck-Medco.[15] Other industries, such as entertainment and banking, also went through a spate of copycat mergers in the late 1990s and are still dealing with the fallout.

Companies making the film producer error aren't necessarily trying to reproduce a rival company's success. Often companies will copy a move by a successful rival even when they have no reason to believe that the particular move was a good one. After America West bought the rights to splash its logo on the home of the Phoenix Suns in 1989, *seven* other North American airlines bought the naming rights to various ballparks and arenas. But how many of these expenditures were an optimal use of promotional money for a company trying to fill airplane seats? The people who fly to other cities to attend sports events are hardly a significant portion of the air travel market. So why were so many airlines falling into the film producer error? Most of these companies were painfully aware that America West was doing better than they were, but didn't know how to emulate it in any deeper way—so they emulated it in a superficial way.

The airline industry is the scene for one of the more blatant, and unsuccessful, attempts to replicate a winning strategy without understanding why it was a winner. After years of dominating the Southern California market, in 1994 United Airlines found itself far behind Southwest Airlines with its industry-leading customer service, quick aircraft turnaround, and low fares. United's solution: Copy Southwest. So out came the ground agents in shorts and golf shirts, matching low fares, and frequent service. Unfortunately, the real secret to Southwest's success was its people—loyal, energetic, creative, motivated people from pilots to flight attendants—and United was still a company whose own employees said things such as, "We've always been treated like angry children who don't deserve what they get."[16] This was a classic example of negative transfer: United tried to replicate some elements of Southwest's strategy without really understanding what lay at the core of that strategy—people.

Businesses can be led into the film producer error not just by failing to appreciate the deeper reasons for their rival's success, but also by failing to appreciate the deeper reasons for their own success. When this happens, a company that has had a success at one venture will embark on similar ventures, believing that "this is the sort of thing we're good at." Sony, for example, had considerable success with its acquisition of CBS Records. This caused its managers to incorrectly assume that Sony had the right policies and capabilities for acquiring and managing another American entertainment industry company. The ironic result was that the film producer error led Sony to get involved in film production.

So ends our stories of negative transfer. It's likely that many readers will see themselves or their own businesses in some of these stories, and that's just the point. Negative transfer is an eye-opener that offers a critical lesson: Not only is knowledge or intellect not always valuable, knowledge can actually be toxic. Negative transfer exists in multiple guises, and is often cloaked in the seemingly unimpeachable logic of core competence, so we need to be especially alert to how the logic can kill when applied superficially. The next section goes beyond negative transfer to zero in on the three final types of mind-set failures we observed in our research, all examples of "one-track mind(-set)."

One-Track Mind(-set)

Have you ever worked in an organization where the answer to every business problem always seemed to be the same? Have you ever looked back at an important decision you made and wondered why everyone didn't think the way you did? Have you ever been surprised by the way customers, partners, employees, and other key stakeholders just didn't seem to get it? It may well be, not that others don't understand you, but that you're operating under incredibly narrow assumptions about what's possible and how people should behave.

It's a Small World

With the benefit of hindsight, the mistakes businesses make often seem *so obvious* that it's hard to see how anyone could have made such an error. "What were they thinking?" people exclaim incredulously. "How could they have imagined, even for a minute, that such a thing could succeed?" The answer in many of these cases is some variation on "it's a small world." This is what befalls companies when executives, senior engineers, and others base their assessments of reality on experiences they've had that are simply not representative of the larger world.

One of the most common ways that a small world comes into play is when a group of technologically sophisticated executives in an engineering-driven company get the "new new thing" in their heads . . . and no matter what it ends up costing, they just can't let go. What was Iridium, after all? An idea hatched by a talented engineer who set out to solve his wife's problem of making phone calls from faraway lands. Here's how one knowledgeable observer saw it: Motorola set out to "design, build, and implement the greatest radio system in the world . . . so, what you had here was a fantasy which had to be implemented notwithstanding the considerable business irrationality associated with it. This is not an issue of strategy . . . this is an issue of fantasy, of hysteria."[17]

When highly paid executives with generous expense accounts imagine that large populations share their values, interests, and priorities, it becomes easier to see where Iridium came from. Iridium executives and design engineers, for example, believed that five hundred thousand people would be willing to pay $3,000, plus up to $8 per minute, to make phone calls with a cumbersome headset from remote places. Whom were they thinking of? They were thinking of tech jocks like themselves, who go gaga for the latest innovation, and other executives with money to burn. Would Iridium CEO Ed Staiano care if a telephone were heavy and cumbersome? No. He wouldn't be carrying it around; one of his assistants would. Would Staiano think $8 per minute was a hefty charge? No. His pay per minute was so high, $8 per minute would have seemed almost negligible. What about the $3,000 charge? The company would no doubt pick up the cost as a standard expense account item. And if someone asked, Iridium could point out that making their communication lines more direct even a few days a year would easily be worth more than $3,000. In short, what seemed reasonable in Staiano's small world was a long way from what would seem reasonable in the world where most people live.

Executives living in particular geographic locations can be just as cut off as executives living in the stratospheres of wealth and power. The family who controlled Barneys, for example, assumed that the tastes and styles popular in their Manhattan milieu would be popular in other American cities. When Barneys' later CEO, Thomas Shull, looked back at the company's failed attempt to expand into places such as Southern California and the Midwest, he said, "Barneys had taken a New York store and placed it in other cities without really appreciating the needs and wants by market."[18] It never occurred to the company that what seemed the height of fashion in Manhattan could seem pretentious or simply inappropriate in the different social and physical climates of other cities.

Despite sending their products directly to all parts of America, the broadcast and print media are constantly plagued by misjudgments founded on their small-world bias. Programs and program segments originating in Washington regularly bore or irritate their national audiences by presenting stories geared too exclusively to people "inside the Beltway." Book publishers living in New York regularly overlook subjects of obsessive interest to people in the Midwest, South, and Rocky Mountain states, while sometimes paying out millions in advances for books that are only of interest to small segments of New York society. Magazine writers working in New York and Los Angeles regularly write condescending articles on the social attitudes, fashions, music, and popular entertainments that the rest of the country loves.

Home Field Rules

When companies begin operating in different regions, countries, or cultures, the notion that "it's a small world" is only one of the assumptions they need to drop. Often the basic conventions for conducting business— the ideas, for example, of what constitutes fair practice or due diligence— will be quite different. If companies don't appreciate these differences, they can easily fall victim to "home field rules." This is what happens when executives assume that their counterparts elsewhere will play by the same rules that they play by at home. They fail to recognize that the field of play is now *someone else's home field* and that different home field rules apply.

Americans and Europeans are used to thinking of this as a problem they face when they try to do business outside the Western world. But it's a problem others are just as likely to encounter when they try to do business in America and Europe.

When Sony acquired Columbia Pictures, Sony's Japanese bosses assumed that American businesspeople would be operating within the same ethical codes as the Japanese. Chief among these Japanese ethical codes are the ones associated with *giri*. *Giri* has no literal translation, but it includes a feeling of moral obligation to superiors and superordinate goals. In effect, the Japanese managers assumed that the American Columbia Pictures management would feel the sort of moral obligation toward their new parent company (a type of *giri*) that Japanese managers would feel. It never occurred to them that the American managers would act as though they *had no* obligations, brazenly putting self-interest ahead of company goals. Yet this is what happened—on a big-screen scale.

In addition to the basic cultural differences, there were particular reasons why home field rules for Columbia Pictures were especially remote from the ones Sony assumed would apply. One is that the specific nature of the movie industry in Hollywood leaves little room for company loyalty or long-term corporate relationships. Another reason is that the particular managers Sony picked to head Columbia Pictures were known for big, high-risk deals, not steady, follow-through work. Finally, Sony's acquisition of Columbia Pictures took place during a wave of anti-Japanese sentiment. Japanese businesspeople had recently been buying American business icons, boasting about Japanese business success, and lecturing Americans on the need to follow the Japanese example. It didn't occur to anyone in Hollywood that the Japanese needed or deserved special protection from American hustlers.

Expansion Fever

The third type of mind-set failure that our one-track mind executive is prone to is a little different than the previous two, but equally important.

This type of failure is specific and remarkably common. Call it "expansion fever." It's what a company is suffering from when it pursues rapid expansion at the expense of profitability and without controlling liabilities. Expansion fever usually involves a mind-set breakdown that goes far beyond a failure to use the right barometers for success. Managers in the grip of expansion fever see every number or fact in terms of its effect on their ability to keep expanding. Creating value for people, doing something worthwhile, and even making profits get pushed aside. To maintain a high or accelerating rate of growth, executives with expansion fever will often destroy value, do things they know will benefit no one, and operate at a loss.

When Maurice and Charles Saatchi were in the grip of expansion fever, they illustrated nearly every kind of misstep that can come from letting rapid expansion take priority over everything else. They went after new acquisitions without pausing to consider how those companies might be integrated into the firm's existing operations. They often paid more for an acquisition than the profits from the acquisition could justify. In the process, they accumulated massive debts and other liabilities. Once a company was acquired, they did little to make sure that they were getting maximum value out of it. As time went on, they increasingly expanded into areas such as business consulting that required different managerial procedures than the ones they had in place. None of these missteps were due to any fundamental lack of managerial ability on the part of the Saatchi brothers or their senior executives. They were simply concentrating so much on expansion that they neglected to consider profitability.

Oxford Health Plans, the health maintenance organization in New York, had an even worse case of expansion fever. Under founder and CEO Stephen Wiggins, growth for the sake of growth dominated everything else, including a reasonable management of liabilities. After thriving with a white-collar clientele, who had low sickness rates, Oxford Health Plans expanded into blue-collar workers, Medicare, and Medicaid patients (groups that tended to run up higher health care costs) without considering whether this was a profitable area of health care to be in. This rapid expansion meant that its computer systems and other administrative apparatus were getting further and further behind. One senior manager described the scene as follows: "We were going out of control. The same check—identical checks—were sent out twice."[19] But even when the attempt to install a completely new software system failed disastrously, leaving customer billings and claims payments in near chaos, the company didn't slow its expansion. It plunged on with new offerings and another major acquisition as though it had everything under control.

So there you have it. Strategic misintent, negative transfer, and one-track mind-sets are behind many of the business breakdowns you've seen, read about, or perhaps even participated in. What can you do to avoid these scenarios in the future?

Make Sure Your Company's View of Reality Is Valid

In all these examples where mistaken perceptions of reality were used to guide large companies, there is one big, recurring paradox: What seems *obviously false* with the benefit of hindsight seemed *obviously true* at the time. In fact, in most cases, the false reality seemed *so* obviously true that *no one thought to question it.*

This is perhaps the biggest lesson of all. If you want to catch your company before a mistaken picture of reality has done too much damage, you have to stop and question the things that seem obvious. You have to take the prevailing assumptions, the things that "go without saying," and scrutinize them to see if they are really true.

But how do you go about doing this? Each type of failure we've described suggests a basic question that every company should periodically ask itself. The resulting list of questions can be used as a tool for scrutinizing each key aspect of your company's perception of reality.

▪▪▪

Is Your Company's View of Reality Valid?

Ten Questions to Help You Make Sure

STRATEGIC MISINTENT

1. Are you in danger of focusing on one principle or model to the neglect of all others? (The Magic Answer)
2. Is it possible that you're pursuing a strategy that isn't attainable? (The Holy Grail)

3. Could you be using an inappropriate barometer for success? (The Wrong Scoreboard)

NEGATIVE TRANSFER

4. Are you assuming that what's worked in the past is what you still need today? (Yesterday's Answer)
5. Has your company moved into an area that requires a different approach than the one it used successfully elsewhere? (A Different Game)
6. Is it possible that you have an inaccurate idea of your own competencies, relative to the competition? (A False Self-Image)
7. Are you in danger of incorrectly attributing your past success or the success of your competitors? (The Film Producer Error)

ONE-TRACK MIND(-SETS)

8. Are your ideas of what your customer needs based on limited models or experience? (It's a Small World)
9. Are you trying to operate in a culture where you might not understand all the unspoken conventions? (Home Field Rules)
10. Have you slipped into pursuing rapid expansion at the expense of real profitability? (Expansion Fever)

Predicting Change

When you have verified, as well as you can, that your perception of reality is accurate, you'll have gone a long way toward preventing a major business failure. But there is still something else to consider when it comes to evaluating pictures of reality—how long the reality will *remain* valid.

A company can have a perfectly unbiased picture of reality, but if the world is about to change dramatically, and the company isn't prepared for that change, it can still be headed for disaster. To prosper for an extended period of time, a company needs to have an adequate understanding of what parts of its reality could change. What are the most common ways in which our perception of reality could be wrong?

The Perfect-Storm Fallacy

In the book, *The Perfect Storm*, author Sebastian Junger describes how three relatively ordinary storm systems came together in the North Atlantic to produce a single storm of immense ferocity. The "perfect-storm fallacy" is the belief that because each of the events contributing to such storms is unlikely, the coincidence of two or more events that could generate a perfect storm is also unlikely.

Perfect storms, however, are a great deal more frequent than people suppose, whether at sea or in business. This is because the total number of possible events that could contribute to a perfect storm is often quite large, as is the total number of combinations of those events and the total number of opportunities for those events to arise. So, while the likelihood of one particular combination that would result in a particular perfect storm might be very small, the likelihood of some unspecified combination that would result in some unspecified perfect storm might be very large.

This might sound fairly obvious when put this way, but even experts in risk and probability regularly get it wrong. LTCM demonstrated how readily intelligent people schooled in probability theory can succumb to the perfect-storm fallacy. The company's executives and advisers were aware that a large-scale market disruption, especially a major devaluation or default, could threaten their investments. So, they allowed for the possibility of such an event in their calculations. What they *didn't* allow for was the possibility of *two or more* such events. But of course they happened. Mortgage-backed securities slumped severely, and Russia defaulted on its loans. Then an unlikely sounding series of smaller events seemed to go against LTCM, one after another. Securities proved unexpectedly hard to unload. Backers were unexpectedly reluctant to invest more. Trading partners were unexpectedly aggressive in taking advantage of LTCM's predicament. Executives within LTCM started making unexpected mistakes.[20] It seemed to be an extraordinary string of bad luck.

Once things started to go wrong, each misfortune LTCM experienced helped to cause further misfortunes. The particular disruptive events that beset LTCM might have each been unlikely. But over any extended period of time, *some* kind of disruptive events, with the potential to have similar consequences for LTCM, were virtually inevitable. The experts in probabilities who were running LTCM estimated their probabilities wrong.

Of course, you don't have to have Nobel Prize winners helping you with your numbers to estimate completely unrealistic odds for a perfect storm. Numerous companies regularly add to their troubles by wildly underestimating the extent to which unlikely events can pile up. Oxford Health Plans, for example, underestimated the number of things that could go wrong as it tried to put a new computer system into operation during a time of rapid expansion.[21] Mossimo, the trendy Irvine apparel company whose cool and breezy line of clothing helped to define Southern California's beachwear culture, underestimated how many things could go wrong as it tried to expand its range of designs, increase production, and deliver to new customers all at once in the mid-1990s.[22] Chrysler underestimated the extent to which numerous business conditions could start changing at the same time, so it had to respond to all of them simultaneously.[23] As these examples suggest, perfect storms are not quite the rare event that some executives imply. Rather, they are quite robust indicators that executive mind-sets are flawed.

The Star Wars Error

If the perfect-storm fallacy makes people too prone to think things *can't* happen, the "Star Wars error" makes people too prone to think things *can* happen. The federal government provides the classic example, beginning when the administration of President Reagan was trying to find a better way to defend America against the ballistic missiles of the evil empire. Senior officials, including the president, were thinking about the great technological initiative that had put a man on the moon. The *Star Wars* movies with their futuristic beam weapons were also fresh in people's minds. So the Reagan administration decided to launch a great technological initiative that would produce futuristic beam weapons to shoot down ballistic missiles. They would make science fiction into reality—just as the Kennedy administration had done.

The only problem with this Strategic Defense Initiative was that the scientific principles that would make it possible had yet to be discovered. Bold though it was, the lunar space program had relied entirely on existing science. The Strategic Defense Initiative, on the other hand, couldn't succeed without some genuinely new scientific breakthroughs. This made scheduling it and budgeting for it virtually impossible.[24] Only now, twenty years and billions of dollars later, are we getting close.[25] The problem is that for businesses that must show a reasonable return on investment, however, twenty years to become operational (no one's talking profitability, of course) is a tough thing to justify.

The Star Wars error occurs when companies fail to distinguish between tasks that require routine engineering and those that require new discoveries. It's when businesses expect research teams to stick to project schedules and preset budgets when they are trying to do something genuinely new. More important, it's when businesses make large investments in expensive systems before all the components of those systems have been shown to be workable. Iridium, for example, failed, in part, because of the Star Wars error. The people planning the venture in 1991 thought that by the time it was operational there would be new technology making the hand-held units cheaper and less cumbersome.

Big corporations are often damaged by the Star Wars error when they base their strategies on basic discoveries that haven't been made yet. But the bulk of the businesses that go under completely because of the Star Wars error are the hundreds of small high-tech start-ups that think they are betting on emerging technologies, when what they are really betting on is emerging basic research.

The Big-Picture Illusion

One of the greatest dangers when it comes to envisioning change can be described as the "big-picture illusion." This is the trap executives fall into when they adopt a strategy that makes sense at the big-picture level, but comes apart at the smaller-scale level where it must be implemented. The most conspicuous sign that someone is vulnerable to the big-picture illusion is a lofty disdain for detail. "Just give me the executive summary," these leaders often say impatiently. "I have to concentrate on the big picture."

It's too much attention to the big picture at the expense of the details, including synergies and integration, that lies behind a large portion of the failed acquisitions that take place each year, as was the case for Quaker. Before the acquisition and after, Quaker failed to pay enough attention to the exact details of the contracts and relationships that Snapple had with its distributors. As a result, Quaker's senior executives were trying to make changes in their distribution policies that weren't even contractually allowable at the level of the individual distributors.[26]

Companies don't need to be involved in acquisitions or corporate restructurings to fall victim to the big-picture illusion. Any thorough attempt to renovate operations is likely to fail if senior executives haven't given enough consideration to exactly what it would mean at the level of the smallest operational units, the specialized employees, and the existing customer and supplier relationships. GM's automation effort was an even bigger disaster than it would have been otherwise because its senior executives failed to determine at the beginning exactly what capabilities the company's different components needed in order to automate. Rubbermaid made its troubles worse because when it eventually responded to the challenges it faced, its executives tried to impose policies the organization didn't have the capabilities to carry out.

None of these cases were failures in execution. They all involved companies adopting policies that *couldn't* be executed, no matter how brilliantly midlevel managers went about their work. The strategies that sounded so convincing at the highest level simply could not be carried out by those companies.

The extent to which managers can succumb to the big-picture illusion is awesome. For years the DaimlerChrysler merger, for example, failed to work operationally by anybody's reckoning. It destroyed corporate value roughly equal to the total purchase price of the Chrysler Corporation. But even after *acknowledging* these disastrous consequences, CEO Jürgen Schrempp continued to defend the merger as "an absolutely perfect strategy."[27]

The Wrong Competitors

One of the simpler ways in which businesses inaccurately predict change is by focusing on the wrong competitors. Usually, this happens because executives assume that the companies that have been their main competitors in the past will continue to be their main competitors in the future. This causes them to underestimate the effects of new competitors entering the market, and it often leads them to overlook the possibility that minor competitors could suddenly become major ones. Executives in businesses that have been the market leader for some time, or have been engaged in an intense competition with a very small group of rivals, are especially prone to make this mistake. The more a business concentrates on winning the competitive battles in which it is already engaged, the less likely it is to be prepared for future battles with completely different competitors.

You may think you know your competitive space too well to make the mistake of focusing on the wrong competitors. But it's the businesses that seem to have mastered a particular competitive space that are actually most prone to identify their future competitors inaccurately. Schwinn was certainly the master of its competitive space. But that is why it overlooked the possibility that its foreign suppliers might enter its U.S. market with lower-priced products. A number of dot-com retailers mastered their competitive space, but it led them to underestimate the threat from traditional retailers, who had been watching the Internet battles from the sidelines.[28]

A Static Business Model

A similar but more dramatic way in which executives inaccurately predict change is by assuming "a static business model" for their industry. This means that they behave as though business in the future will follow the same models it has followed in the past. They neglect to consider the ways in which their entire industry could be transformed or made irrelevant by new technologies or new business practices. When a big change does come, requiring the company to adopt a new business model, these executives are left totally unprepared.

Fruit of the Loom is a classic case of a company assuming a static business model in a time of change. The North American Free Trade Act (NAFTA) of 1995 eliminated the trade barriers with Mexico and Central America. This meant that it was no longer economical to mass-manufacture products such as T-shirts, socks, and underwear in the United States. Companies such as Sara Lee's Hanes unit were ready for this and quickly moved their manufacturing abroad. Fruit of the Loom, however, was slow to respond. Eventually, it was forced to quickly close its U.S. factories and simultaneously open new ones in Central America. The resulting logistics and supply problems were so severe that they contributed to a Chapter 11 bankruptcy filing in 1999.[29]

A company doesn't have to be old and well established to suffer from a static business model. Iridium fell victim to a static business model before it had even gone into full operation. It assumed that once people traveled outside the densely populated areas of rich Western nations, most places they would go would remain uncovered by cell phone systems. It also assumed that roaming privileges across different cell phone systems would be difficult to arrange. But during the years Iridium was being developed and installed, cell phone services expanded at an enormous rate, were extended to many non-Western countries, and managed to set up elaborate roaming arrangements. The environment in which Iridium needed to compete and the things it needed to do to add value changed drastically. Executives at Iridium were well aware of these changes, but they had begun with a picture of reality that didn't allow for the ways reality could change. They were trapped in a static business model and didn't know how to get out.

Making Sure Your Company's Predictions of Change Are Realistic

Companies need to test their ideas of what could change with different questions than the ones they use to test their picture of reality. Making sure that you've got an accurate picture of reality means verifying that the facts you assume to be true really *are* true. Making sure that you've got an accurate picture of what could change means making allowances for things you can't know. It means distinguishing between business conditions that, for better or worse, are likely to remain the same and those that, for better or worse, are likely to change.

There are five questions that can help you to verify that your company is predicting change accurately. Answering these questions is less a matter of collecting new information than a matter of being open to new possibilities.

▪▪▪

Does Your Company Have an Adequate Picture of What Could Change in the Future?

Five Questions to Help You Make Sure

1. Have you taken into account the possibility that several unlikely events could occur at once? (The Perfect-Storm Fallacy)
2. Have you distinguished between projected innovations that require routine engineering and those that require new discoveries? (The Star Wars Error)
3. Have you paid enough attention to the small-scale level at which large-scale changes must be implemented? (The Big-Picture Illusion)
4. Are you focusing on the right competitors, especially newcomers? (The Wrong Competitors)

5. Have you given enough consideration to the ways in which your entire industry could suddenly be transformed or become irrelevant? (A Static Business Model)

Falsehoods Breed Further Falsehoods

One of the more striking things about the pictures of reality employed by failing businesses is the way one false picture tends to generate others. Saatchi & Saatchi, for example, made the film producer error of thinking its success in advertising demonstrated its skills at managing business services. It didn't take much more than this for Saatchi & Saatchi to create a false self-image, where it saw itself as a consummate provider of business services. This false self-image, in turn, reinforced its expansion fever, adding to the distortions created by executive mind-set failures.

Sony's loss of contact with reality in its motion picture venture could almost serve as a summary of the ways companies can adopt inaccurate views of reality. Sony initially entered the entertainment industry because executives there thought that they had discovered a magic answer, namely compatible software. When Sony at first seemed successful, its executives developed a false self-image, and made the film producer error of thinking that they were good at managing entertainment companies. The acquisition of Columbia Pictures was partly due to their big-picture illusion that there would be synergies between the film company and other parts of Sony's empire, when the synergies actually weren't there. Meanwhile, acting on their other misconceptions, the company began watching the wrong scoreboard—market share—and fell victim to home field rules, expecting its American executives to display company loyalty, rather than short-term self-interest. As the financial disasters began to mount, Sony increasingly succumbed to the perfect-storm fallacy, underestimating the number of unlikely things that could go wrong. As you can see from this chronicle of errors, once a business adopts a mistaken picture of reality in one area, its view of reality becomes skewed in other areas as well.

Facing the Big Mystery

The big mystery in all of this is obvious: Why were these sometimes convoluted executive mind-sets allowed to continue? Why weren't the mistaken pictures of reality replaced with more accurate ones as soon as the results were different than expected?

It wasn't that there was a shortage of good information. Most of the companies blinded by a disastrously inaccurate picture of reality had all the data they needed to see that their picture of reality was wrong and to substitute a better one. Most of the companies discussed here—as diverse as GM, eToys, Sony, Motorola, Saatchi & Saatchi, Barneys, LTCM, Quaker, Cabletron, Oxford Health Plans, Food Lion, L.A. Gear, Rubbermaid, the Boston Red Sox, and Schwinn—had data pouring in from their *own* operations that should have easily shown them that their basic business assumptions were wrong. Amazingly enough, the data seemed to have almost no effect.

To understand why no one pointed out that the emperor had no clothes, it is vital to look at the internal policies of the businesses involved. The measures these companies took to encourage and preserve their mistaken pictures of reality were truly remarkable. In fact, as egregious as many of the examples have been in this chapter, there is not a single instance where it was an executive mind-set failure *alone* that pushed these companies to failure. No, it takes more than an inaccurate assessment of reality to fail. In a sense, you have to want to fail, or at least you have to create, build, propagate, or elaborate a culture of close-mindedness that keeps you from doing something about executive mind-set failures. Are there really such organizations where people regularly delude themselves in thinking that everything is just right? The next chapter answers that question.

CHAPTER 7

Delusions of a Dream Company

How Executives Avoid Facing Reality

It's a company most managers would love to work for. From the moment you walk in the door, you can feel the sense of pride and energy. These people are the best in their industry, and they know it. Success isn't something they aspire to; it's what they expect. This company defines excellence—it leads, and it expects the rest of its industry to follow.

The company has an unwavering vision of what it is doing and what it wants to achieve. Its employees have a deep loyalty to the tried and tested products that established their brand. They don't need to wait for customers to tell them what is needed.

It has a sales force that won't take no for an answer. It has employees at every level who will do whatever it takes to get the job done, and managers who keep things running smoothly. When journalists and businesspeople name it one of the most admired companies in America, no one is surprised. And yet, despite the company's positive self-image, it continually strives to do better. There's constant awareness of the company's closest competitor and constant attention to improving internal metrics. There is zero tolerance for major screw-ups.

The most remarkable thing of all is the company's extraordinary team spirit. People from the CEO on down identify with the company to an unusual degree. There is no revolving door for upper-level management. Employees usually stay with the company for their entire careers. Handling the public relations for this company is a breeze. Each employee is a constant promoter of the company goals, and no one speaks out of turn. If one component of the company is attacked or threatened in any way, all the others will spring to its defense.

Does this company sound too good to be true? Something to aspire to, but not something you can realistically expect to achieve?

If you said yes, watch out. This company exists. In fact, there are lots of them that fit this description, some probably within your industry.

But the danger *isn't* that your business will *have to compete* with them. The danger is that your business might *become* a company like this. This company isn't a model to emulate. It's a disaster waiting to happen. In fact, it may be a disaster that has *already* happened, a walking corpse that just doesn't yet know that it's dead.

Zombie Businesses

How could this be? Don't we *want* to strive for all the features of this model company?

Well, yes. But only if certain moderating factors are also present. If you have too much of these qualities, or if you have all of them together, you've got a recipe for a major disaster. Why? Because this company has created an insulated culture that *systematically excludes any information that could contradict its reigning picture of reality.*

Companies that cultivate these positive qualities to excess become "zombie businesses." They might continue to do business the way they always have. They might even do it extremely well. But when a problem develops and things stop working the way they did before, managers have no way of knowing because they are largely cut off from the outside information they need.

What makes these zombie businesses so deceptive is that they are usually *happy* zombies. They are so good at shutting out unwelcome information that they have no idea that they have become zombies. The people employed by a zombie business will make enthusiastic pronouncements about their company's great prospects even after the company has begun collapsing around them. If these people are senior executives, it will seem afterwards that they were trying to con the public. If they are lower-level employees, it will seem that they were hoodwinked. Toward the end, there may, in fact, be conscious acts of deceit designed to cover up what is happening. Mostly, though, the people in a zombie company will be blissfully unaware that they are in the middle of a major business disaster until after it has unfolded. Rather than react and adjust to problems when they occur, managers in a zombie business adopt the delusion that theirs is a dream company.

One of the most interesting things about zombie businesses is that the people who work for them are not themselves zombies. Executives are usually brilliant, dynamic, and impressively attuned to what's happening around them. The technical people will usually have a state-of-the-art grasp of their specialty areas. Practically everyone who works for the company will be carrying out his or her work with competence and intelligence.

The mechanism that makes a business into a zombie consists of "company policies" and "company attitudes" that are ultimately mind numbing, a cumulative effect of so many small and seemingly benign policies that are ultimately destructive.

The entire company doesn't have to be a zombie business for the effects to be devastating. It's enough for a company to have a zombie senior management, a zombie marketing team, a zombie product design department, or zombie attitudes permeating any other essential component. But once a major component of a company goes zombie, the syndrome tends to spread. By the time a formerly successful company has acknowledged huge, irretrievable losses, the post-mortem will usually reveal that there were zombie features almost everywhere.

"Watch Us and See How It's Done"

The first signs that a company is turning into a zombie will often seem like symptoms of unusual health. The company will be thriving, at least in some important respect, and its executives will be justifiably proud of this success. Putting aside false modesty, the company will announce that it's "number one" in its industry in terms of growth or size or revenues or market share or technology or profitability or customer satisfaction or some other important indicator. To make this achievement into a motivator, the company will then express its determination to maintain this level of success or to surpass it. More important, it will make this level of success part of its identity.

Nearly every company whose business failure is examined in this book was glorified as "number one" in some category and made this status part of its self-image. Most of the businesses were celebrated in magazine cover stories, heralded by business gurus, and chosen by polls as being among the most admired corporations in the country. Whether Rubbermaid in *Fortune* magazine, Enron as the poster child of what McKinsey & Company can do, or Motorola with the Baldrige Award, many losers were once winners. More important, almost all of them trumpeted their front-runner status in company slogans, displays, logos, advertisements, and annual reports. They made a point of reminding their employees that they were working for the leading company in their industry, perhaps even the leading company in a number of industries. Enron is a particularly striking example. It actually had a sign inside the entrance to its corporate headquarters that read, "The world's best energy company." Later, this sign was changed to read, "The world's best company." All the other companies and organizations discussed here made similar claims before their fall, although not always in such grandiose terms. It's tempting to think that these claims were fraudulent. But, in fact, nearly all of them were, to some extent, well founded.

The problem is that when a company makes "being number one" part of its self-image, the behavior that made the company number one in the first place starts to change. Instead of trying to achieve something beyond itself, the company starts trying to maintain its own status. The consequences of this inward turn can be seen almost immediately in the way the employees of the "number-one company" begin to treat people from outside the company. They are polite but condescending. Instead of listening and trying to learn from outsiders, employees at all levels will usually be eager to demonstrate their superior knowledge. They know that they don't have to listen to others too closely because they already know better, and it shows in their faces.

Many of the executives whose businesses figure prominently in this book were not only arrogant—they were proud of it. People who dealt with General Motors and IBM in their glory days remember vividly the condescension with which these companies regarded everyone outside their ranks. Daimler-Benz had the same reputation more recently. Saatchi & Saatchi was the probably the most arrogant advertising agency the world has ever seen. The explosive growth of Mossimo, Oxford Health Plans, and L.A. Gear was partly fueled by a belief that they were "rewriting the book" for their industries and, hence, had little to learn from anyone. Webvan, eToys, and most of the other dot-coms made little secret of the disdain they had for traditional businesses. Cabletron, Motorola, and Wang believed that they had the only technology in their industries worthy of being taken seriously. Iridium's arrogance was positively stratospheric, reaching, in fact, all the way into space. At LTCM, when told by a young derivatives trader that its business model couldn't produce the magnitude of profits Nobel Prize winner and LTCM cofounder Myron Scholes was pitching on a sales call, Scholes leaned forward and replied, "You're the reason—because of fools like you we can."[1]

The attitude these companies took toward outsiders was epitomized in the reception Gary Fisher received when he showed his innovative new design for a mountain bike to Schwinn: "This guy in his fifties was looking down at me like I was some kind of jerk kid who didn't know anything. The Schwinn engineers were going 'We know bikes. You guys are all amateurs. We know better than anybody.' "[2]

The air of superiority such companies adopt gradually affects the way people inside a company behave, even among themselves. Often the employees will feel that they have joined an elite brotherhood and will behave as though ordinary business expectations don't apply to them because they are meeting a higher standard. They won't feel a need for so many safeguards, verifications, and outside opinions. Yet at the same time, they'll spend time and resources to achieve operational targets that most businesses would consider excessive or extraneous.

The result in nearly every case is a go-it-alone strategy with nothing to keep it in check. It will hold to its own course, regardless of what other businesses are doing. And by actively deluding themselves into believing that all is well, people effectively avoid facing reality.

"We're Better Than You Are. Period."

Companies with this outlook have no way to learn from others' successes. Even when other firms introduce striking innovations, the self-proclaimed leader views them as desperate attempts on the part of those firms to compensate for their other inadequacies. Schwinn, for example, saw mountain bikes and other innovative models introduced by its competitors as "mere gimmicks" that those companies *had* to resort to because they couldn't provide the superior quality and brand recognition of Schwinn. An Wang and his engineers at Wang shook their heads dismissively at each new product IBM introduced because they found these products so technically inferior to their own. Cabletron saw Cisco as a weak competitor being forced to acquire other companies' technologies because it didn't have the ability to develop the necessary components on its own.

In addition to being unable to learn from other firms' successes, companies with this attitude have no way to learn from other firms' failures. They attribute such failures to the other firm's overall inferiority. They don't recognize that these failures are often due to errors any firm could commit, and that these errors need to be consciously avoided. Hence, they don't make any effort to protect themselves from the same pitfalls. The dot-coms provided some dramatic examples of this. While other dot-coms were crashing around them, many of the better-financed Internet businesses still failed to take corrective measures based on their peer companies' experiences. Dot-coms had come to believe that they were "special," so what could they possibly learn from anyone else?

"Trust Us—We Know What We're Doing"

When a company has an unwavering vision of what it is doing and what it wants to achieve, this vision can easily take on a momentum of its own. After a while, the company will tend to do things, not because they make any business sense, but because they carry out the vision.

No company had a clearer identity or a better-established brand than Levi Strauss. *Levi's* and *jeans* are almost synonymous. Better still, Levi's are regarded as the "most authentic" jeans. They're an icon for the entire spectrum of Western American popular culture, ranging, remarkably enough, from John Wayne to Jerry Garcia. Levi Strauss achieved this status by its commitment to a distinctive, quality product that changed little from decade to decade. Yet this commitment was also its downfall. The company persisted in selling its traditional products despite considerable evidence that customers' expectations were changing. The CEO of one of Levi's major customers said, "We showed them our numbers. We told them what kids were asking for. They even attended some of our focus groups. But they didn't want to believe."[3] As a company spokesperson explained in another press account, "We have a consistent core product that we think appeals to our core consumer."[4] So it's not only that Levi Strauss had a mistaken picture of reality, but also that it was unwilling to question it that accounted for the dramatic fall of the brand.

The more successful a company has been in the past, the harder that company will find it to change the model that made it a success.[5] For example, there are numerous business mottos used to encourage the company to keep on doing whatever it was doing already, the most popular of which is "You can't argue with success." These mottos are regularly invoked to stifle any discussion that could lead a company to make major changes. And, as long as the company appears to be successful, there is little motivation to change.[6] But by the time it becomes undeniably obvious that the old model isn't working and won't start working again soon, the company's fortunes are often past reviving. This is exactly what is behind some of the mind-set failures of Chapter 6. The mistaken picture of reality we called "yesterday's answer," for example, develops in companies whose executives answer every criticism or question with a "we know what we're doing" attitude.

Somewhat surprisingly, the same sense of mission that can lead a company to resist change can also lead it to make changes no one has asked for. Traditional, low-tech companies, such as Schwinn, will often make numerous small changes aimed at perfecting a product that has become increasingly irrelevant. Each year's bicycles, for example, will have features or qualities that the manufacturer believes make them better than last year's. Yet it would often be hard to say what these innovations accomplish, apart from fulfilling the vision of the manufacturer.

Other high-tech companies, such as Motorola, will often be guilty of the same thing on a much grander scale. Motorola was constantly making technological improvements in its analog phones. Its engineers, in effect, were fulfilling their vision of a perfect analog product. Their only problem was that they couldn't see that the whole product category was moving out of favor, fast. The extreme form of this irrational sense of mission is the strategy that could be called "If-we-build-it-they-will-come." A company such as Iridium will forge ahead, fulfilling its vision of what it wants to achieve without pausing to consider whether the vision still makes sense. From the outside, this compulsive drive to make improvements in obsolete products and to complete obsolete projects can look like madness. But from the inside, it will seem like loyalty to the vision that made the company great.

"We Don't Need Customers Telling Us How to Run Our Business"

The single worst aspect of this excessive loyalty to the company mission is that it prevents companies from hearing what their customers are trying to tell them. Businesses that believe too much in their own mission are always in danger of becoming missionaries. Instead of letting customers express what they need, these companies tend to *tell* customers what they need.

In these cases, when middlemen or other collaborators try to point out the differences between what the company is providing and what the customers are requesting, the company's executives tend to be unresponsive. They don't just claim, "We know what our customers want." They go further, claiming, in effect, "We know what our customers want *better* than they do, because we know what's best for them, and eventually they'll see it too." This is exactly the attitude that drove companies such as Motorola and Schwinn to disregard customer preferences.

Once companies get into this frame of mind, they tend to assume that what customers want is whatever the company has to offer. When Barneys was planning its expansion beyond New York, someone suggested that it do a market study to make sure that its offerings would have sufficient appeal to the various local markets. Bob Pressman, who was running the company, thought the idea was ludicrous. "Market studies?" he exclaimed, incredulously. "Why do we have to do market studies? We're Barneys!"[7]

The extent to which high-tech companies will let this attitude shape their behavior can be startling. Cabletron's salespeople actually *lectured* their customers on what their customers needed to buy. Worse, they did this with no appreciation of the fact that their customers didn't want products that were "technologically superior"; they wanted the best overall solution. Motorola kept asserting that its analog phones were the best product, pointing out all the new technological wizardry it had built into them. Neither company understood how to meet the longer-term needs of its customers, even though its customers were spelling out those needs and literally begging the company to supply them.

This "we are the experts" culture is a problem that can afflict any kind of company, high-tech or low-tech, if it has a vision of excellence that takes on a life of its own. Even Starbucks, which has so far avoided the qualities of a zombie business, had a brush with this kind of thinking some years back when customers asked for skim milk in their coffee lattes. Senior executives argued that Starbucks' high-quality dark-roasted coffee did not taste as good with skim milk. One executive even said that offering skim milk "is not in keeping with the quality of our coffee. That is bastardizing it. It's getting to the point that we'll do anything the customer wants us to." Howard Behar, one of the "big three" at Starbucks, but a relative newcomer to the company, was the one who realized that defying the customers' desires was business madness. "Are you nuts?" he finally exclaimed. "Of course we'll do what they want us to!"[8]

Businesses that let their sense of mission take precedence over everything else don't just pay insufficient attention to their customers; they also pay insufficient attention to their suppliers, and this can be just as big of a problem. L.A. Gear didn't consult its suppliers enough about whether its new high-performance shoe designs could be manufactured in a way that would make them sufficiently durable. Schwinn didn't appreciate the fact that the proposals it was receiving from its suppliers showed that those suppliers were ready to move more aggressively into the American market. Lawrence Livermore National Laboratory contributed to a lack of realism surrounding the Strategic Defense Initiative by refusing to listen to what its suppliers, including its contributing labs and researchers, were saying about what was physically possible using lasers. Numerous dot-coms failed to listen to what their suppliers were telling them about the costs of actually delivering what the dot-coms were selling. Like hundreds of other companies blinded by their own vision, each of these organizations moved inexorably toward disasters that could have been reduced or avoided if their executives had listened to what their suppliers were saying.

The swiftness with which a company will be called to account for not listening to customers and suppliers will depend on its competitors. If a company is all alone in its field, it might be able to get away with insular delusions for some time. But as soon as a competitor moves in with a better offering, what looked like market dominance can evaporate overnight. Johnson & Johnson demonstrated this dramatically in its stent business. Its cardiologist customers had asked for circulatory stents that were comparatively easy to handle, that were flexible, and that came in varying lengths. But Johnson & Johnson's 90 percent market share and its "we-are-experts" culture prevented it from paying sufficient attention to its customers' requests. The company got away with this attitude for about two years because there weren't any real competitors. But as soon as rival firm Guidant introduced a product that was closer to what cardiologists had been requesting, it took only forty-five days for Guidant to capture 70 percent of the market. Asked how J&J had lost its seemingly insurmountable lead, cardiologists and hospital administrators pointed to the company's arrogance, lack of respect for customers' ideas, and general inability to listen.

"We Have a Positive Attitude Here"

When businesses start losing touch with reality because of an arrogant belief in their own superiority and their company mission, they tend to adopt a pervasively positive attitude. The more insular the company's outlook, the more buoyant its managers will tend to be about the company's prospects.

An aggressively positive company attitude, once it has become established, rapidly acquires its own momentum. The beliefs that fostered the positive attitude get constantly reinforced because taking a positive, upbeat approach means implicitly endorsing them. The more these beliefs are reinforced, the easier the positive attitude is to maintain. A positive attitude helps to keep everyone happy. No one, least of all the executives, wants to disrupt the resulting positive atmosphere by being negative. In addition to keeping people happy, the positive attitude encourages employees at all levels to do whatever the company asks.

Because a positive attitude helps make people easier to manage, executives who are trying to implement questionable policies will often go to especially great lengths to instill a positive attitude among their employees. When Saatchi & Saatchi, for example, embarked on its highly questionable program of rapid expansion, it consciously created a cult of self-belief among the employees, demanding that they practice "positive thinking" to the point where it became a leap of faith. Just recall the poem in Chapter 4 that was circulated throughout the company. It described the employees going to "the edge," jumping off, and taking flight.

The problem, of course, is that a healthy business doesn't want its employees mindlessly jumping off the edge. It wants its employees to be aware of every significant hazard as it arises and to take steps to avoid it.

Many of the business disasters analyzed in this book could have been avoided or reduced in scale if, instead of taking an unquestioningly positive approach, a senior manager had taken a consciously negative approach, simply to see what this would reveal. Quaker Oats CEO William Smithburg, for example, expressed regret that he didn't have someone develop counterarguments to the Snapple acquisition. Had he done so, Quaker might have gone on with the acquisition anyway, but its managers would certainly have handled things differently. Positive attitudes are a wonderful way to avoid facing reality.

"No Negative Feedback, Please"

A relentlessly positive attitude shuts out critical information from outside the company. This is especially conspicuous when it comes to sales personnel. Maybe it sounds appealing to have "a sales force that won't take no for an answer," but this removes the company's best source of information about its customers' needs and desires. Salespeople with too positive an attitude tend to regard customer and supplier criticisms as "sales resistance," rather than as a source of information that could be used to modify business activities and output. Cabletron, for example, was oblivious to its customers' need for more flexible and more comprehensive solutions in large measure because of the aggressive approach adopted by its sales personnel. Rubbermaid didn't appreciate the need to keep its prices down in part because its sales teams were too confident that Rubbermaid's products were the ones people most needed. Mattel didn't recognize the extent to which retailers were moving to just-in-time deliveries and quick inventory turnovers because its salespeople put too much faith in the durability of Mattel's key brands. Companies such as these can't collect the information they most need from their salespeople unless they find a way to release those people from having to be constantly positive about the company's products and policies.

In addition to shutting out crucial information from outside the company, a relentlessly positive attitude suppresses the most crucial information from inside the company. People will avoid mentioning unsettling information or ideas because bringing up such things sounds negative. No one wants to be a "the nitpicker." There is no reassurance to counter an employee's natural reluctance to be the bearer of bad news.[9] When a company habitually assigns blame for failures, no one is going to speak up when he or she spots a problem. For this reason, when the cola from Coca-Cola's Belgian plant was said to be making people severely ill, the company's employees weren't eager to investigate and were reluctant to inform senior management.

Gradually, the relentlessly positive attitude will change the whole way the business runs. It becomes a company of yes-men. Employees might deliver whatever senior management asks for, but no one in the company will speak up if what is requested turns out to be the wrong thing. Company executives might keep things running smoothly, but they won't be able to introduce the more disruptive innovations necessary to keep the company competitive over the long haul. Any innovations that could result in big improvements will have to come from senior management because everyone else will be uncritically doing what they've been told. But senior management won't have the information necessary to take the appropriate creative action because no one wants to be the one to tell them that things aren't going as well as was expected.

Do these problems sound exaggerated? Isn't the idea of a company suppressing critical data a little farfetched? We saw it happen in case after case that we studied. At microchip manufacturer Advanced Micro Devices (AMD), for example, employees were so careful to maintain a positive attitude when dealing with CEO Jerry Sanders that he never heard about the serious delays plaguing the manufacture of the company's crucial K5 chip. Even when the problems became increasingly obvious at the lower levels, each level in the management hierarchy struggled to put a positive spin on what it was hearing from below. Eventually, as one former employee said, "Everyone in the company knew the thing was in bad shape but Jerry," the CEO.[10]

"Telling Everyone Will Just Make Things Worse"

When people are scared to draw attention to unwelcome information, it's a slippery slope to becoming involved in cover-ups. The problem of cover-ups is far more widespread than businesses like to acknowledge, partly because the obscenely positive attitude that leads to cover-ups also causes the cover-ups themselves to be covered up. Even organizations that depend utterly on accurate technical data can often end up concealing data if the data have negative implications. When the Lawrence Livermore Laboratory was working on laser technology, for example, researchers neglected to inform their administrative superiors each time they fell behind their projected schedules. Then, when Secretary of Energy Bill Richardson kept publicly proclaiming the project "on time and within budget," it became increasingly embarrassing to admit what had happened. Costs mounted and, instead of catching up, the project fell further behind. When the facts eventually were uncovered, the resulting investigation put most of the blame on a lab culture that discouraged scientists from airing problems, a remarkable stance given the scientific ethic.[11]

In publicly traded companies, the desire to maintain stock prices reinforces the other tendencies to suppress any bad news that might otherwise interfere with a positive outlook. For example, when Boston Market was under fire a few years back, the majority owners fired the CEO, Larry Zwain, to try to shift responsibility away from themselves and signal that their house was now in order. Unfortunately, Zwain was one of the few people at the top who really understood restaurant operations; after he took the fall there wasn't much left to stem the bleeding. That the company's problems had much more to do with financing manipulations than operations makes it little surprise that it ended up in Chapter 11 not long afterwards.

"Never Settle for Less Than Perfect"

People often assume that if a business sees itself as the model for its industry, and believes unwaveringly in its company vision, and constantly exhibits a positive attitude, it will inevitably become complacent. Meanwhile, if a business is constantly striving to do better, it tends to assume that it's fundamentally healthy and on the right track. In reality, these assumptions don't hold up. A company can have all the qualities of a zombie business and yet be trying harder than ever. Indeed, one of the features that can be found in nearly all zombie businesses is a kind of company perfectionism.

When companies adopt internal metrics, they tend to settle into an almost irrational perfectionism. They aim for high standards in every operation without stopping to ask if these standards are appropriate. "We do things well," they imply, "because, being the best, anything less would be inappropriate." This determination to excel, regardless of whether it serves any business purpose, can easily get out of control. In extreme cases, it can lead to crazy-sounding expenditures, such as Barneys' bosses importing European craftsmen to lay Italian marble mosaics in their Madison Avenue store.[12] As former IBM CEO Lou Gerstner said in evaluating the problems that beset IBM as it moved into its period of decline, "My view is that the company had been so successful for so long it stopped comparing itself with competitors and started gauging itself by internal measures. That's a recipe for trouble."[13]

The worst aspect of this perfectionism is the way that it encourages executives to expect unrealistically low failure rates. In principle, day-to-day production should be able to achieve an extremely low "failure rate," while prototype ventures need a relatively higher allowance for failure. But companies in the grip of perfectionism quickly lose sight of the difference. They'll often talk about "allowing experiments" and "making room for instructive failures." But in practice, companies that see themselves as the model for their industries usually have trouble allowing even the most trailblazing of failures.

This intolerance for failures of any kind deprives companies of their best opportunity to try out alternative pictures of business reality. The only way to find out if a new product or a new business model will work is to try it out. Companies in the grip of perfectionism are unable to recognize this. They can't distinguish between failures due to negligence and failures due to something innovative that didn't pay off yet. So, they tend to punish the "failures" associated with exploring new possibilities, taking reasonable risks, and offering innovative solutions.[14] In the worst cases, these companies make a habit of finding someone to "take the fall" for each failure. These policies discourage the kinds of innovation that companies most need to stay competitive and profitable. In addition, they cause terrible inefficiencies as employees spend their energies making sure that they're not the ones blamed, rather than getting on with the business itself. One executive we interviewed described how this worked among senior management at one of his previous employers: "We spent more time deciding who would be blamed if things went wrong than setting real strategy."

"Whatever Happens, It's Not My Fault"

Ironically enough, the higher people are in the management hierarchy, the more they tend to supplement their perfectionism with blanket excuses, with CEOs usually being the worst of all. For example, in one organization we studied, the CEO spent the entire forty-five-minute interview explaining all the reasons why others were to blame for the calamity that hit his company. Regulators, customers, the government, and even other executives within the firm—all were responsible. No mention was made, however, of personal culpability.

Perfectionist companies are especially prone to excuse their failures by blaming them on "unforeseeable events beyond our control." When the failure is an especially big one, executives sometimes use the "perfect-storm excuse," directly linked to the "perfect-storm fallacy" discussed in Chapter 6. They'll argue that failure was due to an unlikely combination of factors that won't happen again for a long time. This would mean that, however large the failure may have been, it wasn't anyone's fault, and there's no need for major reforms.

In practice, of course, the perfect-storm excuse will seldom stand up to scrutiny. Chiquita Banana provides a good example. In 2000, Chiquita attributed its losses to a trade dispute with the European Union. This sounds like an unforeseeable event beyond its control, perhaps even a perfect storm. As one senior executive said, "What took us years to develop was wiped out, without any ability on our part to deal with the issue." The only problem is that in eight of the previous nine years the company had used the *same* excuse. Furthermore, it had invoked other events beyond its control to explain additional losses. In 1992, for example, Chiquita said that its $284 million loss was due to "an extraordinary outbreak of disease and unusual weather patterns," rather than their misjudgment of market demand.[15]

"Too Much Team Spirit"

The company attribute that does the most to make the other zombie policies inescapable is team spirit. When team spirit is strong enough, dissent becomes impossible. This isn't because people are afraid to express different ideas; it's because different ideas don't arise in the first place. Employees imbued with a strong enough sense of team spirit delude themselves into thinking alike.

In companies where team spirit is strongest, employees often seem to do everything together. Geography encourages this. At General Motor's Detroit headquarters, for example, all the senior executives ended up belonging to the same closed society because if they participated in any common social activity, it was assumed that they would participate in all of them. In *The Decline and Fall of the American Automobile Industry*, Brock Yates describes this pattern of life very succinctly: "They live together, they work together, they drink together, they play golf together, they think together."[16] If executives were high enough in the GM hierarchy, they worked on or near the fourteenth floor of the GM headquarters building. Getting closer to this center of power geographically was inseparable from getting closer to it socially. At Sears' Chicago headquarters, the situation was much the same. Bill Salter, Sears' executive vice president, later commented on the extent to which Sears employees associated only with their own colleagues: "We used to be so inbred, it's a wonder we didn't have an eye in the middle of our foreheads."[17]

One destructive policy often carried out in the name of team spirit is the habit of breaking up cliques that show signs of going against the grain. Once separated, people with similar innovative insights will no longer be able to support each other or to attain a "critical mass" in any one place. Without sympathetic listeners, they tend to fall silent.

The extent to which breaking up work cliques can eliminate a force for change is apparent when we look at General Motors CEO Roger Smith after the establishment of NUMMI, GM's joint venture with Toyota. Executives from GM who gained experience with this project were bursting with insights and ideas they were eager to put into action. But these insights and ideas all hinged on empowering workers, which ran counter to Smith's obsession that workers were a liability to be eliminated wherever possible. Hence, all these executives with NUMMI experience were dispersed to other parts of GM, with no significant concentration in any one place. In such "hostile" territory, without benefit of a critical mass of colleagues who had all experienced the same thing, the stories of huge productivity improvements through nontraditional management of workers fell on deaf ears.

"I Speak for the Entire Company"

Perfectionist companies tend to reward people who compulsively endorse the company vision, and say things that put the company in the best possible light. Their team spirit makes them ready to jump to the company's defense any time they believe that some part of it is under attack.

The problem is that these people's efforts to protect and defend the company are often counterproductive and go against the company's long-term best interests. One of the worst offenders are liability lawyers and public relations people. Often they have too much influence on company policy. While these professionals can be extremely valuable, they are trained to deal with the effects of company policies, not with the deep and long-term motives for those policies. When managers rely on them, they are thinking in terms of expediency, rather than engaging in the underlying issues. In times of crisis, statements to the press that were written by liability lawyers and concede as little as possible tend to be especially damaging. The public recognizes that these statements aren't addressing the real issues and usually reacts with hostility.

The way Coca-Cola handled the health problems at its Belgian plant illustrates many of the dangers of having employees too thoroughly imbued with "public relations reflexes." When Belgian schoolchildren were reported to be getting sick after drinking Coca-Cola, the local managers' first reaction was to deny that the soft drink was responsible. Then, as the evidence of contamination mounted, executives proceeded to issue a series of statements that conceded as little as possible and attempted to minimize both the problem and Coca-Cola's responsibility for it. Most of the press releases were clearly written by liability lawyers. How else to explain, "It may make you feel sick, but it is not harmful."[18] Senior executives weren't notified in the early stages of the crisis, and they didn't take it very seriously once they did know. No one from the high levels of the company appeared on the scene until ten days after the first incident. By the time the defenders of the company's interests were finished, they had taken a small local problem and turned it into an international setback that would plague the company for years. If this story rings a bell, you might be confusing it with Snow Brand Milk, Bridgestone-Firestone, Enron, Martha Stewart, ImClone, and the entire tobacco industry.

Countering the Forces That Turn Companies into Zombies

What startled us throughout our survey is how often the most destructive policies sound like something a company would want to encourage. All the policies described in this chapter often help to produce willing, enthusiastic employees.

Yet as soon as these policies begin to insulate a company from things it doesn't want to hear, they become a recipe for business failure. Executives who adopt these destructive policies delude themselves into believing that their company is perfect. In truth, they are a symptom of a business organization that allows its reigning picture of reality to become detached from the wider world in which it must operate, and prevent any inadequacies in its picture of reality from being discovered and corrected.

The problem is that you *don't want to eliminate* the qualities that are causing the trouble. You don't even want to undermine them. You *want to balance them* with qualities that will counteract their unwanted effects. How do you do this?

Fortunately, for each of the qualities that tend to isolate a company from critical information, there are policies and techniques that you can use to compensate.

Protecting Your Company from Company Pride

First, if you want to prevent your company from turning into a zombie, you have to counteract any tendency on the part of employees to congratulate themselves too often. Under founders Bernie Marcus and Arthur Blank, Home Depot made a deliberate effort to prevent its managers from becoming too self-satisfied. "You won't often hear us sitting around patting ourselves on the back," its founders explained. "In fact, if you sat in on a board meeting or one of our staff meetings, you would think we were going broke. You might even think, 'Geez, I better sell my stock.'" This was not a feature of Home Depot's culture that developed by chance. It's an attitude these executives carefully cultivated. "Want to know the management secrets of The Home Depot?" its founders offer. "Number one, we are not that smart. Number two, we know we are not that smart."[19]

In addition to making a general effort to avoid excessive pride, there are a number of specific tactics a company can employ to protect itself from complacency. One tactic is to create internal advocates for the competition. These internal advocates are people inside the company whose job is to appreciate or champion *other* firms' strategies and technologies, and present arguments for adopting them. Such advocates are usually most effective if they work in teams that can support each other's efforts. To make the advocate team effective, it will need to be given the same incentives and support as the company's other research and development teams. By critically evaluating the competition's practices, the company's in-house team will be improving on those practices, adapting them to the company's unique needs, and in general making them their own. This should make it easier for the company to put those practices into actual use.

It's also useful to have someone inside your company watching to see what can be learned from competitors' problems and failures. Similar problems regularly sweep across entire industries. Yet unless companies are making an active effort to learn from their competitors' experiences, the ones affected later will be no better prepared than the ones affected earlier. Avoiding other companies' missteps can be just as important as emulating their successes.

An even more effective tool for bringing in new ideas and new practices is to launch joint ventures with partners who have very different strengths. To benefit as much as possible from these joint ventures, your company needs to make clear to its employees that a major goal of the joint venture is to maximize learning from the partner company. Then it needs to follow through by having its employees articulate or demonstrate what they have learned, with suitable rewards when they do this successfully. This is what Toyota did when it partnered with GM to launch NUMMI. While GM was busy shutting out the unwelcome lessons about the value of empowering workers, Toyota was learning all the practical skills it needed to run automobile factories in America.

Protecting Your Company from Its Own Idea of Excellence

The biggest problem with a "company vision" is that it tends to take on its own momentum and becomes extremely difficult to change. Yet small changes need to be made constantly and big ones periodically. As Michael Dell of Dell Computer said, "You have to be self-critical to succeed. If you sat in on our management meetings, you would find that we are a remarkably self-critical bunch with a disdain for complacency that motivates us."[20] Bill Gates of Microsoft issues similar warnings. "Companies fail," Gates says, "when they become complacent and imagine that they will always be successful."[21]

The answer, according to such leaders, is to stay alert for information that could signal how the company vision might need to be changed. This means constantly making sure that the improvements the company most wants to provide are the ones that customers most want to have. It means never creating new offerings simply for the sake of creation, but always considering customer needs.

To reinforce this kind of thinking, it is extremely helpful to make each top executive personally responsible for dealing with real customers. While some might complain that this takes executives away from their administrative duties, that is exactly the point. Why does John Chambers of Cisco talk to customers several times a week? Why did Jack Welch of General Electric get involved in the details of selling things such as jet engines? Why does Michael Dell spend about half his time with customers? It isn't because these successful leaders want to "micromanage" things. It's because they know that taking responsibility for individual customer relationships—and making other senior executives do the same—is one of the best ways to discover what a company is doing right and what it should be doing differently.

Protecting Your Company from Its Positive Attitude

Even if executives are in close touch with customers, there's no way they can spot all the developments that might have a drastic effect on the company's future. This means that it is extremely worthwhile to reward any employee who finds flaws or potential problems in the company's policies and procedures. DuPont has demonstrated how effective such systems can be in its safety program. For many years, its employees have been actively encouraged to report near-miss incidents without fear of disciplinary measures against themselves or their coworkers. As a result of this program, DuPont has one of the lowest rates of occupational injury of any company.[22] Programs with a much broader focus can maintain a high level of return by convening "devil's advocate" groups that are assigned the task of spotting vulnerabilities in past and current policies.

David Klatt, president of the Rubbermaid Group of Newell and one of the key people charged with bringing Rubbermaid back to its old glory, relates a story about his "mentor":

> One of the mentors I have is the guy who runs HR here. They call him "the Godfather" and for some reason people just open up to

him. Nicest man you ever want [to meet] yet he's still tough-minded about business. . . . He's also not afraid to come in here and shut my door and say, "You know, David, you just missed this one. You screwed it up and here's how I suggest you fix it and he'll let me fight back on some of them where I think I was right and a lot times . . . most of the time unfortunately . . . he's right. But it's great to have somebody like that around me.[23]

Once you know about potential problems, you have to bring them to the attention of the people who need to act on them. This means that it's vital to find ways to disseminate *unpopular* knowledge quickly across the organization. One way to do this is make heroes of the "Paul Reveres," who ride through the company warning that "the British are coming." Of course, it's important to distinguish these "Paul Reveres" from "Chicken Littles," who ride through the company announcing that the sky is falling. The difference is that the "Paul Reveres" are not spreading doom and gloom, but prompting people to take practical, cost-effective actions.

Protecting Your Company from Perfectionism

There are several ways to counter the irrational perfectionism that can cause a company to focus obsessively on standards that are becoming increasingly irrelevant. One of the most effective is simply *to change goals* whenever the old goal is being fully met, not just "raise the bar." This isn't to say that continued development and regeneration of core competencies is a bad idea. Rather, it highlights the risk in constantly looking for incremental improvements in old models that may no longer be the right ones given changing competitive and customer dynamics.

Meanwhile, to facilitate any change in policies, you have to allow for mistakes, as long as these mistakes are part of an effort to do something differently. But how can senior executives get lower-level employees to believe that small failures really won't be held against them? The answer is to have executives set the example by acknowledging their own small failures and by participating in discussions of how those particular failures might be avoided in the future. This isn't some utopian dream. At eBay, for example, top managers explain what they did right, wrong, and very wrong, all in public forums. At IDEO, managers who never seem to have any failures to report are warned that they aren't being ambitious enough. With top management setting the example, employees at these companies soon learn that it's OK to make mistakes. In addition to facilitating change, this tolerance helps people take responsibility for their actions, rather than make excuses.

When companies abandon their perfectionism and begin setting more realistic goals, they need to make sure that they are measuring themselves by *external* benchmarks, rather than by some internal standard. If a company doesn't do this, especially for routine operations and centralized support services, it will have no idea whether its operations are successful or not. On the other hand, if a company does use external standards, it will be well on the way to seeing what it's doing in a realistic light. In rebuilding IBM, for example, Lou Gerstner said, "The first thing we had to do is reorient ourselves from a highly introspective view of the world to an obsession with the marketplace, both customers and competitors."[24] Giving IBM a more realistic idea of where it was genuinely delivering value was a key step in bringing it back from disaster.

Finally, to protect itself more fully from perfectionism, your company should establish a policy of rewarding experiments that are unsuccessful when it comes to producing financial returns but that are highly successful when it come to producing knowledge returns. Charles Schwab did this with its Internet-based business ideas, launching many that it knew would drop by the wayside. It called these ventures "noble failures," because they allowed the company to learn quickly what would and wouldn't work on the Net.[25] Fred Smith, CEO of FedEx, told us that the failure of ZapMail in the early 1980s (the idea was to send documents via FAX; the only problem was that these machines appeared on everyone's desk much sooner than anticipated) exposed the company to new technical skills that eventually led to its industry-leading hand-held routing scanners.[26] Other companies even pick a "Mistake of the Month." In a staff meeting, the group will have each person acknowledge a mistake. Mistakes are then listed on a whiteboard and a vote is taken on which mistake taught the company the most.[27] By awarding a prize to the winner, the company can make the point that it's serious about getting rid of irrational perfectionism.

Protecting Your Company from Too Much Team Spirit

All these methods of preventing a company from turning into a zombie will only succeed if the company can counteract the groupthink associated with too much team spirit. This means finding ways to foster and preserve any opinions that differ from the prevailing one. It's these differing viewpoints, after all, that provide the means to challenge, revise, and ultimately replace the company's reigning picture of reality.

One technique for fostering dissent is to request a "minority report" whenever the company is considering an important new course of action. The job for those drafting this report is to make as strong a case as possible for whichever alternative seems to be the *second*-strongest candidate. This practice tends to expose unexpected aspects of each course of action.

Another technique is to build these contrasting visions into routine operations so that, much of the time, minority reports aren't even needed. One of the most effective ways to do this is to create crossfunctional teams and diverse work groups whose members will see things differently. Such heterogeneous groups have been shown to be much better than homogeneous groups when it comes to developing new knowledge.[28]

You also might appeal to genuine outsiders, such as critical evaluators from other business units in the same company or from other noncompeting companies, or even nontraditional evaluators, such as people who are *not* specialists in the process or operation under consideration. Sometimes these outsiders can make valuable contributions to an organization's thinking merely by asking basic questions.

Whenever an organization has developed potentially innovative groups within its own ranks, it needs to preserve these groups so they can support each other's efforts. This means keeping the people together "who see things differently" or have a passion for some alternative strategy. Toyota demonstrated how productive this policy can be in its handling of the NUMMI venture. Instead of breaking up the cliques, as GM did, Toyota kept executives with NUMMI experience in groups of thirty to sixty, transferring them into the project together and keeping many of them together when they were moved to other plants. It also encouraged NUMMI executives to hold regular meetings afterward to discuss their special insights. These practices made it easier for NUMMI executives to move on to other American Toyota plants and still apply what they had learned.

Protecting Your Company from Its Public Relations

Protecting a company from its own public relations is one of the more paradoxical problems a company must face if it wants to avoid turning into a zombie. After all, you don't want your employees bad-mouthing your company. And you don't want them damaging the morale of your entire work force by undermining what the company is doing.

Fortunately there are two simple policies that can help a company avoid causing itself a great deal of damage. One is to keep liability lawyers and public relations people out of basic planning and decisions. Among other things, this helps a company to concentrate on what really needs fixing, rather than getting distracted by the problem of managing appearances. Communicating what you're doing is important, but it can't take the place of substantive action.

The other policy is to avoid thinking in terms of "damage control" and instead to concentrate on *eliminating* the damage *and* its causes. Instituting this policy can be difficult unless the CEO and other top executives make a point of setting the right example. But with the proper leadership, "solve the problem" reflexes can replace public relations reflexes.

Policies and Techniques to Keep Your Company Responsive to Outside Developments

COMPENSATE FOR COMPANY PRIDE

1. Create internal advocates for strategies and technologies introduced by competitors and by other outside firms that are tackling analogous tasks.
2. Give someone the job of monitoring competitors' missteps and making sure that they're avoided.
3. Use partnering to bring in new ideas and new practices.

COMPENSATE FOR THE COMPANY'S VISION OF EXCELLENCE

1. Make sure that the improvements the company most wants to provide are the ones the customers most want to have.
2. Make each top executive personally responsible for dealing with important customers.

COMPENSATE FOR THE COMPANY'S POSITIVE ATTITUDE

1. Reward employees who can find flaws or potential problems in the company's procedures.
2. Make heroes of the "Paul Reveres," who ride through the company warning that "the British are coming." (As long as they're not really "Chicken Littles" announcing that the sky is falling).

COMPENSATE FOR COMPANY PERFECTIONISM

1. Change goals when the old goal is being fully met, rather than simply "raising the bar."
2. Get senior managers to set the example when it comes to acknowledging and learning from failures.
3. Use external benchmarks, especially for routine operations and centralized support services.
4. Use devices such as "Mistake of the Month" to reward experiments that are unsuccessful when it comes to producing financial returns but highly successful when it comes to producing knowledge returns.

COMPENSATE FOR TEAM SPIRIT

1. Request minority reports and reports that aim at presenting the strongest contrasting position.
2. Create crossfunctional teams and diverse work groups whose members will see things differently.
3. Seek critical evaluations from genuine outsiders.
4. Preserve potentially innovative groups, so they can support each other's efforts.

COMPENSATE FOR PUBLIC RELATIONS REFLEXES

1. Keep the liability lawyers and public relations people out of basic planning and decision making.
2. Don't think in terms of "damage control." Think instead of eliminating the damage and its causes.

Being a Zombie Isn't Just a Matter of Attitude

Get your company to actively embrace information that could require it to change its reigning picture of reality and you'll have gone a long way toward keeping your company healthy. In fact, if the company has already turned into a zombie, you'll be well on the way to bringing it back to life. But despite these healthy attitudes and policies, the company might still be seriously at risk.

The reason is that the delusional attitudes that turn a company into a zombie will affect every part of its operations. It might be doing everything right to turn itself around, but if it's already a zombie, even the routine procedures that businesses use to monitor and control what they are doing on a day-to-day basis will stop functioning properly. The relevant information might be there, and managers might be willing and able to act on it. Yet there might still be a complete disconnect between the incoming information and that action it would seem to require.

To understand how this is possible, we have to look more closely at the procedures companies follow when it comes to handling strategically important information.

CHAPTER 8

Tracking Down the Lost Signals

Why Businesses Don't Act on Vital Information

Think about how it works in spy thrillers. The secret agent discovers information vital to national security. She finds some way to get the message out. A junior clerk at some government agency receives the message and immediately recognizes its importance. "We need to verify its authenticity," the clerk says, tense with excitement. "But if this message checks out, the president and the prime minister need to be informed at once." Within hours, national policy has been changed, all of NATO has been mobilized, and the world has been saved from a major catastrophe.

Real life is far more disappointing. The French foiled a terrorist plot to crash a hijacked airplane into the Eiffel Tower. They warned the FBI that a similar plot would soon be directed at American targets. A few months later, the FBI received information that a number of foreigners with terrorist associations had enrolled in American flight schools. The students wanted to learn to fly big commercial jets, but weren't interested in learning how to land the planes. Among the students were people the French said were connected with the terrorist plot they had foiled. Meanwhile, sources in the Middle East warned that a major attack on an American target was being planned. Earlier reports had identified the World Trade Center as one of the most likely targets.

FBI field agents in Minnesota and Arizona put some of these facts together and tried to initiate action. But nothing was done. The search and wiretap requests that the field agents submitted were first edited, so that they seemed less urgent, and then denied approval. The FBI field agents were reassigned to something else. In a work of fiction, the amount of relevant information supplied to the FBI would have seemed like over-kill. Yet all this information was essentially ignored by an agency dedicated to dealing with such matters. A few weeks later, the World Trade Center was destroyed.

Now ask yourself which of these two scenarios your own business would be more likely to follow. It's easy to get indignant about the FBI's bungling. It's easy to imagine that none of the people responsible would have been able to survive in the private sector. But can we really be confident that a large commercial enterprise would have done any better?

Imagine that one of the most vital pieces of information your company will ever receive has just entered the system. This information could take a number of forms. Customers could be making persistent inquiries about products your company isn't producing—as with Johnson & Johnson's cardiovascular stents. The accounts reported by your company's most profitable subsidiary might show strange inconsistencies—as with Barings' Singapore trading house. The licensing fees that your company is collecting from competitors' sales might be soaring, while your own sales are leveling off—as with Motorola's cell phone division. Key competitors with healthy balance sheets might suddenly be shifting their supply chains to foreign manufacturers—as with Fruit of the Loom. Components from other firms, on which your products are dependent, might be experiencing abnormally high failure rates—as with Ford Explorers and Firestone tires.

Whatever the information, most people with a little imagination could see how it might have drastic consequences for your company's future. Yet are you confident that the information wouldn't be lost or ignored? Would the information get to the right person in your business? Would that person initiate the appropriate action? And would the action, once initiated, actually be carried through?

Tackling the Big Mystery

There are simply too many examples of companies and other organizations that have failed to recognize a vital piece of information and act on it. Yet there are some businesses—and some government agencies—that are much more likely to recognize and act on vital information. What makes some organizations receptive and responsive and others not?

This is a major puzzle. It's not plausible simply to blame the size of the bureaucracies involved. It's not convincing, for example, to say that the organization in question simply had too many layers, or that it was swamped with too much information. Many huge corporate and governmental organizations, with many superfluous layers, still manage to cope with awesome quantities of information every day. If they couldn't do this with a high level of reliability, things such as our public health system, with its programs for monitoring and controlling infectious diseases, would leave us with a steady stream of disasters. Fortunately, with today's information technology, it doesn't take an especially efficient organization to process information efficiently. Furthermore, the kind of information we're talking about isn't the sort that can be easily lost in a flood of similar items. Information that points to the possibility of a major disaster should be relatively easy to flag and to handle with special dispatch.

It's tempting to say that the managers involved in the cases we listed at the beginning of this chapter were simply incompetent. But this isn't convincing either. In all the organizations we've discussed, including the FBI, the people making the key decisions regarding the vital information were in fact highly qualified, hard working, extremely skilled, and strongly motivated to succeed. There is no sign that they were drunk or absent or sleeping on the job or that their mental faculties were in any way impaired. In each case, practically everyone making the crucial calls had a long history of competent decision making. How is it, then, that they all proved so disastrously unreceptive to the information that mattered most?

Undirected Information . . . or "Information? What Information?"

To discover how vital information goes astray, we need to follow the trail of the information from the moment someone in the organization becomes aware of it to the moment someone decides what appropriate measures should be taken. Somewhere along this path, we'll find the spot where the vital information typically stops getting passed along, is lost, gets destroyed, or is made inactive. This critical location, where the information trail ends, will differ across organizations. Some organizations will be riddled with them; others will have a single category of bottleneck that is so restrictive that it makes the entire organization unresponsive.

The first step in following this information trail is to look at what happens to the information when it first comes to the attention of an employee. Usually, the vital information will enter the system not once, but many times. The employees who receive the information will typically have several opportunities to assess its importance. The crucial question then is: Does the employee who is likely to receive the information have a basis for recognizing that it is truly important? Does the employee, for example, know that the danger signaled by the information is a real possibility?

All too often, employees are slow to recognize the importance of new information because no one has ever shown them that they need to take the implied danger seriously. It never occurred to Coca-Cola employees, for example, that a handful of complaints from school children in Belgium could represent a serious threat to the value of Coca-Cola's brand in Europe and even, to some extent, around the world. It never occurred to the employees of Johnson & Johnson, Cabletron, Levi Strauss, Nissan, Schwinn, and a host of other companies that requests from customers for different product designs could be indicating a potential for abrupt, mass defections of customers. In part because these companies portrayed themselves to their employees as enduring, almost invulnerable institutions, their employees failed to recognize the importance of information pointing to major vulnerabilities.

If the organization ignores the information for a while without disastrous consequences, employees often begin to think that nothing bad will occur. This happened with the London Underground. For years, smokers on their way out of the stations had been accidentally starting fires by lighting up and dropping their matches while still on the escalators. Each little "non-event" added an organizational antibody that reduced the likelihood that a major event would be noticed in a timely fashion. Then, because no one was actually killed, information about the fires gradually ceased to seem urgent. It was only in 1987, when a fire in the King's Cross Station killed thirty-one people and injured many more, that safety measures were finally taken.[1]

Once employees recognize the importance of some information they've received, they need to know where to direct it. Often the employee's immediate superior will be no better equipped to deal with the information than the employee. The appropriate person to take charge has to be someone who can act on the information or who can get the information quickly to another person who can act on it. When there's a lack of clarity about who's responsible for what, especially outside the employee's own department, this in itself can prevent a vital piece of information from being acted on until it's too late.

Sometimes the problem is that there isn't any person appropriately placed who's ready to act on the vital new information. Research departments often find themselves with this problem. They spot a new trend or invent a new product, but find that there is no one in the company who is prepared to act quickly enough on the new information. The Xerox Corporation's Palo Alto Research Center (Xerox PARC) constantly found itself in this predicament. It created dozens of "killer ap" products, including the graphical user interface that Apple adopted for the Mac, the computer mouse, and the Ethernet. But the only significant Xerox PARC invention ever put into production by Xerox was a laser printer. Why? Because there were no personnel elsewhere in Xerox with the skills and vision necessary to take Xerox PARC's other discoveries and run with them. Steve Jobs of Apple later said that Xerox "grabbed defeat from the greatest victory in the computer industry. Xerox could have owned the entire computer industry today. Could have been, you know, a company ten times its size . . . the IBM of the nineties . . . the Microsoft of the nineties!"[2] But when its Palo Alto Research Center invented the products of the future, it had no one in the company to tell.

Missing Communication Channels . . . or "I Have It; You Need It. Now What?"

Let's assume that the employee who received the vital information knows that it's important. Let's assume, further, that the employee has some idea of whom to tell about it. The next question is whether there's an easy way to reach the person who needs to act on the information. This might sound simple. After all, if someone works for the same company, it's relatively easy to find out that person's phone number or email address. But the problem, of course, is that employees usually only communicate with people outside their immediate working group when they've been told they should and when some sort of precedent has been established.

The result is that many companies can't act on vital information because there are no regularly established communication channels between the people receiving the information and the people who need to act on it. Nissan, for example, operated for years with a rigidly bureaucratic culture that required its sales, manufacturing, and R&D divisions in the U.S. to report separately to Japan, and not interact with each other. In effect, all the corporate communication channels led only to Tokyo. To make matters worse, there was no direct interaction between regional managers in America and top corporate executives in Japan. This meant that if the Nissan salespeople discovered customers were rejecting an automobile because of a small but irritating design feature, the design department was unlikely to ever hear about it. A spokesman for Nissan North America said the entire company behaved as though it had been "hit with a 'stupid stick.' "[3] But the problem was mostly that the large numbers of intelligent people employed by Nissan were trying to function with missing or inadequate communication channels.

Even when the communication channels seem adequate, they can't cope effectively with urgent information if they are too rigid and hierarchical. NASA provided a classic example of this. None of its employees could go over their immediate manager's head and managers didn't interfere with anyone not directly beneath them. Employees reported problems to their immediate supervisors, but felt that they could take no further action if their supervisors ignored the problem. Supervisors at all levels relied solely on the information given to them by their immediate subordinates.[4] The result was that specific pieces of information that could have prevented most of NASA's major failures, such as the *Challenger* explosion, were regularly ignored, even though these pieces of information existed somewhere in the organization.

To make sure that crucial information has some chance of being acted upon, an organization should establish a way to flag any potentially vital information so that it gets special attention. There should be an easy way for "ordinary" customers and employees who would know about possible problems to get their observations directly to senior management. Confirmed information with the potential to affect several departments should be automatically forwarded to those departments. Then the person responsible for making sure that the information is acted upon should follow up with a phone call. Once the relevant person receives the information, that person has to accept responsibility for the vital information and agree to take appropriate action.

Missing Motives . . . or "Why Should I Tell You?"

This brings us to motivation. If employees know how to recognize and direct vital information, and if communication channels exist so that they can easily reach the appropriate people with that information, the next question is whether they are adequately *motivated* to get the information to the appropriate person. This can't be taken for granted. Indeed, a close examination of companies that *assume* their employees would automatically pass on vital information shows that not only is there usually no incentive to do so, there is often an incentive not to.

Sometimes employees are reluctant to share vital information because they fear being ridiculed or taken less seriously in the future if the information doesn't turn out to be so vital. New recruits, in particular, tend to be afraid that seasoned veterans will regard them as laughably green, naïve, or unsophisticated if they flag worrisome information unnecessarily. This is one of the reasons that the first signs of the attack on Pearl Harbor weren't immediately reported to the base commander: No one wanted to be seen as a "nervous Nelly." Even veteran employees are often reluctant to contact senior executives for fear of being told that they're overreacting. "Disturbing the boss" with information that is even potentially important needs to be actively rewarded. Otherwise, senior executives will have little chance of being told if their company faces its own Pearl Harbor.

Employees are often even more reluctant to pass on vital information in companies that encourage intense competition between their managers and divisions. In Motorola, for example, the decentralized structure and heavy incentives for business-unit performance made executives wary of cooperating with other business units. The occasional efforts to encourage interdivisional cooperation at the corporate level were never reinforced by powerful enough incentives to be effective.

Incentives play out in another way as well. When a company is structured on a divisional basis, incentives must also match this divisional level of autonomy. At Motorola, however, the power of divisional incentives so overwhelmed other compensation that, as former CEO Robert Galvin noted in Chapter 3, critical investments in digital cell phones were not undertaken because executive pay would have taken a hit.

Call it business school logic gone bad. Without limit or constraint, even the most basic notions about management can go awry. Incentives are an especially dangerous example of this. At Oracle, for example, the typical 2 percent sales commission would skyrocket to as high as 12 percent on the last day of each quarter, creating perverse incentives to delay sales or discount prices to close the deal on that magical day.[5]

If executives have too much to gain from the success of a project, they tend to have difficulty providing balanced information on what its chances of success might be and whether it should be canceled. This problem becomes even worse when managers are rewarded largely in stock options. Unlike actual stock grants, options have no downside risk. If the stock goes down, the option is simply never exercised. On the other hand, if the stock goes up, the option holder can collect all the gain. Iridium CEO Edward Staiano, for example, received a huge number of stock options that would be worthless if he pulled the plug on Iridium, saving investors from further losses. Meanwhile, if Iridium soared, Staiano would become very rich. This kind of situation can make an executive extremely reluctant to pass on information that puts his or her project in a bad light.

If the CEO is the one who wants to suppress adverse information, other managers may find that they no longer have the information they need to correct failing operations. This was one of the factors that contributed to the disastrous decline of Rite Aid. The board of this giant drug store chain gave CEO Martin Grass a $100 million incentive, to be awarded if he could get Rite Aid stock above $49.50.[6] Grass also had an estimated $83 million in exercisable stock.[7] Under these circumstances, it's not too surprising that Grass not only chose a high-risk strategy of rapid expansion, but also presided over a period of wildly inaccurate financial records in which "bad news" was regularly lost. "It was ludicrous," said a leading analyst, commenting on the compensation scheme, "I think it contributed to his being aggressive on accounting."[8] "Aggressive on accounting" in this case was a monumental understatement. After the chaotic condition of Rite Aid's books was discovered, two hundred accountants spent $50 million tackling the momentous task of recalculating the erratic accounting records for fiscal 1999 and 1998. They simply gave up on 1997, which proved to be too overwhelming.[9] When the dust had settled, it was clear that in addition to misleading investors, Rite Aid had no accurate idea of how much money it was making or losing or where. The company had not only managed to lose track of obscure vital information; it had lost track of its routine vital information as well.

Missing Oversight . . . or "I Hear What I Want to Hear."

When all the necessary pieces for the proper handling of information are in place, someone still needs to check to make sure that they're actually working the way they're supposed to. This means that executives overseeing each facet of a business must do more than examine the reports that are routinely forwarded to them. They must actively seek out potentially important information that might not otherwise be coming to their attention.

Many executives fail to discover the extent to which their picture of reality is mistaken simply because they assume that people working for them are relaying information accurately. Tom Yawkey, the owner of the Boston Red Sox, provides an all-too-typical example. When his scouts reported that African-American players were not good enough or simply not ready for big league play, he accepted their reports without question. Yet any serious attempt to verify these evaluations might have caused Yawkey to question his picture of baseball reality.

It's especially easy for executives to accept good news unquestioningly and to investigate further only when there seems to be a problem. If an operation is yielding spectacularly high returns, their instinct is to leave it alone. Yet sizable profits aren't always "healthy profits." No one demonstrated this more dramatically than Barings Bank, whose Singapore-based derivatives trader Nick Leeson racked up such impressive gains that he was hailed at Barings as the "Michael Jordan of trading."[10] The only problem was that he was reporting only his profitable trades, not his unprofitable ones. When the numbers were finally recorded correctly, it turned out that Leeson was responsible for trading losses of 860 million U.K. pounds, which brought down the entire Barings Bank. There had been no shortage of early warning signs. Senior bank officers in London as well as junior staff people in the Singapore office knew—one such person told us, "Of course we knew; everyone knew"—about secret account #88888 that hid Leeson's trading losses. Yet nothing was done to reign in the rogue trader. On one occasion, when a fifty million pound shortfall was uncovered, Leeson came up with three conflicting explanations that were never seriously challenged.[11] The vital information that might have saved Barings from going under kept getting waved aside because no one wanted to look too closely at an operation that appeared to be so profitable.

Corporate boards fall into this trap time and time again. The Rite Aid board, for example, accepted CEO Martin Grass's aggressive expansion unquestioningly because the stock price went up 300 percent. Enron, WorldCom, and a long list of dot-coms all had corporate boards that refrained from questioning their policies or even looking too closely at what they were doing, because their stock prices were soaring. After all, why argue with success, especially if you happen to own a piece of it?

Even if a corporate board is interested in scrutinizing the company more closely, many of them are ill equipped to do this. Sometimes the board members are celebrities and figureheads who simply aren't spending enough time and effort on their directorship. At General Motors, for example, the outside directors during Roger Smith's time averaged eight directorships apiece. Research shows that if a company's directors are on multiple boards, the company is significantly more likely to become a defendant in a securities fraud lawsuit, a result suggesting that directors with less available time tend to be less vigilant.[12]

One of the most striking things about oversight breakdowns at all levels is that organizations are especially likely to bypass their routine checks and controls in the urgent and exceptional situations where they are most needed. NASA, for example, was usually meticulous about its verification procedures. But it abbreviated these procedures prior to the *Challenger* disaster and prior to launching the out-of-focus Hubble Telescope.

In their haste to close an exciting deal, companies negotiating acquisitions are especially prone to attempt shortcuts involving due diligence. After First Union bought the Money Store, it discovered so many accounting problems that it began operation "Search for the Bottom" to find out what was wrong. David Carroll, who headed up the investigation for First Union, said it eventually discovered that it had "bought a company that was devoid of rigorous processes, credit quality and audit" controls.[13]

Bypassing critical controls is a problem endemic to many small companies, and once again, Internet start-ups during the boom years provide the quintessential example in their goal to stamp out bureaucratic encroachments. But how did "bureaucracy busting" work in practice? Unlimited open lines of communication across hierarchical levels created inefficiencies and even a sense of entitlement for lower-level personnel; long hours at work, with few rules, risked burnout and almost certainly generated wasted time; a "no-rules" entrepreneurial atmosphere diffused accountability and responsibility. There's a reason why virtually all large organizations adopt some bureaucratic systems: They create stability, accountability, and efficiency. While *bureaucracy* is a dirty word for many, the truth is that few organizations can survive—as Max Weber realized years ago—without some degree of structure.

The Ungovernable Organization . . . or "Sorry, No Time to Worry About That."

Sometimes the CEO and other senior executives will manage to foster a company culture so disdainful of any proper procedures for handling information that certain aspects of the company become almost ungovernable. This can especially happen in highly innovative, rapidly growing companies that encourage employees to be revolutionary and creative. Oxford Health Plans, for example, believed that to keep a creative edge it needed to avoid everything associated with bureaucracies—including proper oversight. Saatchi & Saatchi regarded rapid expansion as so crucial that keeping track of its day-to-day operations seemed much less important. Rubbermaid was so caught up in the quest for new products that internal systems for assessing and managing operations were greatly neglected. Bankers Trust encouraged its derivatives salespeople to do whatever it took to make the sale, paying little attention to what they said or what promises they made. Enron cultivated a "break the rules" culture that excused careful controls as wasteful bureaucracy, a logic that many dot-coms also adopted as their own. All of these companies were in some respects operating out of control. No one was compiling the information that would have shown what kind of trouble they were in.

The Ungovernable Board or . . . "This Board Just Works, OK?"

Some organizations are ungovernable simply because of fundamental breakdowns in their boards of directors, the group most responsible for vital information and the ultimate governance mechanism in a company.

Remarkably, such board failures aren't due to the "usual suspects" that academics and governance experts keep highlighting: demographics such as the prevalence of outsiders or directors who own significant stock, or even whether the CEO also holds the chair position. Our own research indicates that for companies in the S&P 500 there are no performance differences *at all* between firms that follow the party line— many outsiders, who own lots of stock, with a director who holds the chair position separate from the CEO—and those that do not.

What really counts for board effectiveness is something that isn't so easily captured in statistics and averages, yet is inherently understood by many directors. How boards function as a group—the nature of their interactions among themselves and with the CEO, and what they consider important to look into and what they don't—plays a huge part in board effectiveness.

Most modern boards don't make the cut. Here's how the present-day CEO of Saatchi & Saatchi, Kevin Roberts, describes directors on many boards: "Their average age is ten years off the pace, experience is pretty similar. Generally speaking, they are don't-rock-the-boat guys at the end of their careers who have been there, done that . . . aren't driven or hungry anymore and . . . haven't seen a consumer for so long that they are totally out of sync with what the company is trying to sell."[14] That's Enron under Ken Lay, WorldCom under Bernie Ebbers, Adelphia under John Rigas, Tyco under Dennis Kozlowski, and Conseco under Steve Hilbert.

Boards played a role in many of the business breakdowns we studied. At General Motors, as Roger Smith was spending $45 billion on robotics, the board looked the other way for years. At Mattel, directors backed CEO Jill Barad even after a series of missed targets and disastrous acquisitions. The board troubles at Enron are also now well documented.

Stanley Gault, the former CEO of Rubbermaid, described how that board handled his successor, Wolfgang Schmitt, in the last years before the company was sold to Newell:

> It was his incompetency and the board's procrastination and incompetency that let the company go down the drain. The problems and issues could have been addressed and they could have been fixed expeditiously. The board just decided to take the easy way out and

sell the company. I fault Schmitt, of course, for poor performance but I also certainly fault the board because they could have made a change years earlier and, if so, the company still would be independent today. The collapse of Rubbermaid has to be the greatest commercial disappointment in my fifty-year career and especially because it could have been avoided.[15]

What can help? Boards must understand that it's OK to just say no. Adequate debate, both during and outside board meetings, and both in venues where the CEO is present and in those where he or she isn't, is critical. Having the right (read: diverse, strategically relevant) directors on the board will also help. Chemistry among board members counts too; the constructive conflict that diversity can generate shouldn't spill over into interpersonal conflict that splits the board apart and reduces its effectiveness. One approach that can help is to actively involve incumbents in selecting new directors.

The biggest challenge for boards may well be to identify those early warning signs that something might be amiss and then act on it. The experience of boards in companies such as Enron, Kmart, Global Crossing, and WorldCom suggests that the burden of proof has shifted toward ever-closer board involvement.

Excessive Oversight . . . or "Don't Worry; Everything's Under Control."

When it comes to managing the flow of information, the only thing as bad as insufficient oversight is excessive oversight. One of the reasons that excessive oversight is so devastating is that it tends to keep everyone communicating in routine channels and operating in routine ways. But the whole point about truly vital information is that it *isn't* routine. Often, acting on vital information means not only deviating from routine procedures, but changing them, decisively and dramatically.

Companies suffering from excessive oversight often reward smooth, routine functioning to the point where it becomes impossible to take account of special circumstances or to take corrective measures that go beyond the ordinary. When this emphasis on smooth functioning is combined with the relentlessly positive attitude that characterizes zombie businesses, the results can be devastating. After all, the established management teaching, articulated by Frederick Winslow Taylor early in the twentieth century, is that the job of all employees is to find out what their boss wants and give it to him or her.[16] Managers who are in the habit of questioning or innovating are gradually weeded out, because these activities threaten to disrupt the smooth functioning of the system. At the highest levels, this means that the boss's financial or operational "right-hand man" is likely to become his or her successor, even though this person usually lacks the abilities necessary to choose new directions for the company. As an aside, consider how tightly coupled CEOs and CFOs in such stellar companies as Tyco (CEO Dennis Kozlowski and CFO Mark Swartz), WorldCom (CEO Bernie Ebbers and CFO Scott Sullivan), and Enron (CEO Jeffrey Skilling and CFO Andrew Fastow) became before their fall. People seldom realize it at the time, but they are actually offering a chilling diagnosis of this whole syndrome when they describe a company as "operating like a well-oiled machine."

In the real world, where unexpected hitches and obstacles crop up all the time, the last thing you want is a company that constantly behaves like a well-oiled machine. Because, at some point, it's going to crash.

General Motors provides an extraordinary example of just how destructive excessive oversight can be when combined with zombie attitudes. All the communications in the company were required to follow rigidly established channels that had no provisions for handling information that wasn't routine. Information that didn't fit in a box on an existing form tended to be ignored. Everyone was expected to agree with every statement a superior made. As one GM executive put it, "If you raised a problem, you got labeled as 'negative,' not a team player. If you wanted to rise in the company, you kept your mouth shut and said 'yes' to everything."[17] A 1988 memo by a senior GM executive admitted, "Our culture discourages frank and open debate. The rank and file of GM personnel perceive that management does not receive bad news well."[18] Before any new action was taken, it had to be studied, checked, and rechecked. If you were an engineer with an improved design for any product or process, "You [had] to produce 50,000 studies to show that it [was] a better solution, then you [had] to go through 10 different committees to have it approved."[19] The people with the final say on most proposals were known for their lack of imagination and often claimed to do merely what the numbers told them. In this corporate environment, it was not only extremely difficult to challenge GM's overall picture of reality; it was difficult to correct even its tiniest details.

A corporate board can be prevented from dealing with vital information by excessive oversight, just the way the rest of the company can. During Roger Smith's tenure, for example, the conventions for board meetings at GM didn't allow board members to speak unless they were formally charged with giving an informational report.[20] This procedure by itself rendered the GM board almost completely ineffectual.

The great paradox, where oversight is concerned, is that insufficient oversight and excessive oversight often go together. Rubbermaid, for example, was a company that operated with insufficient oversight where production and distribution efficiencies were concerned. Yet it simultaneously suffered from excessive oversight when it came to the supervision of its middle and senior managers. It was a company that prided itself on innovation, yet it effectively suppressed any innovative thinking when it came to its own business model.

Companies that realize that they are in some respects out of control often manage to achieve the worst of both worlds by imposing controls indiscriminately. This kind of "blind oversight" is especially destructive because it wastes resources and distracts employees from more productive activities at the very moment when they most need to be increasing their efficiency. During its downward spiral, Control Data provided an especially striking example of this. Many of its employees said that they were suddenly being required to spend as much time filing reports on what they were doing as doing their actual work. In an attempt to get a better grip on what was happening to the foundering computer company, top executives succeeded in pushing it under.

The Exceptional Personality . . . or "Don't Mess with the Big Guy."

Sometimes many of the breakdowns in oversight that cause vital information to be neglected are due to the special treatment that is given to exceptional personalities. The personalities who are most often exempted from normal supervision and controls are the ones who have a history of delivering spectacular successes. Executives generally feel that these personalities deserve extra latitude because they are likely to bring off successes in circumstances where lesser talents wouldn't be able to do it. Since many of the personalities involved feel that they have earned this extra latitude, executives with the job of supervising them also have to make sure that they treat them with sufficient deference. After all, if executives don't handle these special talents carefully, they risk losing the company's share in the future profits these personalities might generate.

Investors and corporate boards who think that the best way to judge a business venture is to look at a person's track record should remember that the biggest business disasters are usually created by the personalities with the most impressive track records. It's not just because they're the ones given the biggest opportunities to create business disasters. And it's not just because they have personality traits that have a downside as well as an upside. It's because when they are put in charge of major projects, they usually aren't required to operate with the same degree of scrutiny and with the same checks and balances that constrain lesser mortals.

Look at a few examples and it's easy to see why. Between them, Peter Guber and Jon Peters could claim credit or partial credit for a string of hits that included *The Way We Were*, *The Last Detail*, the Barbra Streisand remake of *A Star Is Born*, *Close Encounters of a Third Kind*, *The Deep*, *Midnight Express*, *Caddyshack*, *Shampoo*, *Missing*, *Flashdance*, *The Color Purple*, *Rain Man*, and *Batman*. Is it any wonder that Sony left them alone to work their magic at the helm of Columbia Pictures? Executives at Motorola's cell phone division built a business with more than 60 percent share, making it the most lucrative and fastest-growing part of the company.[21] What CEO would want to mess with a record like that? Jill Barad built Barbie dolls from $250 million in annual sales in the mid-1980s to almost $2 billion in 1998.[22] By the time she got through segmenting and diversifying the Barbie line, the average American girl had eight Barbie dolls.[23] Why should anyone be surprised that the Mattel board gave her more than a little leeway when she took charge of the entire company?

In cases like these, it's not just the personalities themselves that escape scrutiny. Middle management assumes that with such impressive talent on hand, the accuracy and validity of the details can be taken for granted. Lockheed Martin and NASA's Jet Propulsion Lab had celebrated rocket scientists coordinating their respective contributions to the Mars Climate Orbiter project. But it never occurred to anyone to ask whether they were all supposed to be using English measures or the metric system, a miscalculation that cost the Orbiter its life.[24] Nick Leeson was being celebrated by Barings Bank around the world for his prowess as a derivatives trader. But despite numerous warning signs, it never occurred to anyone outside the Singapore office to rein him in for questionable trading practices, and inside the Singapore office, no one thought to challenge him because he was the boss. These kinds of slip-ups sometimes seem like little things at the time, but in each of these cases—and in many others—they had terrible consequences.

Sometimes the exceptional personalities are exempted from normal oversight not because of their past accomplishments, but because of nepotism, old loyalties, and other emotional biases. Ingvar Kamprad of IKEA is one of the few CEOs who has written about an occasion when he damaged his business by nepotism: "My involvement as part owner of a television factory was perhaps the worst mistake of all. That was in the 1960s, and it cost IKEA 25 to 30 percent of the firm's assets at the time. I had put the husband of a relative in management, but both he and the managing director of the firm were more interested in flying airplanes. The unforgivable part of the fiasco is that I saw the way things were going, but did not have the courage to make the decision to settle the matter in time."[25] Even when executives have the best of intentions and try to uphold the most rigorous of standards, it is almost impossible for them to make sure that their relatives aren't being exempted from the kinds of oversight that would be applied to any ordinary employee.

When people out for personal gain subvert those "best intentions," the trouble really begins. At Adelphia, for example, the Rigas clan allegedly took turns looting the company in the most brazen manner. Manhattan apartments? No problem. Condos in Cancun? Step right up. How about your very own golf course? Absolutely. Perhaps the *pièce de résistance* was the homestead John Rigas constructed, a veritable rambling Ponderosa replete with Norman Rockwell barns and lawns worthy of Augusta.[26] At Enron, CFO Andrew Fastow ran roughshod over any and all who dared to get in his way.[27] The story has repeated itself in many places over the past scandal-plagued years: Tyco's extremely well-paid CEO Dennis Kozlowski scamming to avoid New York State sales tax on multimillion-dollar art work;[28] ImClone's Sam Waksal's insider trading;[29] CEO Ken Lay pushing Enron's stock to workers while privately selling off big chunks of his own shareholdings.[30] Exceptional personalities, no matter how exceptional, must not be exempt from oversight.

Overly Distant Overseers . . . or "Let's Just Leave Them Alone."

When outsiders acquire a company, especially if they are foreigners, there are special factors that can prevent them from receiving vital information about the business and acting on it. Part of the problem, of course, is that they don't know as much about the milieu in which the company operates, and they don't have their own network of contacts within the company. But often a bigger problem is something that might be called the "fear of fixing" syndrome. Outsiders spend millions or billions on the assets, but do little after the acquisition to manage, let alone integrate, the acquired firm into the parent company. Foreign acquirers—particularly in very big acquisitions—tend to adopt an especially "hands-off" manner. The catch is that by acquiring the business, they will often have greatly reduced the incentives for local managers to run the business well.

Watch how this all played out in the difficult acquisition of Chrysler by Daimler-Benz. Despite the "merger of equals" press releases, Chrysler wasn't granted equal status after the deal closed. Yet it was not decisively taken over either. Instead, the company floated in a kind of oversight limbo. Some senior managers withdrew because they felt eclipsed by the Germans in Stuttgart. Others left for opportunities at GM and Ford. Many others began distancing themselves from the company, both financially and emotionally. According to one German executive, "[Chrysler CEO Bob] Eaton went weeks without speaking with Jürgen [Schrempp]. He preferred to maintain lower-level contact. Jürgen, meanwhile, was afraid of being labeled a takeover artist. He left Chrysler alone for too long."[31]

A well-placed former Chrysler executive described why:

> Jürgen Schrempp looked at Chrysler's past success and told himself there is no point in trying to smash these two companies together. Some stuff was pulled together, but they said, "Operationally let's let the Chrysler guys continue to run it, because they have done a great job in the past." What they didn't take into account was that immediately prior to the consummation of the merger or shortly

thereafter, enough of the key members of that former Chrysler management team left. They saw the forest, but they didn't realize that removing four or five key trees was going to radically change the ecosystem in that forest. It was a misjudgment.[32]

Finally, some thirty months after Daimler-Benz announced it was "merging" with Chrysler, the German company began to move aggressively to fix Chrysler's problems. It sent in German managers, started examining the operations in detail, and scrambled to make changes that should have been made before the sale had even taken place.

Lost Lessons . . . or "Can We Just Move on Already?"

There is one last situation in which businesses lose track of vital information that's worth special attention. This is when a business neglects to use the information that can be gained from a business breakdown itself (the sort of information that you are gaining by reading this book).

One reason to make a special effort is that small failures often precede large failures of a similar nature. By learning how to prevent that type of failure the first time it occurs, a company will often protect itself from a much worse catastrophe in the future. Saatchi & Saatchi is a good example of a company that didn't learn from its previous breakdowns. Instead of learning what to do differently when some of its first acquisitions went bad, it continued to overpay, conduct insufficient due diligence, and engage in minimal and ineffective integration activities. Businesses that suffer any scale of breakdown can salvage something important from the experience if they learn how to prevent similar failures in the future.

Another reason is that somewhere in the failed enterprise are valuable intellectual assets. Frequently these assets were costly to acquire and represent a hard-to-replace resource. By transferring these assets to new or surviving operations, the company will often be able to use them to create new value. FedEx's failed ZapMail project is a perfect example. This venture, designed to send FAX messages between clients, proved impractical from a business standpoint. But by the time FedEx had finished learning the lessons of the failed venture, it had introduced a new engineering-driven cohort to the firm, boosted the firm's technological capabilities, and enabled the company to implement sophisticated tracking systems ahead of its rivals. Instead of simply writing off the project, the firm mined it so effectively that it yielded some of FedEx's most valuable competitive tools.

But when businesses are too quick to move on to new projects, they often fail to learn the most basic lesson of any failure, which is simply that such failures are possible. This, in turn, leads them to make the error of not allowing for errors. The result is that executives fail to allow themselves enough latitude to correct mistakes and change course. When this is the case, one small slip is often all it will take to send the whole enterprise hurtling toward disaster. The huge upfront investment in Iridium made that project particularly vulnerable to the "no mistakes allowed" standard, one that no company can meet. Bary Bertiger, the Motorola engineer who dreamed up Iridium, drew an interesting parallel in our conversation with him:

> There were no mistakes allowed because the smallest of mistakes could put you in deep trouble in a hurry because it was all leverage. 3G cellular operators are going to be looking at a very similar landscape . . . because they spent billions on licenses, billions on infrastructure, and if they guess wrong on what it's going to take to sign people up to this new service, we're going to see a lot of operators fail as a result.[33]

Many of the businesses and government agencies that we studied turned out on investigation to be operating without a safety net. Enron and LTCM each exposed themselves to huge downside risks that they could neither cover nor rapidly reduce. NASA's biggest failures all came when the backup systems and apparently redundant test sequences had been bypassed. Snow Brand Milk was seduced by the D-0 delivery standard that left absolutely no room for error. Each of these organizations had experienced earlier failures that could have taught it about the larger hazards it needed to plan for. But each organization had procedures in place that made learning from those failures almost impossible.

Who's in Charge Here, Anyway?

When we track vital information that's been ignored at companies suffering breakdowns, we find in case after case that it wasn't an isolated slip-up or instance of incompetence on the part of an individual employee. In virtually every example, it was *the way the system had been set up* that was to blame.

Who is responsible for letting a company get into this condition? A mistaken picture of reality will contribute to this state of affairs, and this state of affairs will help preserve a mistaken picture of reality. The delusional policies and attitudes that make for a zombie business will help support the mistaken picture of reality, encouraging employees to ignore any vital information that would threaten it. In fact, all three of these things—the mistaken picture of reality, zombie attitudes, and bad procedures for handling vital information—could be described as three sides of a terrible triangle, where each side supports the others.

But someone has to be responsible for putting this terrible triangle into place. And someone has to be responsible for dismantling it. That someone is the subject of the next chapter.

CHAPTER 9

Seven Habits of Spectacularly Unsuccessful People

The Personal Qualities of Leaders
Who Preside over Major Business Failures

To be spectacularly unsuccessful requires some very special personal qualities. We're talking about people whose failures were breathtakingly gigantic, who have taken huge, world-renowned business operations and made them almost worthless. They have caused thousands of people to lose their jobs and thousands of investors to lose their investments. They've managed to destroy hundreds of millions or even billions of dollars of value. Their destructive effect is so beyond the range of ordinary human beings that it's on a scale normally associated only with earthquakes and hurricanes.

The personal qualities that make this awesome scale of destruction possible are all the more fascinating because they are regularly found in conjunction with truly admirable qualities. After all, hardly anyone gets a chance to destroy so much value without also demonstrating a potential to create it. Most of the great destroyers of value are people of unusual intelligence and remarkable talent. They are almost always capable of being irresistibly charming, exercising great personal magnetism, and inspiring others. Their faces have typically appeared on the covers of *Forbes*, *Fortune*, *BusinessWeek*, and other business publications.

Yet when it comes to the crunch, these people fail monumentally. The list of leaders who have failed spectacularly is not a list of people who weren't up for the job. It's a list of people who had a special gift for taking what could have been a modest failure and turning it into a gigantic one.

How do they do it? What's the secret of their destructiveness? Remarkably enough, it's possible to identify seven habits that characterize

213

spectacularly unsuccessful people. Nearly all of the leaders who preside over major business failures exhibit five or six of these habits. Many of them exhibit all seven. Even more remarkable, each of these habits represents a quality that is widely admired in today's business world. As a society, we don't just tolerate the qualities that make leaders spectacularly unsuccessful; we encourage them.

Let's look, then, at The Seven Habits of Spectacularly Unsuccessful People. Although these habits are most destructive when it's the CEO who exhibits them, other managers with these habits can do terrible harm as well. Learning to recognize these habits is the first step toward finding ways to compensate for them.

Habit #1: They see themselves and their companies as dominating their environments

"Wait a minute," you might say. "Where's the harm in that? Don't we want leaders who are ambitious and proactive? Shouldn't a CEO seize the initiative and create business opportunities, not just react to developments in his or her industry? Shouldn't the company try to dominate its business environment, shaping the future of its markets as well as setting the pace within them?"

The answer to all these questions is, of course, yes. But there's a catch. Successful leaders are proactive because they know that they *don't* dominate their environment. They know that no matter how successful they have been in the past, they are always at the mercy of changing circumstances. They need to generate a constant stream of new initiatives because they *can't* make things happen at will. To be successful for more than a fleeting moment, every business venture needs to be one that customers and suppliers interact with voluntarily. This means that no matter how successful the company, its overall business plan will need to be continually readjusted and renegotiated.

Leaders who see themselves and their companies as dominating their environments forget these things. They vastly overestimate the extent to which they are controlling events and vastly underestimate the role of chance and circumstance in their success. They think that they can dictate terms to those around them. They think that they're successful and that their company is successful *because they made it happen*.

There are some deep psychological reasons why many leaders begin thinking this way, the most important of which is the human need to feel responsible for what happens to us. We need to feel that we can influence our fate when things are going wrong, and that we deserve our success when things go right. Yet CEOs are constantly faced with threats that are in some respects beyond their control, and they are successful in some respects beyond what they deserve. Under these circumstances, many business leaders *need* to believe that they are dominating their environments in order to cope with the stresses of their jobs.

The Illusion of Personal Preeminence Many a CEO believes that he or she is personally able to control the things that will determine the company's success or failure, a tendency labeled the illusion of personal preeminence. Rather than scrambling to keep track of changing conditions, the CEOs who succumb to this illusion believe that they can create the conditions under which they and their company will operate. What's more, they believe that they can do it by their own personal genius and force of personality. Like certain film directors, they see themselves as the *auteurs* of their companies and sometimes even as the *auteurs* of their industry. They imagine that their job is to realize their creative vision, imposing their will on unruly collaborators and inert raw materials. As far as they're concerned, everyone else in the company is there to carry out their personal conception of what the company should be.

When CEOs actually do possess a measure of genius, they are especially prone to slide into this illusion of personal preeminence. An Wang, for example, knew that he was a technical genius. This led him to believe that he could master business situations by employing the same intelligence and diligence that had allowed him to master technical problems. Mossimo Giannulli had a touch of genius when it came to expressing popular trends in clothing designs. This led him to believe that he was also a business genius, one who had little need for qualified and experienced managers. In the opinion of Merrill Lynch analyst Brenda Gall, Mossimo "bought into his own image too much" and believed that he could do anything.[1] It wasn't until his rapid growth plan fell victim to cost overruns, late shipments to major customers, and inadequate systems—stripping his company's stock price by 90 percent—that he finally stepped down.

Executives with a degree of business genius are just as susceptible to this illusion as those with a more technical kind of genius. Samsung CEO Kun-Hee Lee was so extraordinarily successful with semiconductors and electronics that he thought he could repeat this success with automobiles. Webvan CEO George Shaheen had been so successful in his earlier job as CEO of Andersen Consulting that he was completely oblivious to the fact that he wasn't communicating effectively with his managers in Webvan. "He operated twenty thousand feet above everyone else," explained a former Webvan executive. "I liked him," commented another Webvan manager, "but he was the wrong man, particularly for a public company."[2]

Behavior That's a Little Too Preeminent Leaders who suffer from the illusion of personal preeminence often reveal this in the way that they treat the people around them. To these leaders, the people they interact with are instruments to be used, materials to be molded, or audiences for the leader's performances. When business leaders think this way, they often use intimidating or excessive behavior to dominate the people who surround them. In most cases, it's not unconscious or unintentional. They want to be "larger than life," "legendary," "awe-inspiring." The subtlest practitioners of this intimidating personal style are those who achieve it while speaking softly and making small gestures. They revel in the contrast between the little things they do and the huge effects they can get by doing them. But there is no shortage of leaders who prefer the other alternative—speaking loudly and carrying a big stick. Whichever style they chose, leaders who believe in their personal preeminence can achieve a remarkable level of intimidation.

As cofounder and CEO, Bob Levine of Cabletron was famous for his flamboyant, confrontational style. He was also famous for his bodybuilding regimen, right-wing politics, and survivalist mentality. He purchased an abandoned grocery store near the company's offices so he could lift weights during his lunch hour. His lighter side is illustrated by the fact that he bought a working army tank to keep in his yard. Legend has it that he once used it to scare a pizza deliveryman. As a salesman, he was known for aggressive motivational stunts. At one Cabletron sales meeting, he arrived brandishing a knife to teach employees about killing the competition. At another, he appeared dressed in combat fatigues and swinging a machete.[3]

Few CEOs could match Bob Levine when it came to colorful antics, but many CEOs whose companies suffered major breakdowns could match him when it came to sheer intimidation. Roger Smith of GM had such a ferocious disposition that the EDS executives who witnessed one of his outbursts say he turned red, shouted, and pounded on the table.[4] Jerry Sanders of Advanced Micro Devices (AMD) intimidated those around him by his temper to such an extent that they were afraid to tell him any news that they thought might upset him.[5] Enron leaders Jeffrey Skilling and Andrew Fastow were known for their toughness and arrogance.[6] Sir Richard Greenbury was feared for years by his underlings at Marks & Spencer.[7] Rubbermaid's Wolfgang Schmitt could be "a very engaging and personable guy," but he adopted a personal style at work that was described as "very blunt and intimidating in dealing with people." Inside the company Schmitt "was known as the 'U-boat commander' because he had a very tough, take-no-prisoners style about him."[8] These aren't people who occasionally get angry; they are people who have made displays of anger and other intimidating behavior part of their basic management style.

The Illusion of Corporate Preeminence Executives who succumb to an illusion of personal preeminence often succumb to an illusion of corporate preeminence too. This is a belief on the part of the CEO that his or her company is absolutely central to suppliers and customers alike. Rather than looking to satisfy customer needs, the CEOs who believe they run "preeminent companies" often act as though their customers are the lucky ones, fortunate to be able to have their needs satisfied so effectively. It's almost as if the entire customer relationship is turned on its head so that it is the customers' job to please the company by showing themselves worthy of the company's products.

Leaders who suffer from an illusion of corporate preeminence often believe that the superiority of their company's product makes it invulnerable. An Wang, for example, believed that Wang would eventually dominate its markets because its products were simply so much better than any others. Bob Levine believed that rivals such as Cisco were producing such inferior products that he had little need to take them seriously. If the customers didn't immediately see this, he thought it was the job of Cabletron's sales force to *make* them see it.[9] CEOs such as these become so proud of their company's product that they believe that its sheer excellence will give them the latitude to do anything they please. After all, they tell themselves, if you make the best product in the world, customers must either come to you or settle for something inferior.

Even when competitors who offer better designs or better prices challenge the company's products, executives who suffer from an illusion of corporate preeminence will continue to believe that their company is secure simply because of its status in the business world. Kun-Hee Lee, for example, believed that Samsung's corporate preeminence more or less guaranteed its success. "We, at Samsung, used to believe that we could do better than anyone else," one of Samsung's managers later confessed. "Samsung believed that it could not fail."[10] Wolfgang Schmitt of Rubbermaid has said, "Our success had its own form of seductiveness. It made us pretty self-satisfied and not inclined to ask the tough questions."[11] At Schwinn, managers boasted, "We don't have competition. We're Schwinn."[12]

Habit #2: They identify so completely with the company that there is no clear boundary between their personal interests and their corporation's interests

Like the first habit, this one can readily seem innocuous or beneficial. After all, don't we want our business leaders to be completely committed to their company? To see the company's best interests and their own best interests as one and the same? To be as careful with company money as they would be with their own?

Yet, in case after case, a deeper examination of the factors contributing to major business failures suggests that *the failed executives were not identifying too little with the company, but too much.*

What is going on here? In Chapter 2, we already pointed out some of the problems that arise when the primary shareholder is also the primary manager. For one, giving an executive too large a stake in the company also gives the executive too much power. If the CEO controls too large a block of stock, there will be no one in a position to take corrective action if the CEO chooses a dangerous or destructive course.

Here we are concerned with something quite different. Identifying too much with the company encourages CEOs to make unwise decisions. Instead of treating the company as something they need to care for, nurture, and protect, CEOs who identify too much with their company treat the company as an extension of themselves. They cause the company to do things that would make sense for a person, but do not make sense for a company.

This is a habit that can be remarkably easy to slip into. CEOs are especially prone to identify too much with a company if they believe that they are personally responsible for the company's success. This means that leaders who succumb to the illusion of personal preeminence are also likely to fall into this related trap. If the CEOs are company founders or have taken a small company and helped turn it into a very big one, they are in particular danger of confusing their company's achievements with their own. In extreme cases, the CEO will actually believe he or she IS the company. Mossimo Giannulli liked to say, "I am Mossimo." Kun-Hee Lee was rumored to be quite pleased to be referred to as "Mr. Samsung." For many years, in his own mind and in the minds of his employees, An Wang *was* Wang.

When CEOs and their employees are unable to separate the CEO from the organization, they're well on their way to a "private-empire" mentality. The CEOs begin to behave as though they own their companies, even when they don't, and they begin to act as though they have the right to do anything they want with them, which isn't true.

CEOs who succumb to this mentality often use the corporation to carry out personal ambitions when these are not a good way to generate profits. Samsung CEO Kun-Hee Lee decided to enter the automobile industry mostly because he liked cars. The Saatchi brothers pushed their company to become bigger and bigger, regardless of whether or not this resulted in more profits, because of their own aggressively expansive egos.

Once they've launched a project, such leaders often invest in it with no sense of proportion or restraint because they feel that betting on the project is betting on themselves. Roger Smith's plan to make GM factories as worker-free as possible became so much a part of his own identity that he was incapable of stepping back and evaluating it critically. A succession of Motorola CEOs made Iridium so much a symbol of their imaginations and boldness in envisioning the future that it became difficult for them to stop and reevaluate the venture when circumstances changed. Mossimo Giannulli couldn't get any critical distance whatsoever from the company he had named for himself, so its activities all became an expression of his own megalomaniac ego. In cases such as these, the CEO becomes unable to acknowledge that the pet project has become a losing proposition, because to do so would seem like a declaration of personal inadequacy.

Legendary automotive executive John DeLorean provides a stunning demonstration of how thoroughly identification with a company can ruin its chances of success when he tried to launch a new car company. At first, the prospects for his venture seemed excellent. But as soon as DeLorean decided to name the car he would manufacture after himself, the whole enterprise took on a different tone. He changed the design of the company's first model from a vehicle for the middle classes to the "supercar" later featured in the *Back to the Future* movies. He also greatly increased the amount he was spending to build his automobile factory in Northern Ireland. Essentially, his ego demanded that everything associated with his own name be first class. This made the environment he created for his workers into a model for factories everywhere. But it also made him almost psychologically incapable of controlling costs. Later, when it became increasingly obvious that DeLorean's automobile company was in serious trouble, DeLorean couldn't bear to recognize it because it would have seemed as though he was betraying himself.

Decisions Express the Executive's Personality When CEOs identify too much with the company, they tend to make business choices to suit themselves, not the company. Cabletron neglected marketing largely because cofounder Craig Benson (who is now governor of New Hampshire) never liked marketing. Stephen Wiggins, CEO of Oxford Health Plans, saw himself as too much of a computer expert to be running a company that would settle for mass-market software. Said Michael Kornett, Oxford's president in 1992 and 1993, "He's computer-literate and a systems jockey. His mind-set was 'We aren't a vanilla company and we can't buy a vanilla managed-care processing system.' "[13] This fixation on avoiding vanilla ended up costing Wiggins his job, and almost cost the company its life.

Executives who adopt this general frame of mind regularly confuse their personal adversaries with the company's adversaries. An Wang, for example, hated IBM because he felt that it had cheated him early in his career, so for a long time, he refused to cooperate with IBM, even indirectly. This is one of the reasons why he delayed entering the PC market and ultimately did it with proprietary software. Jerry Sanders of AMD hated Intel and attacked it for years, sometimes to the obvious detriment of AMD.[14] Stephen Wiggins of Oxford Health Plans hated the government so much that he often seemed more eager to score points in his ongoing battles with government agencies than to accept the compromises that would have allowed his company to get on with business. The racist attitudes that permeated the Boston Red Sox in the age of integration is a particularly heinous example of how personal hatreds can get translated into corporate hatreds, and the price you pay for crossing that line.

Perhaps the most surprising thing that happens when CEOs identify too much with their company is that they become *less* careful with the company's assets. They take big risks with other people's money, *not* because it's *other* people's money, but because they are treating it as their *own* money and *they happen to be big risk takers.* Very often, it's making big bets and managing to collect on them that got the CEOs into their top jobs in the first place. Once in charge, these CEOs aren't likely to abandon the risk-taking style that made them rise above their peers. Bankers Trust CEO Charles Sanford, Jr., is a perfect example. Not only did he have a risk-taking attitude himself; he encouraged it among employees by basing their pay entirely on their recent performance. In the mid-1990s, his high-flying recruits were paid to trade aggressively, innovate aggressively, and sell aggressively.[15] They weren't paid to safeguard company assets. So they didn't. The push to sell derivatives led to lawsuits, lost business, and Charlie Sanford's job.[16]

Unfortunately, this sort of attitude toward company money is more the rule than the exception. Even Peter Guber and Jon Peters, despite their violation of other codes, were mostly guilty of treating Sony Pictures as an extension of their own personalities. If they were extravagant and reckless with Sony's resources, it was mostly because they were extravagant and reckless with their own resources.

The Darkest Side of Identifying with the Company When leaders identify with their companies too much, they become increasingly likely to use corporate funds for personal reasons. At the time, most CEOs aren't aiming to do anything illegal. In nearly every case, they slide down a slippery slope. Executives get used to traveling in a cocoon of constant luxury and having their every expenditure on the road treated as a business expense. They work such long hours that they feel they've given up their private lives for the company. So eventually they come to believe that everything they do is "for the company" and should be paid for by the company.

CEOs find it especially easy to rationalize the use of corporate funds for private purposes when these purposes are philanthropic and involve causes the corporation would generally support. In June 2000, for example, Fruit of the Loom began investigating former CEO William Farley for directing the company to make charitable donations dating back to 1994 to "satisfy his or his family's personal obligations under pledge agreements."[17] The nonprofit organizations in question ranged from educational institutions such as Boston College, to hospitals such as New York Presbyterian. All of these contributions would have seemed beneficial to the world and at least vaguely in the interests of Fruit of the Loom. Yet they involve questionable expenditures of corporate funds and equally questionable expenditures of the executive's time and attention.

Once executives are covering some of their personal expenditures with company money, it becomes increasingly difficult to keep the personal and the corporate separate. This accelerates the blurring of boundaries between personal identity and corporate identity. After John DeLorean named the new car his company was going to manufacture a "DeLorean," people started to call the company DeLorean, and employees said that they worked for DeLorean. When listening to DeLorean's own speech, it was often hard to tell whether he was talking about the car, himself, or his company. Under the circumstances, is it any wonder that he tended to forget which checkbook was which?[18]

If the executives have been on the job long or have overseen a period of rapid growth, they may come to feel that they've made so much money for the company that their expenditures on themselves and those dear to them, even if extravagant, are trivial by comparison. In fact, by their very extravagance, these executives often seem to be demonstrating to themselves how great the services were that they performed for their company. This twisted logic seems to have been one of the factors shaping the behavior of Dennis Kozlowski of Tyco. His pride in his company and his pride in his own extravagance were not in conflict, but seem, in fact, to have reinforced each other. This is why he could sound so innocent and sincere, making speeches about the need for ethical conduct in business, while simultaneously using corporate funds for personal purposes to an extent that is now becoming legendary. If Kozlowski seemed utterly shameless, it was because in his own mind, these things demonstrated his worth to his company and to society.[19]

Being CEO of a sizable corporation is probably the closest thing in today's world to being king of your own country. The Pressman brothers demonstrated how kings could live if their kingdom were Barneys. Gene Pressman lived in Bugsy Siegel's former twenty-five-thousand-square-foot home with accessories that included a collection of fine wines—estimated at one hundred thousand bottles—and a number of antique cars.[20] While Barneys slid into a financial crisis, Pressman's daughter Nancy spent $1.2 million remodeling her home, made a practice of removing money from the store's "money room" for personal use, and regularly gave her boyfriends extravagant outfits she had helped herself to from the store racks. In 1994 and 1995, as the company operated tens of millions in the red, the Pressmans took what a former executive estimates to be "at least $14 million to $15 million out of Barneys and possibly much more." Gene embarked on a million-dollar renovation of his Westchester home. Then, right before declaring bankruptcy, Gene and Bob Pressman went on vacation and withdrew an additional $5 million from the company for supposed retroactive salary increases.[21] From an ethical and business standpoint, this might sound self-destructively insane. But it is really just an extreme case of executives failing to distinguish between themselves and their company.

Habit #3: They think they have all the answers

It's hard not to be impressed with business leaders who continually dazzle us with the speed with which they can zero in on what's really important. They always seem to have a deep acquaintance with the relevant facts. They can instantly make sense out of complex situations. Above all, they have a gift for sheer decisiveness.

Altogether, this is the image of executive competence that we've been taught to admire for decades. Movies, television shows, and journalists all offer us instantly recognizable vignettes of the dynamic executive making a dozen decisions a minute, snapping out orders that will redirect huge enterprises, dealing with numerous crises at once, and taking only seconds to size up situations that have obviously stumped everyone else for days. At the higher levels of business, there actually are many people who resemble this stereotype or seriously aspire to resemble it. Their personal styles may vary, but underlying all their conduct on the job is this ideal of an executive who has all the answers and who can articulate those answers as fast as his or her associates can ask the questions.

The problem with this picture of executive competence is that it is really a fraud. In a world where business conditions are constantly changing and innovations often seem to be the only constant, no one can "have all the answers" for long. Leaders who are invariably crisp and decisive tend to settle issues so quickly that they have no opportunity to grasp the ramifications. Worse, because these leaders need to feel that they already have all the answers, they have no way to learn *new* answers. Their instinct, whenever something truly important is at stake, is to push for rapid closure, allowing no periods of uncertainty, even when uncertainty is appropriate.

People around the CEO sometimes encourage this sort of "decisive behavior" because they find it reassuring. They want to follow a leader who has all the answers. The fact that they are invariably following a leader who doesn't have all the answers—even though they know logically that this has to be the case—is very frightening.

Leaders who accept this ideal of executive competence tend to relish the sort of performance they are able to give, where they make snap decisions and issue orders at high speed. Rubbermaid CEO Wolfgang Schmitt was especially fond of demonstrating his ability to sort out difficult issues in a flash. A former colleague told us that around Rubbermaid "The joke went, 'Wolf knows everything about everything.' " This attitude of having all the answers permeated Schmitt's entire management style. "I remember sitting in one discussion," this colleague said, "where we were talking about a particularly complex acquisition we made in Europe and Wolf, without hearing different points of view just said, 'Well, this is what we are going to do.' He made it sound as if it was obvious to him and should have been obvious to the rest of us."[22]

No industry seems immune from choosing CEOs who exhibit this executive style. Roger Smith of GM visibly reveled in being crisp and decisive, even when he had only a limited idea of what the implications of his decisions might be. George Shaheen of Webvan was at his best when demonstrating his ability to be quick and incisive. The only problem was that he had never stopped to figure out if his company's business plan was a workable one. Dennis Kozlowski of Tyco not only seemed to have an instant answer for every issue his company faced; he also seemed able to articulate the management principle that each decision illustrated. In company after company, the executive leading the way to disaster seems the living embodiment of what the media have taught us a decisive executive should look like.

All of these paragons of decision making share another quality—they learn only what is a direct extension of what they already know. Wolfgang Schmitt is a good example. When describing him, John Mariotto, former president of Rubbermaid's office products unit, said, "Wolf's problem is he will not listen and really hear people telling him things he doesn't agree with, and he has few left who will dare to disagree with him anyway."[23] Stanley Gault, the earlier Rubbermaid CEO, stated Schmitt's problem even more simply: "He refused to accept advice and suggestions."[24]

One of the critical side effects of a CEO's fixation on being right is that opposition can go underground, effectively closing down dissent. Once this happens, the entire organization will grind to a halt, *whether or not these CEOs were actually right or wrong in their judgments.*

Interestingly, Schmitt saw himself as an agent of change at Rubbermaid and was frustrated by people who "gave you lip service, and [others] who actively undermined the efforts." As he told us with evident irritation, others in the company said, "We've been extraordinarily successful. Why would we need to change? One of America's most admired companies, blah, blah, blah."[25] The difference in perception between Schmitt and his staff at Rubbermaid is striking, and characteristic of many of the executives described in this chapter. For Schmitt, the problem wasn't his approach. He knew that the company needed to change, and he knew how it needed to change. Unfortunately, he was a leader without followers.

Control Freaks Leaders who adopt the ideal of executive competence usually try to have the final say on everything their company does. If, like so many spectacularly unsuccessful leaders, they also feel personally responsible for the company's success and identify strongly with it, this will increase their desire for control. The more these leaders can control their companies, the less they feel threatened that their success depends on things outside their control. Thus, personal control for these leaders is both an extension of what they see as their executive role and protection against their own vulnerabilities.

It would be hard to find anyone who illustrates this compulsion to control everything better than An Wang. "Control was a big issue," one of his salespeople emphasized. Employees knew that An Wang had to bestow his blessing on just about everything that happened within the company. And if an issue seemed important, Wang would intervene to make the decision himself, often in an ad hoc manner. "There was an autocratic management style from the top down."[26]

In personality, Mossimo Giannulli seems at first glance to be as different from An Wang as anyone could be, yet in his compulsion to control everything, he is much the same. Besides designing and marketing the merchandise, he made every key decision himself, rather than delegating to other managers.[27] "I don't think anyone is as capable of running this company as [I am]," he explained, admitting that some have called him a "control freak."[28]

Ultimately, executives "with all the answers" trust no one. Only they can be relied upon to make the final call on any issue where the answer isn't obvious. This is how they put their personal imprint on every aspect of their company's operations.

Habit #4: They ruthlessly eliminate anyone who isn't 100 percent behind them

Like the other habits of spectacularly unsuccessful people, this one can seem like an essential part of the leader's role. CEOs with a vision believe that a major part of their job is to instill a belief in their vision throughout their company, getting everyone working together to achieve the goals they've set out. If a manager, for instance, doesn't rally around the cause, these CEOs feel their vision is being undermined. After a short grace period, these CEOs will ultimately confront hesitant managers with the choice of "getting with the plan" or leaving.

The drawback of this policy is that it's both unnecessary and destructive. CEOs don't need to have everyone in the company unreservedly endorse their vision to have the company carry it out successfully. By eliminating all dissenting and contrasting viewpoints, they cut themselves off from their best chance of correcting problems as they arise.

Executives who have presided over major business disasters have regularly removed or ousted anyone likely to take a critical or contrasting position. Roger Smith of GM was especially successful at getting rid of any executives and board members who saw things differently than he did—sometimes by having them fired, but often by sending them to some distant outpost where they'd have no further influence at headquarters. Jill Barad at Mattel removed her senior lieutenants in relatively short order if she thought they had serious reservations about the way she was running things. At Fruit of the Loom, an insider reported, "It almost became a badge of honor to get fired by Bill Farley."[29] At Rubbermaid, Wolfgang Schmitt created such a threatening atmosphere that firings were often unnecessary. When new executives brought in to effect change realized that they'd get no support from the CEO, many of them left almost as fast as they had come on board. Ed Schwinn simply left the room when some senior Schwinn executives began outlining what they saw as the problems in the company. Upon his return, he announced, "Guys, this is not going in the direction that I wanted it to. We'll pick this thing up at a later date." One week later, the executive who was most forceful in describing Schwinn's problems was asked to resign.[30]

Habit #5: They are consummate company spokespersons, obsessed with the company image

Leaders who adopt this fifth habit become the sort of high-profile CEOs that are constantly in the public eye. They spend a lot of time giving public speeches, appearing on television, and being interviewed by journalists, performing with remarkable charisma and aplomb. They brilliantly inspire confidence among the public, employees, potential new recruits, and, especially, investors.

The problem is that amidst all the media frenzy and accolades, these leaders risk allowing their management efforts to become shallow and ineffective. Instead of actually accomplishing things, they often settle for the appearance of accomplishing things. Their best energies and attention go into crafting a public image, rather than into running the company. In fact, in extreme cases, they can no longer tell the difference. A meeting where they turn in a great performance seems as good as a meeting that actually gets something done.

The public tendency to judge a CEO's success by the current price of the company's stock greatly reinforces this fifth habit, because the fastest and easiest way to improve the share price is to put on a good show for the media and for investors.

The unholy alliance of business media and stock markets also encourages companies to choose "great communicators" for their top positions. William Farley of Fruit of the Loom, for example, was known throughout his career for his ability to dazzle potential investors. As one Chicago columnist wrote, "There has always been something attractive and optimistic about Farley that otherwise savvy investors cannot resist. And there is something about the showman in him that has entranced otherwise sober spectators."[31] Dennis Kozlowski of Tyco had a similar ability to impress investors and journalists. He maintained a heavy schedule of speeches and interviews in which he held up Tyco as a model of management practices, often, ironically enough, emphasizing the importance of ethical standards.

Most CEOs achieve this level of media success not by some stroke of luck, but by devoting themselves assiduously to public relations. Jerry Sanders of AMD is just one of the many CEOs who have loved making public appearances and being covered by the press. Maurice and Charles Saatchi devoted so much of their energies to promoting and shaping the public image of Saatchi & Saatchi that it sometimes seemed that the main thing their agency was advertising was the advertising agency itself. Sam Waksal, the former CEO of ImClone who pleaded guilty to insider trading charges, was a master at drumming up media interest in his company's cancer-drug Erbitux.

Even CEOs such as GM's Roger Smith, who are not ordinarily thought of as media darlings, often fall into this fifth habit of spectacularly unsuccessful people. Despite his famous reluctance to be interviewed for the movie *Roger and Me*, Smith was proud of his ability to "wow the audience" at business gatherings by presenting a dazzling vision of how GM's new technological and business innovations were supposed to work. Unfortunately, this vision had little to do with how the innovations actually did work. While Smith was describing how precisely programmed robots would smoothly perform complex tasks, back at GM's Hamtranck paint facility the real-life robots were spray-painting each other.[32]

Pitching the New Vision When a company is being genuinely innovative, it's especially tempting for the CEO to concentrate most of his or her energies on selling the new vision animating the company's efforts. During the years when General Magic was struggling to develop a viable product, for example, CEO Marc Porat seemed to be in every magazine and news show. During Enron's period of rapid innovation and growth, both Jeffrey Skilling and Ken Lay seem to have been more concerned with creating an appearance of trading initiatives at their energy company than with actually implementing these initiatives. But the kind of all-out public relations efforts these CEOs managed to mount not only distracted them from the job at hand; they also raised expectations impossible for their companies to meet. Rather than admit that they have fallen short of these expectations, and weaken their standing in the capital markets, CEOs in this predicament often fall into a vicious circle. They bolster each unrealistic conception of what the company is doing with another unrealistic conception. They don't dare let up on their public relations efforts for fear that investors and the media will start viewing the company in a more skeptical light.

Becoming Pop Icons Even though their companies may be in a state of crisis, many of these CEOs find time to make themselves not just corporate spokespeople, but lifestyle spokespeople, appearing in TV ads and celebrity news columns. Ed Schwinn seized the opportunity to star as himself in an American Express commercial. William Farley appeared in TV ads for Fruit of the Loom underwear, lifting weights, and he briefly considered running for president in 1988.[33] Mossimo Giannulli played a role in Janet Jackson's "You Want This?" video. He signed autographs in department store appearances, dated and later married television actress Lori Loughlin, and was seen around Hollywood with his actor friends Steven Baldwin and John Stamos.[34] Are these CEO types really the best media icons to use in promoting the company? And if they *are* the best icons, should they be trying to run the company at the same time?

Some CEOs achieve a similar celebrity status by making high-profile donations and lavish public expenditures. Steve Hilbert of Conseco was renowned for his philanthropy and his spectacular social affairs. The Indianapolis Symphony's Hilbert Circle Theater now bears his name, and the local NBA team plays in Conseco Fieldhouse.[35] The huge parties Hilbert threw included one where he chartered a jumbo jet to fly guests to St. Martin for his sixth wife's birthday. The Saatchi brothers made themselves into public figures, not just in the world of business, but also in the worlds of art and politics. They created an important modern art museum from their private collection and Maurice was knighted by the Queen. If the scale of the philanthropy doesn't trigger suspicions, the ostentation of the contributions and the way they are so often combined with personal extravagance should.

Don't Bother Me with Details In the midst of their public relations blitz, these CEOs often leave the mundane details of their business affairs to others. Dennis Kozlowski of Tyco sometimes intervened in remarkably minor matters, but he left most of Tyco's day-to-day operations unsupervised. "There is no limit to how big the company could get because of the way we manage it," explained one of his lieutenants. "It's a very decentralized company and Dennis will tell you his most difficult job is to get the best managers in the world to manage these companies."[36] Roger Smith, as CEO of GM, was oblivious to what many of his decisions meant at the factory level and to the lives of the workers.[37] CEOs obsessed with image have little time for operational details.

Financial Statements as Public Relations Tools When CEOs make the company's image their top priority, they tend to encourage financial reporting practices that promote that image. In other words, instead of treating their financial accounts as a control tool, they treat them as a public relations tool. This, of course, puts the executives on another slippery slope. The resulting examples of creative accounting exist in many variations. Steve Hilbert of Conseco authorized financial procedures that moved acquisitions on and off the company's balance sheet at the company's convenience. Ken Lay of Enron presided over a more aggressively creative accounting system that attributed many unprofitable deals to other "partner companies," so that these deals wouldn't appear on Enron's balance sheet at all. Tyco's Dennis Kozlowski had his financial officers list an intangible "asset" of nearly $35 billion on the company's books, which was described as the "goodwill" of the companies Tyco had acquired. When this sum was added into the company balance sheet, it made it look as though Tyco was accumulating assets at an impressive rate, even though what it had actually accumulated was $27 billion worth of debt. Companies such as these that distort their financial reports seldom do it to deceive the public. They do it as a result of a general mind-set, put in place by the CEO, in which everything the company does is seen as a matter of public relations.

Habit #6: They underestimate major obstacles

CEOs who succumb to this sixth habit tend to wave aside obstacles as though they are minor difficulties, when many of them are, in fact, major hurdles. They become so enamored with their vision of what they want to achieve that they overlook the difficulty of actually getting there. They assume that all problems are solvable, when many problems, in fact, are either insolvable or else solvable at too great a cost.

Roger Smith, for example, treated every obstacle to his goal of workerless factories as though each were just a minor difficulty that GM would soon take in its stride. In a characteristic blunder, he assumed that the computer systems necessary to manage robotic factories could be obtained by acquiring a first-rate software house, even though, in practice, the entire resources of EDS were not enough to provide GM with what it needed. Often it seems that the more fully CEOs can visualize the way they want their companies to look in the future, the less fully they can visualize the obstacles along the way.

Executives coming off a string of successes are particularly prone to underestimate obstacles. Stephen Wiggins is an example of a CEO who got into trouble partly because his previous successes had come so easily. In six years, he transformed Oxford Health Plans from a guest room start-up to the second most profitable HMO in New York. At every stage in this process, he employed innovative, technically savvy operating procedures. Computer systems were things he was personally familiar with. So, when he heard about the problems involved in creating the sort of software he wanted, he repeatedly treated them as minor hurdles any competent programmer should be able to handle. He didn't deny that bad software could be a serious hazard, but he saw it as something that could be easily remedied. Growth was critical, and nothing could slow his company down. After all, how tough could it be to remake a company's computer systems while maintaining ongoing operations?[38]

Executives who are used to solving technical problems are especially likely to underestimate problems that don't seem technically intimidating. In the case of An Wang, for example, it wasn't ever the difficulty of the technical problems that the leader underestimated, but the business problems. Having conquered the technical obstacles, he repeatedly made the mistake of thinking that the business obstacles would be trivial by comparison.

In some cases, the habit of treating all obstacles as minor is an essential part of the leader's personal style. Executives who employ this approach are able to glide over many obstacles through a combination of charm and momentum. They draw people into their projects, inspire them with the self-confidence to do whatever's necessary, and let those associates scramble around to keep the enterprise rolling. By refusing to get rattled by potential setbacks, they help others to do the same. Mossimo Giannulli was one of these leaders, which explains why he could treat the huge logistical problems of adding tailored suits and expanding into department stores across the country as if they were almost incidental to his creative vision. Dennis Kozlowski was another leader of this kind. This is why he could wave aside as a minor matter the fact that parts of his company were experiencing declining profits even though the whole rationale for Tyco's acquisitions was to get more profits out of individual business operations. Later, when his personal expenditures of company money surfaced, this personal style was one of the reasons why he waved those matters aside as well, even though the amounts involved apparently ran into hundreds of millions of dollars.[39]

Full Steam into the Abyss When CEOs find that the obstacles they had casually waved aside are proving more troublesome than they anticipated, they tend to deal with the problem by escalating their commitment. While the evidence mounted that Roger Smith's expenditures on robots and other technology were failing to improve productivity, the GM chief kept increasing those expenditures, ultimately wasting much of the $45 billion dedicated to the effort. While Webvan's existing operations were racking up huge losses, George Shaheen was busy expanding these operations at an awesome rate. While Tyco was struggling to maintain profitability in many of its divisions, Dennis Kozlowski responded to every setback by simply increasing the pace of his acquisitions, earning himself the nickname "Deal-a-Month Dennis."

Why do these executives respond this way? Why not hold back for a while until it becomes clear whether that line of activity will produce an adequate return on investment? The answers to these questions are once again partly psychological. Some CEOs feel an enormous need to be right in every important decision they make, partly for the same reasons that they feel responsible for their company's success. If they admit to being fallible, their position as CEO seems frighteningly precarious. Meanwhile, their employees, business journalists, and the investment community all want the company to be run by someone with an almost magical ability to get things right. Once a CEO concedes that he or she has made the wrong call on an important issue, there will always be people who'll say that they weren't up for the job.

The effect of these unrealistic expectations is to make it exceedingly hard for a CEO to pull back once he or she has chosen a particular course of action. What's more, if your only option is to keep going in the same direction, then your response to an obstacle can only be to push harder. This is why leaders at Motorola and Iridium kept on investing billions of dollars to launch satellites even after it had become apparent that land-based cell phones were a superior alternative. "People do not like to admit that their past decisions were incorrect," explains a management expert who has studied the problem in detail. "What better way to affirm the correctness of those earlier decisions than by becoming even more committed to them?"[40] Proceeding with the same course of action, but with new resources, removes, for the time being, any need to admit that this course of action was wrong in the first place. The renewed investment seems to introduce a new element, so that it becomes easier to believe that the renewed effort will result in success. If there are any doubters, the other habits of spectacularly unsuccessful people will either eliminate them or make them ineffective.

After each round, it becomes harder to pull back or change direction. The psychological scale of the mistake, should the CEO admit to making one, will have grown larger. The financial losses that would have to be declared, should the project be a failure, will have become greater. Meanwhile, since the project has been scaled up, the rewards for bringing it to a successful completion are likely to have increased as well. All the pressures on the CEO that led to the problem in the first place still exist, but most of them are now intensified.

Escalating Commitment A classic example of escalating commitment in the face of insurmountable obstacles was RJ Reynolds' "Project Spa," the massive development effort that resulted in the launch of the Premier, the first "smokeless" cigarette. The concept sounded brilliant. People liked cigarettes, but hated the health risks associated with tobacco smoke. So RJ Reynolds' brainstorm was to produce a product that delivered the qualities people wanted in cigarettes—but without the tobacco smoke! To provide more of the flavor, the cigarette would also contain an aluminum capsule that would slowly release appropriate chemicals when it was heated.

Hundreds of millions of dollars were invested in the project. When the first samples were tested on customers, however, they reported that the cigarette smelled awful and tasted even worse. In Japan, researchers learned to translate one sentence in Japanese, "It tastes like shit."[41] Nevertheless, having invested so much time and money into the project, the product development team—who were smoking Premiers constantly and convincing themselves that the product was great—worked the numbers to paint a better picture of the market data. The go-ahead came from CEO Ross Johnson, and the Premier made its market entry in October 1988.[42]

The roar of controversy that met the introduction of the Premier was deafening. Federal government safety regulators, including the Surgeon General and the FDA, branded the product a "nicotine-delivery system" and proposed banning it. RJ Reynolds was accused of perpetrating a sinister plot, and state courts were petitioned to outlaw the device. Meanwhile, word got out that the smokeless cigarette tasted terrible. By December, retail outlets were already returning the product to distributors and discontinuing in-store promotions. Unable to deny that the product was a disaster after spending $1 billion on Project Spa, RJ Reynolds canceled the Premier.

Recognizing the point at which escalating commitment is getting out of hand can be almost impossible for the person responsible. This behavior can be mistaken for determination or stick-to-it-ness. Quaker CEO William Smithburg, for example, publicly stated that he would not give up on Snapple, because, as he put it, "I've never run away from a challenge, and I'm not running away from this one."[43] We are all taught to admire courage in the face of adversity. In the case of Snapple, it simply meant that inappropriate policies were kept in place longer, doing further damage both to Snapple and to its parent company.

Stephen Wiggins of Oxford Health Plans was caught in this predicament when the software he had commissioned kept taking longer to complete than expected. At each juncture, it seemed that with just a little more money and a little more time, Oxford would have the problems solved. During the five years of the project, Oxford employed more than one hundred outside systems contractors and spent more than $100 million.[44] Yet it *still* failed to produce a software system that could do the job. When should Wiggins have called it quits? Obviously, at every moment from the time the project was launched. But for someone whose reflexive response to difficulty was to escalate commitment, it was impossible to see this.

Habit #7: They stubbornly rely on what worked for them in the past

Many CEOs on their way to becoming spectacularly unsuccessful accelerate their company's decline simply by reverting to what they regard as the tried and tested. In their quest for certainty in a world grown unpredictable, they persist in using the wrong scoreboard. In their effort to achieve stability in a world of change, they seize on yesterday's answer. In their desire to make the most of what they regard as their core strengths, they cling to a static business model. Like Ed Schwinn of the bicycle company, they insist on providing a product to a market that no longer exists. Like William Farley of Fruit of the Loom, they fail to consider innovations in areas such as sourcing because that's not what made their company successful in the past. CEOs like these all end up choosing the wrong option because they almost automatically fall back on a "default response," an answer from the past.

In place of considering a wide range of options, CEOs with this habit choose their course of action with reference to *themselves* and the things that made them successful in the past. For example, Jill Barad relied on the same sort of promotional techniques that had been effective for her when she was promoting Barbie dolls. She tried to use them with educational software, a product category that's distributed and consumed very differently than dolls and doll clothes. Worse, she tried to use them with Wall Street, an audience that's not as easily swayed as seven-year-old girls. "Jill is and was very bright, a brilliant marketer," commented her rival at Hasbro, *but*, he added, "I am not sure Jill came to grips with some of the difficulties of being a CEO, where it's not that you can spend all your time on product or talking to Wall Street, but there are many, many other things that go into it."[45]

Defining Moments Executives often revert to harmful or inappropriate strategies as the result of a "defining moment" earlier in their careers. At one point, they chose one particular policy that resulted in their most notable success. This becomes their "defining moment." It's usually the one thing they are most known for, the thing that gets them their subsequent jobs, the thing that makes them special. The problem is that once people have experienced this "defining moment," they tend to let it define them for the rest of their careers. And if they become the CEO of a large company, they let their defining moment to some extent define their company as well.

When confronted with a crisis later in their career, these executives tend to do whatever they did in their defining moment. For William Smithburg of Quaker, the defining moment had been his successful promotion of Gatorade. The problem was that he tried to repeat that behavior when it came to dealing with Snapple. For An Wang, the defining moment was probably his successful launch of a word processor with systems that were all proprietary. Unfortunately, he tried to repeat that behavior when it came to PCs.

A particular hazard of defining moments is that they can lead to fallback strategies that are not only inappropriate but inherently high-risk. The Saatchi brothers are a good example of business leaders who learned a risky style of management from their early defining moments. They won their first big clients by violating the standard operating procedures associated with the British Advertising Association. They did this by aggressively raiding the client and employee rosters of other advertising agencies. Because this worked so well for them, they later assumed that they didn't have to follow standard operating procedures in other areas either.

Several of the other top executives discussed here developed high-risk management policies as a result of their early successes and the defining moments that produced them. Charles Sanford, for example, the CEO of Bankers Trust, tried to handle every aspect of banking with the same fast-paced, transaction-oriented style that had made him a successful bond trader. Stephen Wiggins of Oxford Health Plans believed that he had to rethink and redo each aspect of the managed health care industry, including the software necessary to run operations, because it was this policy that had made him successful in the first place. These and many other high-flying CEOs failed, not because they couldn't learn, but because they had learned one lesson all too well.[46]

Psychotherapy for the CEO?

What can be done about these Seven Habits of Spectacularly Unsuccessful People? A whole book could be devoted to ways in which people counter their effects, but, to start with, just making CEOs, managers, journalists, and investors aware of them should be a big help. There are many opportunities for CEOs themselves to stop and question their own behavior if they notice themselves slipping into one of these habits. It would also help enormously if those reporting to CEOs realized that these habits shouldn't be admired or accepted as normal. Instead, wherever CEOs fall too conspicuously into one of these habits, they should be met with raised eyebrows and, whenever possible, a warning. Finally, whenever these habits begin having too great an influence on the CEO's behavior and on the direction of the company, it is the corporate board's job to intervene. The Seven Habits of Spectacularly Unsuccessful People are too dangerous to be left unchecked. Investors in particular need to be on the alert for signs of these habits, as we discuss in the next chapter.

The Seven Habits of Spectacularly Unsuccessful People

1. They see themselves and their companies as dominating their environments, not simply responding to developments in those environments.
2. They identify so completely with the company that there is no clear boundary between their personal interests and corporate interests.
3. They seem to have all the answers, often dazzling people with the speed and decisiveness with which they can deal with challenging issues.
4. They make sure that everyone is 100 percent behind them, ruthlessly eliminating anyone who might undermine their efforts.
5. They are consummate company spokespersons, often devoting the largest portion of their efforts to managing and developing the company image.
6. They treat intimidatingly difficult obstacles as temporary impediments to be removed or overcome.
7. They never hesitate to return to the strategies and tactics that made them and their companies successful in the first place.

LEARNING FROM MISTAKES

Part III presents the most forward-looking part of our analysis. We've pointed out why executives are vulnerable during the four challenging transitions of Part I, and we've described the underlying reasons for executive failure in Part II. In these final two chapters, we explicitly develop two critical ideas that have stayed in the background to this point. First, can we use the findings of our study as an early warning system? Can our results tell us how to predict when trouble is coming? And second, how do successful executives create organizations that can learn from, and better yet, avoid, disaster? What can we learn from them?

As I said in Chapter 1, this book is about people. And it's people who are willing and able to face up to reality, end the delusional attitudes that protect flawed thinking, address informational breakdowns that scar organizations, and purposely move away from the habits of unsuccessful leaders, who will provide the strongest defense against the great corporate mistakes that bring down great institutions.

CHAPTER 10

Predicting the Future

The Early Warning Signs

The stories of failure and the underlying reasons why they occurred contain an important lesson that has been implicit throughout. How can we know? What should we be looking for to warn us of impending disaster? How can we apply the lessons of General Magic, Rubbermaid, Quaker, Wang Labs, Mattel, Schwinn, Fruit of the Loom, and the rest to make sure that we don't make the same mistakes?

Of course, there's no vaccine for failure, and no smoke alarm that's sure to go off in time to save a business. But there are many clues, some of which we've already seen in earlier chapters, and others that we're about to examine more closely. We need to be on the lookout for these clues whether we are a manager in a company; on the board; a prospective employee; a potential acquirer; or an investor. From all of these points of view, it's vital to know how to recognize the critical signals that foreshadow business failure.

There are two things to keep in mind as we begin. First, whenever possible we'll try to identify those warning signs that are most visible to outsiders. There will be no neon signs blazing with the words "DANGER—DO NOT ENTER," but there are a surprising number of insights available when we're on alert and know what to look for. And second, if we see a warning sign, it is nothing more or less than that—a warning. One way to put this in perspective is to consider how the government or military evaluates threats. As the severity of the threat increases—presumably because of an accumulation of warning signs—we shift to a higher level of alert. So as we see the warning signs for potential company failure, we need to pay even more attention and be ready to act, if necessary, to protect our investment or our careers.

The box below summarizes the major warning signs our research uncovered. It provides a good diagnostic to assess the potential for trouble. Each question directs you to a different facet of your business, and we will use the issues these questions raise to structure the entire chapter. While we won't always have all the data we need to make a positive ID of a warning sign, and different people will no doubt see different things, together all of the questions provide a road map of some of the biggest potholes and suggests how to find them.

■ ■ ■

Questions to Ask When Looking for Early Warning Signs

UNNECESSARY COMPLEXITY

1. Is the company's organizational structure convoluted or complex?
2. Is its strategy unnecessarily complex for an otherwise simple problem?
3. Is its accounting overly complicated, nontransparent, or nonstandard?
4. Is it employing complicated or nonstandard terminology?

SPEEDING OUT OF CONTROL

5. Does the management team have enough experience to handle growth?
6. Are there small, yet nontrivial, details or problems that seem to be getting overlooked by management?
7. Is management ignoring warnings now that could lead to problems later?
8. Is the company so successful or so dominant that it's no longer in touch with what it needs to do to remain on top?
9. Do the unplanned departures of senior executives signify deeper problems?

THE DISTRACTED CEO

10. Do I have unanswered questions about the CEO's background and talent?
11. Is the CEO spending too much money to fulfill personal missions that don't necessarily benefit the company?
12. Are company leaders so consumed by money and greed that they're taking questionable or inappropriate actions?

EXCESSIVE HYPE

13. Is it possible that the excitement around the company's new product is just hype?
14. Could the excitement around the company's merger or acquisition be hype?
15. Is the excitement around the company's prospects just unfulfilled hype?

16. Is the latest missed milestone part of a pattern that could signify deeper problems?

A QUESTION OF CHARACTER

17. Are the CEO and other senior executives so aggressive or overconfident that I don't really trust them?

Unnecessary Complexity

Some things are by their very nature quite complex (such as the theory of relativity and derivative-based hedging strategies), while others are made complex. You can make structures, strategies, accounting practices, and even the terminology employed to talk about the business more complicated than necessary. Whatever form it takes, unnecessary complexity is a warning sign because it tends to create bigger problems than it solves.

But why make something complex in the first place? Occasionally, executives rely on complexity to provide legitimacy to a course of action. In other words, it provides cover. For example, when Motorola relied on a sophisticated, complex forecasting model to assess the potential of digital cell phones (rather than relying on direct customer feedback, of which there was plenty), it may well have been because the company didn't really want to go to digital.

More often, though, unnecessary complexity occurs without anyone realizing what's happening until it's too late. In some cases, over a period of time it creeps into a process or into an organization's structure, as poor decisions are layered one on top of the other. So how do you spot unnecessary complexity when those closest to the situation often can't see it themselves? It starts with knowing where to look and what to look for.

Complicated Structures and Processes

All organization systems are subject to breakdown. For example, one of the reasons why U.S. fighter jets accidentally shot down two U.S. Black Hawk helicopters over the no-fly zone in Iraq in 1994 was because personnel in the AWACS (Airborne Warning and Control System) radar plane assumed that someone else was watching the flight zone at the time of the accident. Why would they make this assumption? Because of the principle of "diffuse responsibility," which translates into having more than one person responsible for the same coordinates in a hostile region. With two people paying attention, the logic goes, there's much less likelihood that something will get overlooked. Unfortunately, it was precisely because personnel knew there was someone else with over-lapping responsibility that they felt empowered to pay less attention.[1] This is exactly the same phenomenon that accounted for the Kitty Genovese incident in Queens, New York, in 1964. On a hot summer night, Kitty was attacked in full view of dozens of people, but no one called the police because they assumed, with so many other people viewing the same scene, that someone else had already done so.[2]

The first place you can analyze for unnecessary complexity is the process behind a merger or acquisition (M&A). For example, when Pharmacia and Upjohn combined in 1995, fears that one side would dominate if corporate head offices were consolidated in one country prompted the merged business to set up a new head office in London. Unfortunately, since Pharmacia and Upjohn didn't close down corporate offices in Sweden or the U.S., this only served to create a new layer of management that duplicated existing structures. The net result of mis-steps like this: several senior executives (including the new CEO) and top R&D people departing and M&A restructuring costs mushrooming to $800 million, one-third more than originally anticipated. It wasn't until 1998 that the company finally settled on a single corporate head-quarters in New Jersey.

The best (or worst) example of creating unnecessary complexity in M&As is the classic story of co-CEOs. Why is this a good idea? Is there anyone who really believes that two people, each having made it to the top through enormous dedication, sacrifice, and ambition, will do better when they share responsibilities? How long did Bob Eaton of Chrysler last with Jürgen Schrempp of Daimler? John Reed (Citicorp) and Sandy Weill (Travelers) barely shared the executive suite at Citigroup before Reed moved on. The creation of co-CEO positions following a merger should be seen for what it is—a temporary face-saving way to get both eight-hundred-pound gorillas to say yes.[3]

Complicated Solutions to Simple Problems

If you were traveling in Southeast Asia in 1990 and you needed to make a call, but you couldn't because there was no cell phone service, surely the first solution you'd think of is a constellation of low-Earth-orbiting satellites. You might think briefly about just building some more cell towers and expanding service, but though that seems easier, it's not nearly as sexy as the satellites.

Now let's say you're back home in the U.S. in 1996 and you don't have time to drive to the grocery store, but you need to stock up on a few basics. You come up with the perfect solution. You'll build twenty-six high-tech distribution centers each costing $50 million and offer home delivery over the Internet without a delivery fee. Of course, you could just hire young, low-wage delivery people for $6.50 an hour to do it, but that's too simple. Better to spend the $1 billion plus instead.

Complex solutions can be appropriate, and powerful, when they are employed to solve very complex problems. For example, Intel's microchip fabrication plants are marvels to behold, but they enable Intel to compete not just on technical specs but on low costs as well. In that industry, dual capabilities are important, and there aren't a heck of lot of reasonable alternatives if you want to be a big-time player. It's when a company adopts a solution way out of proportion to the problem it's trying to solve that trouble occurs.

Unnecessarily complex strategies or solutions are good warning signs to watch out for because they often hide flaws or overshadow simpler options. Management or investors can get so caught up in the grandness of the plan or the details of the execution or the gee-whiz factor of the technology, that they forget to ask whether it's a good idea in the first place. For example, Marc Porat, the former CEO of General Magic, told us that the company took on too many related strategic initiatives at once and was unable to succeed at any: "We tried to create an operating system, a hand-held device, and the communication network software— and thereby tried to create two markets."[4] The best defense against such seductive strategies is to keep an open mind and ask, is this the best way? Is there a simpler, perhaps even more effective, solution?

Complicated Accounting

Despite many who believe otherwise, accounting rules are not intentionally designed to be complicated. The goal of accounting is to illuminate the true financial performance of an organization, not to confuse or hide it. If it's confusing or unusual or inconsistent, it's time to take a closer look. Don't be fooled by those who call it innovative; Enron's use of off–balance-sheet partnerships was very innovative, after all. A good rule of thumb is this: Nonstandard or unusual accounting can make a company look better than it is, but it will rarely make the company better than it is, and it often is a warning sign that the company is actually worse off than it appears.

Three of the biggest U.S. bankruptcies ever—Enron, WorldCom, and Conseco—followed a pattern of aggressive and creative accounting arrangements ranging from off–balance-sheet manipulations (Enron) to systematic capitalization of expenses (WorldCom) to shifting acquisition accounting to and from the income statement (Conseco). Internet companies were notorious for pushing the accounting envelope. One common practice was to trade ad space with other dot-coms, booking the barter as revenue. Other times, companies recorded noncash revenues by swapping services for stock. Since the valuation of most dot-coms was based on revenues and not cash flow, let alone earnings, this practice could give a quick boost to a company's stock price.[5]

Nonstandard accounting isn't always easy to see; however, if you understand where a company is most likely to benefit from it, you will have a better chance of spotting it. For Internet companies, the emphasis was on revenues more than profits, so revenue recognition games became a hot button. For companies such as Enron, the strength of the balance sheet was a particular concern, thus the off–balance-sheet partnerships. Pay attention to the prominent metrics in an industry, because if nonstandard accounting is going to appear anywhere, it will be there.

Complicated Terminology

Internet entrepreneurs and managers created a whole new vocabulary of business terminology. Rather than "strategy," Internet start-ups boasted "business models." Online companies and venture capitalists emphasized the importance of "reach" and "stickiness," when what they really meant was that Internet start-ups needed "customers" to make "repeat purchases." They didn't compete in a "market"; they competed in a "space." In some ways, you can understand the appeal. After all, what would you rather tell your shareholders—that your "burn rate" was $500,000 per month or that you were going to lose $6 million next year?

To go along with their new terminology, many of the dot-coms of the late 1990s asked Wall Street and their investors to use a new set of accounting standards to evaluate their businesses. They talked about how the "new economy" needed new rules to accommodate a changed world, since the old accounting standbys such as EPS and P/E ratios weren't very effective when you had no "E." In the end, of course, the standard accounting principles were just fine, as they accurately captured the fact that these companies were not creating value for shareholders.

Even several large technology companies tried to play the terminology game. For example, Nortel Networks asked investors to focus on a measure it called "net earnings from operations," which excluded amortization of goodwill and development costs, and gains and charges. In 2000, Nortel reported "net earnings from operations" of $2.31 billion, or seventy-one cents a share, while according to generally accepted accounting principles the company actually lost $3.47 billion, or $1.17 a share.[6]

Speeding Out of Control

How many times have you read about a company where insiders looking back describe the organization with phrases such as "speeding out of control" or "we couldn't get out of our own way" or "complete chaos"? Now think about how often executives describe their current situation that way? Not nearly as often, right? So why is it that no one seems to notice that their company is out of control until it's too late?

Companies that are speeding out of control make costly mistakes because executives are overwhelmed. This most commonly occurs in companies that are experiencing rapid growth, but it can also take place in companies that are adjusting to technological change or are dealing with management turnover or are in any situation that can create frantic behavior.

Racing Before They Can Walk

Picture a company that is growing at breakneck speed. Now add in an inexperienced management team, and give them lots of money and little adult supervision. Each of these elements can bring a company to grief, but when all four are present at the same time—as they were in many of the Internet start-ups during the boom years—watch out.

In 1994 Dale Sundby founded PowerAgent, an online start-up poised to revolutionize advertising by matching companies with customers in a classic one-to-one marketing scheme. Sundby, a law firm CEO and former IBM executive, had never worked in advertising, yet he managed to raise $16 million by 1996. In search of the elusive first-mover advantage, PowerAgent went haywire employing multiple software developers doing redundant work in an effort to get a customer interface in place, and hiring experienced sales executives before the product was even available. Despite a burn rate that reached more than $2 million a month (slick promotional video for $500,000; high-profile parties; well-furnished offices in several cities), the product never did become available. As one industry veteran brought in to make sense of the mess put it, "I took one look at the product right after getting there and said, 'You've got to be kidding. We can't launch anything that looks like this. This is awful. Awful.' "[7] And the board of directors in this story? Mostly absentee investors hoping to cash in on the Internet gravy train.[8] From there, it was only a matter of months before the company folded.

While some early warning signs are more shrouded than others, outside investors can read the S-1 statement the SEC requires in advance of IPOs, and the 10-K for companies that are already public, both of which contain information on management experience, capitalization and funding, the board of directors, and management plans moving forward. The business press—while far from accurate in the subjective assessments of a company's prospects—occasionally does publish actual facts. If anyone had paid attention to any of these sources, they would have seen the danger in Webvan's strategy to raise hundreds of millions of dollars and adopt an extraordinarily aggressive growth strategy. The fast-paced rise of Mossimo was well chronicled by the press, as was the lack of experience founder Mossimo Giannulli brought to the CEO job.

Most of all, there was a whole community of big spenders at loose running Internet start-ups, leaving a trail of high-octane expenditures. For example, Boo.com, the high-profile European Internet start-up that raised $135 million, boasted six luxurious offices set up in different cities and insisted that management—traveling with an entourage—stay at the best hotels. One prospective investor said in describing the elaborate efforts the company went through to build its Web site, "It was like they were trying to build a Mercedes-Benz by hand." In the end the start-up declared bankruptcy, selling its back-end shipping technology for $375,000.[9]

Broken Windows: Little Mistakes That May Foreshadow Big Ones

You don't have to tour a company's facilities to see broken windows. As with any warning sign, it's all about knowing what to look for. For manufacturing companies, it might be a minor quality problem now that leads to a bigger one later. For service companies, it might be the loss of a smaller client that foreshadows bigger client failures. Execution errors may not be the root cause of failure, but they can be symptomatic of something more serious. You might not know that WorldCom was systematically overcharging customers by switching millions to more expensive plans without their knowledge, or refusing to adjust billing errors[10]—practices that cost the company hundreds of millions in class action suits and proceedings brought by several state attorney generals[11]—but you could have paid attention to such things as (1) WorldCom's number-one ranking in long-distance slamming complaints to the FCC or (2) PlanetFeedBack's[12] rating of several of WorldCom's business units in the top ten worst companies for customer service and billing errors.[13]

Follow the cash. Don't be deceived by relying on a company's net income as the only measure of financial health. You have to look at a company's ability to cover its debt. In much the same way that banks assess personal income and expenses when writing home mortgages, corporate lenders issue covenants to ensure that a company has adequate resources to cover the cost of debt. When companies go bankrupt, it's usually because lenders have decided to cut their losses because loan covenants have been violated.

Finally, don't be afraid to look at an even simpler measure—cash in the bank. It may well be the single most important indicator of health for a company, especially in technology and biotech.

Unheeded Warnings

Companies do not have to be small, fast-growing dynamos like some of the Internet start-ups we've discussed to succumb to the pitfalls of speeding out of control. Large companies with experienced management teams have sped past a lot more than mere broken windows. At J&J's stent business, management failed to notice that the building was on fire before it was too late. The smoke was there for anyone to see—the erosion of European market share and the lack of ongoing innovation in a business that requires it. As a manager, these are your warning signs. But as an investor or board member, the real warning sign is when conditions such as these are present, and no one seems to be doing anything about it. As John Keogh, president of an insurance company that writes policies to cover corporate directors and officers (D&O insurance) told us, "My experience anecdotally is that where there is smoke, there is fire. So if you find a problem in one piece of the business, it's probably an early indicator of a bigger problem. When management finds there is a bigger problem, the sooner they deal with and manage it, obviously the better. It's the ones that take longer to come to the surface that tend to be the ones that destroy companies."[14]

We saw plenty of examples of what Keogh was referring to: RJ Reynold's Project Spa was a smoker's fantasy that never should have moved as far as it did. Customers hated the taste and told the development team exactly that in no uncertain terms. Customers sent overt warnings to Motorola as the company stonewalled against digital, and to Rubbermaid as it tried to pass along ever higher costs to retailers. The warnings need not come from customers—people inside a company sometimes summon the courage to speak out, but executives at the top don't always listen, as was the case at Enron.[15]

Unheeded warnings are common in M&A transactions. Companies become so focused on the end result or on getting to the next deal, that they gloss over potential differences. Unfortunately, the one certainty in acquisitions is that whatever you don't resolve before the deal is completed, you end up addressing one way or another afterwards. Whether it is a critical erosion in market demand (which Mattel missed in acquiring The Learning Company) or potential account conflicts that mean the loss of Colgate as a client (which Saatchi & Saatchi disregarded), the facts are usually staring the company in the face. Often, the unheeded warning you see may not lead to the downfall of the company or the deal, but it may be indicative of a pattern that will.

In the case of Snow Brand Milk, by the time anyone noticed that warnings were going unheeded in the milk business, it was too late. But it wasn't too late to notice the culture of unheeded warnings and the impact that this might have on the rest of the business. In the director-and-officer insurance industry, insurers typically look at lawsuits that have been settled in a very different way than do investors. Investors often think of a suit settlement as a sign that the company has put these problems behind them. Insurers look at it as a warning sign that the company may well have committed offenses that will eventually lead to more lawsuits.[16]

Success and More Success

Here's a surprise. Want to know one of the best generic warning signs you can look for? How about success, lots of it! Leaving aside the unfortunate reality that many of the companies we studied were quite successful before the really bad stuff happened—Rubbermaid, Motorola, Wang Labs, Sony, Conseco, Johnson & Johnson, Snow Brand Milk, LTCM, Barneys, the list goes on—there are several reasons to always be on the alert. First, the zombie businesses of Chapter 7 were uniformly successful at one time, but developed a host of delusional policies and attitudes that were an outgrowth of that success. Second, companies that are successful in their marketplace act as an advertisement for others to enter the same arena. Third, success breeds arrogance. Even a company as powerful as Microsoft wasn't immune to the perils of success, and probably should count itself lucky that the antitrust suit ended up where it did. Fourth, it's easy to let our guard down when we're awash in profits. It's only natural; "there is a common failing of mankind, never to anticipate a storm when the sea is calm."[17] Finally, success creates its own momentum that in the scheme of things is remarkably difficult to maintain. One of the reasons why WorldCom turned to fraudulent accounting was because that was the only way that it could keep the great numbers up; the regular course of business was no longer doing it.

Few companies evaluate why business is working (often defaulting the credit to "the CEO is genius"). But without really understanding why success is happening, it's difficult to see why it might not. You have to be able to identify when things need adjustments. Otherwise, you wake up one morning, and it looks like everything went bad overnight. But it didn't—it's a slow process that can often be seen if you look. For example, as the retailer GAP began its downfall, there was more bafflement than analysis. CEO Mickey Drexler had made the right calls before, and it was assumed that he would continue to make the right calls to turn things around. Unfortunately, the triggers for turnaround—critical dissent, bench strength, and open-mindedness—were all missing. Drexler's personal style coupled with his successful track record made it difficult for management to challenge him, and the company's "We set fashion, we don't respond to it" ethic shut down debate.[18]

The extreme case of a successful company that loses all semblance of constraint and responsibility to standard norms of business conduct may well be Adelphia. When we think of Adelphia, we think of the classic Mel Brooks movie, *Blazing Saddles*. There's a scene in that film when everyone converges on a town where the saloon, the stores, the bank, and even the sheriff share the same name—Johnson. The town is totally dominated by this one man and his family, and while in the film Mel Brooks used the name Johnson, in the business world the name was Rigas. John Rigas and his family were the kings of the town of Coudersport, Pennsylvania. Most of the people in town worked for Adelphia, and Adelphia and the Rigas family owned most of the town. The real estate, the restaurant, the movie theater, the golf course—all were part of the family. And perhaps the defining principle of the company, and the family, was that you took care of your own. So, John's wife Doris decorated the Adelphia buildings with $12.4 million in furniture from a Rigas family business;[19] son-in-law Peter Venetis ran a venture capital fund with company money; when the company needed a vehicle, it bought it from the family car dealership; snow removal, lawn mowing, maintenance—that's right—all from family-run businesses.[20] The Rigas family created Adelphia—the word itself means "brothers" in Greek—as an island unto itself, but when they ventured to the outside world in search of capital, and proceeded to abuse that capital, the game was up.[21]

We saw some of this behavior in Chapter 9 when we discussed the illusion of preeminence. It's not always easy to see this spectacularly unsuccessful habit from the outside, but the Adelphia story provides a window to that world. When a company shuts itself off from common norms of behavior; when a company takes the positive of a "family business" and turns it into a kingdom with little access to the outside world; when a company owns too much, and controls too much, and dominates too much; when all of these things are happening it is time to take a closer look. Fantastic success or overwhelming dominance doesn't mean that bad things are happening or will happen. However, there are an extraordinary number of times when precisely these attributes are in place in companies that run up against failure. So it's worth paying attention if you work for, or invest in, such a company.

Executive Departures

Between 1999 and 2001, four of five senior executives at GAP left the company, culminating in the resignation of CEO Mickey Drexler as the company's year-over-year same-store sales continued to decrease. Over a two-year period (1999–2000), six direct reports to Mattel CEO Jill Barad resigned for "personal reasons." Not long afterwards, CEO Barad stepped down. CEO Jeff Skilling left Enron in August 2001, just three months before Enron's problems made front-page news. Kmart averaged 38 percent annual turnover in the top executive ranks throughout the decade of the 1990s. Silicon Graphics lost 40 percent of its top management team in the two years preceding its 1996 stock meltdown. Almost all of the top sixty-four executives at Cordis left following the 1995 acquisition of that company by Johnson & Johnson.

How clear can a pattern be? A revolving door at the top is often a strong signal that there has been executive failure at a company. It may be an indication of Unsuccessful Habit #4 ("They ruthlessly eliminate anyone who isn't 100 percent behind them.") or it may reflect inside information senior executives are acting on. It's standard practice for analysts and many investors to track insider sales of stock, but what stronger statement can an executive make than to leave his or her job and the company entirely?

Even when a company appears to be strong, or at least a stalwart in an industry sector, executive departures can still be informative. Consider Sun Microsystems. On May 1, 2002, Sun Microsystems announced that President Edward Zander was resigning from the company, making him the fourth senior executive to leave Sun in a two-week period. Sun CEO Scott McNealy characterized these moves as "positive and planned out," yet just five months later Sun announced an unexpected revenue decline for the first-quarter of fiscal 2003 along with layoffs of 11 percent of its work force, or forty-four hundred people. Interestingly, McNealy continued to defend the company's position ("Sun is in great shape. I am having a blast."); in the five months between Zander's resignation and the layoff announcement, Sun's stock price went from $8.18 to $2.99, a decline of 73 percent.[22]

The Distracted CEO

The next time you attend an annual meeting of a company whose stock you own, there's something you can do to prepare. Look up the section of the proxy statement that describes the activities of board committees and compare the number of times the compensation committee met in the past year to the number of meetings of the audit committee. If the compensation committee is convening more often, *much more often,* look out. When asked why, board members will say that executive compensation is very complex and merits in-depth consideration. But does that imply that the company's financials aren't complex and, hence, merit *less* attention?

The easiest way to spot a company that is distracted is to look at the CEO. Organizations take their lead from the top, and distraction or misdirection at the CEO level can have serious consequences. Studying a CEO for signs that he or she has become sidetracked will never yield a black or white answer, but there are some patterns that emerged in the failures we studied that provide some clues. In Chapter 9 we described the habits of unsuccessful leaders, some of which we will echo here, but this time attending much more closely to the clues that might indicate that a CEO has gone over the line.

The People

Sam Waksal was the founder of ImClone and the man Bristol-Myers Squibb (BMS) decided to bet $2 billion on when it took a 20 percent stake in the biotech firm and its only product, the cancer drug Erbitux. When the FDA turned down ImClone's application for the drug, BMS was left to explain what happened. When it was subsequently revealed that ImClone had known about FDA concerns months beforehand and had apparently provided inaccurate data to the FDA,[23] more explaining was necessary. And when the related insider trading scandal broke (eventually leading to Waksal's indictment and drawing in such pivotal figures of the New York social scene as Martha Stewart), BMS was left to explain why it decided to partner with Waksal in the first place.

While no one could have predicted exactly what did happen, there were big clues that Sam Waksal might not be the best business partner for a prestigious pharmaceutical company. There's no question that Waksal had the brains and the charisma, but a look into his past might have revealed some disquieting concerns about just how these prodigious talents were used.

After earning a Ph.D., Sam Waksal went through a succession of prestigious jobs, but he left under a cloud each time. His first job was at a lab at Stanford, but it ended when Waksal was asked to leave after he misled the top scientist there about how he had procured a supply of difficult-to-produce antibodies. Afterwards, he managed to land at the National Cancer Institute for a sojourn that lasted less than three years. This time his contract wasn't renewed because of a series of experiment-ending problems that mysteriously occurred just when Waksal was due to deliver his work to his collaborators.

His next stop was Tufts University, where once again the same pattern of charm and questionable ethics spilled out. The last straw for Tufts was when Waksal's brother, Harlan, a medical resident at Tufts, was arrested for the possession of cocaine and Sam, though not a medical doctor, covered for his brother by seeing his patients while Harlan was "indisposed." A few years later, while working at Mount Sinai School of Medicine in New York, he was accused of falsifying data in an experiment, which ended his time at that institution. Finally, Sam Waksal was ready to go into business for himself. That's when he founded ImClone in 1985, bringing his brother Harlan with him soon afterwards.[24]

There is of course no certainty that a CEO with a checkered past will be untrustworthy in the future, but if we don't pay attention to the data we collect, the odds are that we'll be unhappily surprised. Just as careful underwriters of D&O insurance find that past lawsuits are a predictor of lawsuits still to come, we've got to go with the pattern of data we discover. That is the essence of what an early warning sign is, after all.

And when we consider the data emerging from the companies we studied, one other fact that seems to stand out is the high number of family-run businesses that ended up in ruins. Schwinn, Barneys, and Rite Aid were run by follow-up generations to the founders, and all went bankrupt or close to it. Samsung and Levis were controlled by their founding families when they ran into trouble as well. As we noted in Chapter 2, it *is* possible for a CEO to own too much stock, because after a certain level of ownership there is virtually no limit to a CEO's power. Whether this power is turned into positive or negative outcomes cannot be predetermined, though the fact remains that CEOs in a family line have not been vetted in the same way that executives working their way up a hierarchy have been. The one thing we should expect with some confidence, however, is that companies run by a founder's family are likely to produce more volatile results because their power gives them the freedom to choose high-risk strategies that can yield widely varying outcomes.[25]

The Behavior

The second type of early warning sign requires even less effort on the part of investors, managers, board members, and other watchdogs. This is because the types of behavior that are exhibited by CEOs in the throws of Napoleonic fervor tend to be so blatant that they can't be missed.

They often start by making sure that they're the center of attention, ideally with a very cool crowd. So, the Saatchi brothers are active with the Tory Party in the UK. Sam Waksal buys a swank SoHo apartment, decorates it with expensive art, and joins the Manhattan smart set. Edward McCracken, the former CEO of Silicon Graphics, was a regular at White House events in the 1990s. Ken Lay was never more than a phone call away from close friend President George W. Bush. The list of CEOs profiled in Chapter 9 prescribing to this "hobnob" ethic is not inconsequential.

What's remarkable about all these people is that while they chose to live the high life, socializing with celebrities and politicians, and spending lavishly on pet projects or misdirected strategies, the companies for which they had fiduciary responsibility suffered huge losses. Being a CEO is more than a full-time job, and perhaps the same can be said for being a jetsetter, Hollywood celebrity, or well-connected Washington lobbyist. While there is a role for CEOs to play on issues of public interest, when this segues from making a contribution to adopting a lifestyle, bad things tend to happen.

How about when a company begins building a striking new headquarters, designed to serve as a corporate symbol? In addition to distracting the CEO from his or her most important tasks, this kind of project can absorb most of the attention of senior executives for months on end. Whose design ideas will be incorporated into the final plan? Whose department will get what space? Which executives will be assigned which offices? The possibilities for disputes and plotting are almost endless. Yet none of the efforts the new building absorbs are likely to have anything but a negative effect on corporate performance. The executives at the Money Store provide a classic example. During the period before their 1998 acquisition by First Union, they were so preoccupied with building a new headquarters shaped like a Mayan pyramid that internal controls all but lapsed, and the business was running almost as though it had no senior management at all.[26]

My personal favorite Big Fat Warning Sign is when a company decides to acquire the naming rights for a new sports arena or stadium. For example, when CMGI (an Internet holding company with a variety of businesses under different names) ponied up a cool $114 million for a fifteen-year deal to plaster its name on the New England Patriots' new stadium in 2000, there wasn't much of a business case to support it. After all, as a holding company it had no consumer brand to market, and there was no product or service called CMGI that anyone could purchase. Add to this the little fact that CMGI lost more than $5.4 *billion* in 2001 and continues to struggle in the post-Internet era, and the folly of buying stadium-naming rights is rather apparent.[27]

Remarkably, CMGI is not alone. A surprising number of companies that paid millions of dollars to have their corporate logo and name adorn sports stadiums and arenas in the past five years ended up with severe financial difficulties. Beside the no less than eight airlines making such investments, some of the other "winners" and what they spent were:[28]

Fruit of the Loom	Pro Player Stadium	Florida Marlins, Miami Dolphins	$20 million
Enron	Enron Field	Houston Astros	$100 million
Conseco	Conseco Fieldhouse	Indiana Pacers	$40 million
PSINet	PSINet Stadium	Baltimore Ravens	$100 million

The Money

When we asked Russell Lewis, the CEO of the New York Times, what warning signs he believes are potential markers for trouble, the first thing he mentioned was "If the compensation is disproportionately high to the size of the business and the performance, I'd get the hell out of that investment in a hurry."[29] Good advice, echoed by some other experts we spoke to, but we'd go even further. When the company itself becomes consumed with money and with greed, it's time to take a closer look, if not get out altogether. And the poster children for the "greed is good" fixation are none other than those kings of bankruptcy, WorldCom and Enron.

WorldCom under CEO Bernie Ebbers and CFO Scott Sullivan reminds us of the movie *Chocolat*, whose climax featured one of the main characters totally engorged with chocolate. Unable to stop eating, unable to control his obsession, he finally falls asleep in the window display of the chocolate shop. At WorldCom, money and profits took the place of chocolate, and there was no limit to their hunger. The board authorized loans to Ebbers of $400 million; sales representatives systematically double-billed customers, boosting their commissions; during analyst meetings, Ebbers would only discuss the company's stock price, showing a graph of an increasing share price and asking, "Any questions?" The company boosted earnings by taking down reserves whenever it wanted to goose the numbers; operating expenses were regularly capitalized (one employee was even told to capitalize plane tickets when visiting company sites); when all else failed, CFO Sullivan allegedly invented financial numbers to boost earnings.[30]

The Enron story is even more well known than WorldCom's. The Enron saga that has emerged is also of a company that lost control, had no limits, and cared for nothing but money—for individual executives, and for the company as a whole. The off–balance-sheet partnerships are now well established as a remarkably brazen tool to enrich CFO Andrew Fastow and a select few at the company. Actually, the idea that money comes first dates back to as early as 1987, when auditors uncovered a huge oil-trading scandal at Enron. Traders, who were found guilty of generating false transactions to increase volume and, not incidentally, their bonuses, were not fired by then-CEO Ken Lay until the scam became public.[31] Within Enron, this was considered business as usual.

These types of egregious actions by key executives are not always as visible to outsiders as excessive compensation, but when it takes over the culture of a company, then virtually everyone on the inside probably has some inkling. This includes board members as well as managers up and down the hierarchy, who have special insight to warning signs such as these. For investors, the lesson is that as easy as it is to get caught up in the excitement of a company such as Enron that is breaking all the rules, or such as WorldCom that is building the new AT&T via astute acquisitions, the reality is never as straightforward. In this regard, it's also a story of hype, which brings us to the next type of common warning sign.

Excessive Hype

The world of hype peaked with the Internet bubble, yet this practice is far from gone. Why would hype be a good warning sign? Let's start by looking at the definition of the word.

> Hype: noun (1) Excessive publicity and the ensuing commotion; (2) Exaggerated or extravagant claims made especially in advertising or promotional material; (3) Something deliberately misleading; a deception.[32]

It doesn't sound so harmless when you look at it this way, and it wasn't so harmless to the countless investors who got caught up in the hype of the Internet boom.

The danger is that hype can hide problems or mask intentions that if known would lead people to make different decisions. Hype can cloud investors' judgment of the value of a stock. It can lead managers to misguidedly rely on a new product or technology. So whether you're an investor, board member, CEO, or middle manager, it pays to watch for the warning signs that something, or somebody, is all hype.

Hyping Products Before They Exist

Marketing a product before it comes out and creating a little hype for its release is common practice in business. Think no further than the film business, where the promotion machine goes into high gear even before a movie opens. However, the last time we looked, there weren't too many films being hyped before shooting even begins! But that's what happened with General Magic and Iridium. To some extent the engineers in charge couldn't help it; remember, these were both classic stories of "techtosterone." But when something sounds too good to be true . . . it usually is.

One of the businesses that is most vulnerable to hype gone wild is the pharmaceutical industry. When your health and the health of loved ones is at stake, there's little that you won't do, and even less that you won't believe in. In other words, it's the perfect setting for making outlandish claims that generate free publicity. The remedy within the industry is the FDA, which is charged with overseeing and approving drugs.

Enter Sam Waksal, scientist, CEO, and Manhattan socialite. As his company, ImClone, was developing the cancer drug Erbitux, the hype machine went into overdrive. Waksal declared that Erbitux "is going to be the most important new oncology launch ever."[33] He made the cover of *BusinessWeek*, ImClone's stock took off, and Bristol-Myers Squibb announced it's $2 billion investment in the high-flying biotech. The only problem was that the FDA rejected ImClone's application for Erbitux on December 28, 2001, sending the stock of both ImClone and Bristol into a tailspin. One of the most amazing things about the story is that in its seventeen years in existence, ImClone had not produced a single drug or had a single profitable year, yet this never seemed to concern anyone as its stock price skyrocketed. For an investor, the lessons of the post-Internet boom are clear. Holding onto a stock whose value is predicated on the hype of its "product to be" can be disastrous. In many cases, most of the upside is already factored in due to the hype, leaving only significant downside exposure. As one short seller put it, "When I hear management make overstatements, I get interested."[34]

Hyping M&As

The one place where dishing out hype has been elevated to an art form is in the merger-and-acquisition game. With a losing track record, a pattern of underestimating costs and overestimating benefits, big acquisition premiums, and hero CEOs pushing for deals, the pressure to make the big picture look good is enormous. To see an uptick in the stock price in the first couple of days after the deal is announced is an immediate affirmation that this acquisition is different. Often involving a coordinated attack by the acquiring company's CEO, investment bankers, and professional public relations firms hired solely for this purpose, the goal is to get a favorable spin in the first press articles that appear after the deal is announced.

In a fascinating article in *The Wall Street Journal*, journalists Nikhil Deogun and Steven Lipin compared statements the acquiring company's CEO made when a deal was proclaimed, and then later statements when the subsequent sale of the acquired company was announced.[35] As these examples attest, hype is alive and well in the M&A business. The good news is that we can be on the alert for this type of hype and recognize it for what it is—a transparent attempt to manipulate investors.

Deal	Dates Bought and Sold	CEO's Words at Time of Purchase	CEO's Words After Sale
AT&T buys NCR	1991, 1995	"Ours will be a future of promises fulfilled."	"The world has changed."
SmithKline Beecham buys Diversified Pharmaceutical Benefits	1994, 1999	"Unique alliance . . . positions us to win."	"We [need] a sharper focus."
Eli Lilly buys PCS Health Systems	1994, 1998	"Jewel at a very attractive price."	"Business can benefit from new ownership arrangements."
Quaker Oats buys Snapple	1994, 1997	"Tremendous growth potential."	"Remove financial burdens and risks Snapple brought."

Hyping the Company

While it's certainly not always the case, we can't help but be struck at the number of times that business and trade publications anoint saint-hood on a company or individual that stumbles shortly thereafter. We've already seen Rubbermaid fall from America's Most Admired Company in *Fortune* magazine, but did you know that former Enron CFO Andrew Fastow, who was at the center of the off–balance-sheet partnerships that contributed to his company's downfall, earned the CFO Excellence Award for Capital Structure Management from *CFO Magazine* in October 1999, a little more than two years before Enron's bankruptcy declaration? Not to be outmatched, *Chief Executive* magazine named Enron one of its top five corporate boards around the same time. And the Newspaper Association of America honored Kmart as the "Retailer of the Year" on January 21, 2002—unfortunate timing to be sure as the following day Kmart filed for Chapter 11. Mattel's Jill Barad was feted on the cover by *BusinessWeek* in 1998 (almost exactly one year before Mattel acquired The Learning Company), while other cover stories on Dennis Kozlowski of Tyco (*BusinessWeek* in 2001) and Mickey Drexler of GAP (*Fortune* in 1998, just before GAP began its losing streak) have also appeared.

The End of Hype: Missing Milestones

One of the best warning signs that a company may be relying on hype is the missed milestone. Whenever a company announces that its quarterly earnings are below forecast, the market reacts negatively to the news. The magnitude of the reaction will depend on the track record of the company or CEO. As with our criminal justice system, first-time wrongdoers are treated more leniently than repeat offenders.

Jill Barad went through a streak of missed earnings targets (four quarters in a row), yet each time she would pronounce that better times lay ahead ("We continue to be confident in the future of this company"[36]). Her penchant for promotion and publicity (she did, after all, rise to the CEO position on her amazing success at building Barbie dolls into an almost $2 billion business) didn't play out so well on Wall Street, however. Her assurances to investors were taken at face value, and when she couldn't deliver, her credibility was gone and so was she.

By the time a company reports a missed earnings targets, it's often too late for investors to save their money. However, there is another type of missed milestone that can precede the disastrous earnings report. Advanced Micro Devices, for example, has a long history of product development and production delays that have led to poor earnings. The launch of its K5 chip in 1996 was a full year behind plan, leaving its new production facility greatly underutilized and unprofitable.[37] Given AMD's track record and the early warning signs for this chip, the problems AMD has encountered in competing against Intel should not be surprising.

A Question of Character

Perhaps the single most important indicator of potential executive failure is the one that is hardest to precisely define—the question of character. A person who has high ethical standards and deep competence, who desires to succeed by helping others to be better than they would otherwise be on their own, who can face reality even when it's unpleasant and acknowledge when something is wrong, and who engenders trust and promotes honesty in the organizations they create and lead. That may sound like a tall order, but the real problem is that some of the executives at the helm of companies we've profiled in this book weren't even close. Tony Galban, a D&O underwriter at Chubb, zeroed right in on this issue: "The three things behind every bad D&O liability situation are greed, cronyism, and denial. And if you were to watch people on the [witness] stands over the last six or eight months you would see an extraordinary amount of denial, some of which is almost not credible."[38]

Even many of the scrupulously honest executives we studied—and there were many—stumbled when they couldn't accept the reality of a changed world. For these executives, the problem wasn't one of ethics, but of defensiveness. How can we spot this warning sign? Here's one suggestion from Tony Galban:

> Always listen to the analysts' calls because that gives you a sense of how an individual thinks on their feet. They give you a sense of whether they're in denial or whether they're being professional. I've seen even the most polished people make very revealing comments

in the heat of press questioning. . . . you know, where you want to concentrate on subject A and you touch upon subject B, but they keep grilling you on subject B. . . . By the time the third question comes on subject B, watch how testy the CEO gets. "I thought we covered that," or "It's just what I said earlier" . . . Just very unresponsive, testy remarks which means, "I'm here to talk about subject A. I've been rehearsing subject A all night and now you're going to sit here and poke me on this marginal subject B and I don't want to talk about it."[39]

While many investors will never get a one-on-one audience with the CEO or CFO of a company, both analysts' calls (often available in real-time through a company's Web site) and the annual report provide some insight to character. John Keogh, another big-time underwriter of D&O insurance, pointed out what he looks for when CEOs are in the hot seat: "How well [do] they understand their business? . . . [Was] the management team incredibly arrogant? . . . [Did the CEO or CFO] have all the answers and is [he or she] pretty [much] on top of his or her game?"[40]

The letter to shareholders is one of the few direct windows to a CEO that many outsiders can access. Implicit in some of the warning signs we've discussed is a degree of aggressiveness or overconfidence, and the letter can sometimes provide clues. Tony Galban teaches the D&O underwriters who work for him to

[G]o through the letter and circle all the adjectives because, remember, that's been distilled. . . . [T]hat letter has been distilled through General Counsel, that letter has been distilled through all the other people who looked at it to make sure they're being careful. What you are wary of are people that have an excessively aggressive sense of control, and people that are cowboys. They tend to be the worst personality fits for what I call a sanguine CEO. You're looking for people that speak in overly aggressive terms about what they will accomplish, people that have a self-righteous indignation about failures, people that are defensive about having bad years, people that are in simple denial. I mean, you'll see these . . . "Well, sales are off 60 percent this year, but so are everybody's," or "Sales were off 60 percent this year, but that was an aberration," or "Sales are off 60 percent this year, but believe it or not we're in better shape than ever." These are the . . . sort of mass denials that you want to get to, so the letter to the shareholders is a good place to find it.[41]

In some ways the ultimate warning sign is that we don't trust the CEO and other senior executives. Clearly there are clues to what might happen in a company, and while there is certainly a great deal of uncertainty around these clues, they offer investors, board members, managers, and others important insights to the future. The question of character may well be the most important of them all.

Predicting Is One Thing, Doing Something About It Is Quite Another

Hockey superstar Wayne Gretzky was said to have the uncanny ability to "see" where the puck was going to be before anyone else. Larry Bird and Magic Johnson were said to have similar abilities on the basketball court, knowing where players would be and threading passes to them as if they had eyes in the backs of their heads. No doubt, some of this ability was built into the genetic code of these athletes, but there was a tremendous amount of hard work and study put in as well. Most great professional athletes are known to be students of the game. Appreciative of the sport's history, yet keenly aware that the learning process never stops, they are constantly looking for new trends or patterns that can make them better players.

The business world is not all that different in this respect. CEOs such as Lou Gerstner, Jack Welch, Andy Grove, and Bill Gates may have certain qualities of greatness in their genetic codes, but much of their success can be attributed to hard work and a study of their crafts. By examining the failings of so many great leaders, we've evaluated the reasons for their downfalls, but we've also discovered patterns of behavior that precipitate a great many of these disasters. These patterns are valuable, not only because they are direct causes of company failure, but because they can provide insight to what might happen, giving us an opportunity to step in to change the course of events before it is too late.

Of course, opportunity is not the same as action. While we might expect investors to be vigilant in responding to potential trouble, how confident are we that managers within our own companies will take to heart the lessons of this book? What are the challenges that keep managers from learning from their mistakes, and what can we do about it? The next, and final, chapter tackles a problem that has been behind the scenes throughout this book—how do smart executives learn?

CHAPTER 11

How Smart Executives Learn

Living—and Surviving—in a World of Mistakes

In the hit movie *The Firm*, Tom Cruise plays a young attorney who joins a powerful and successful law firm. It's the job of his dreams, and Cruise is on top of the world—until he makes a discovery. There's been a cover-up, the firm is involved in unscrupulous and illegal activity, and someone has died mysteriously. As our protagonist begins to make inquiries, he is counseled to look elsewhere. When he persists, he is blackmailed. When his investigation gathers steam, his own life becomes endangered.

Now imagine a real-world organization—absent the violence, to be sure—but still a place where asking questions only gets you into trouble. A company with a long record of attacking insiders and outsiders alike who don't toe the party line. A firm that actively seeks to cover up or destroy potentially damaging information, and ruin the careers of those who try to bring that information to light. If that organization sounds familiar, it should. *The Firm* mirrors Enron.

Consider the evidence. At Enron, the cutthroat culture that forced out the lowest performers also made it very dangerous to be wrong. CEO Jeffrey Skilling and CFO Andrew Fastow were described as "intimidating" and "arrogant" by whistle-blower Sherron Watkins in her testimony to a Congressional committee investigation.[1] Enron repeatedly shuts down negative assessments of its accounting and its prospects. For example, in a letter to Chairman Ken Lay, a senior executive writes with evident frustration, "I am incredibly nervous that we will implode in a wave of accounting scandals." This same executive also notes that several other senior Enron employees raised questions about the firm's ac-

267

counting methods to former CEO Skilling, but were stonewalled.[2] When the company does investigate the allegations in that letter, it turns to its own law firm, which is instructed by senior executives not to review the underlying accounting for the partnerships, the very area that is at the heart of the concerns.[3] As one former employee says to *Fortune* magazine, "People perpetuated this myth that there were never any mistakes. It was astounding to me."[4]

The culture of retribution at *The Firm* has few boundaries. Enron executives involved in one of the major off–balance-sheet partnerships push to have an Enron attorney who is negotiating with lawyers for the partnership fired for incompetence. What's going on here? These senior Enron executives playing the private-partnership game actually try to use their positions to attack an opposing lawyer, who is in fact an Enron employee looking out for Enron's corporate interests![5]

And pressure isn't only applied internally: A Merrill Lynch research analyst rates Enron's stock "neutral" in 1998. Merrill executives complain to the company president that the analyst's call on Enron is costing them investment-banking business. The analyst is replaced that summer.[6] *Fortune* writer Bethany McLean prepares perhaps the first major story on Enron that raises questions about the firm's accounting machinations; she calls Ken Lay for a reaction. He denigrates her logic and sends her on her way. But wait. The Enron corporate jet quickly arrives in New York with Andrew Fastow and two others, who proceed to pressure her to back down. When she refuses, appeals are made to senior management at Time Warner (*Fortune*'s parent) to dismiss her; they stand by her account.[7] How's that for hardball?

The pattern is clear: This was a company that purposely shut down alternative and conflicting views of reality to protect the status quo. In the name of preserving success and being in hard-nosed pursuit of greatness, an inflexible, intolerant culture developed in which new ideas were ignored, concerns were dismissed, and critical thinking got you fired. Just like the movie *The Firm*, this story is so extreme that it's almost impossible to believe. This is a real-life, modern-day, perfect case study in how not to create a learning culture.

In many ways, Enron was a scam—a series of double-deals perpetrated on customers, consumers, investors, and employees. Supporting it all was a system that was one part closed culture, one part perverse incentives, one part "no-holds-barred" people, and one part immense hubris, but even with all this going on, it was still possible to rein in the damage. But nobody wanted to; there wasn't a culture of openness that could have fostered a different path; and there were no systems in place to compel people to stop the train before it was too late.

The scariest part of the story is that while it's easy to write off Enron as an aberration, a genetic mistake in the evolution of business, we know that we're not quite as different from Enron as we insist in public and maybe even believe in private. For example, how would you answer these questions?

- Do you believe that the CEO and other senior executives in your company are open to different ideas?
- Does the typical employee or manager believe that he or she can bring mistakes to the attention of the bosses without personal repercussions?
- Does your company have a formal or informal process for learning from mistakes?
- Is it standard practice in your company to challenge people who say, "This is the way we've always done it!"?
- Are there a set of corporate values that people really believe in and use to decide how to handle the "gray" areas of business?

If you answered honestly and came out with "Yes" for each question, you live in a very happy world indeed. Unfortunately, the evidence from this research project suggests something quite the opposite. After all, it wasn't as if Motorola didn't have the technology for digital cell phones or the talent to implement a new strategy based on digital. And it wasn't as if the company was unaware of the shift toward digital while it was happening. Smart executives at Motorola simply chose not to do anything about it. They chose to be close-minded, they chose to close down dissenting views, and they chose not to face up to their mistake even when confronted with clear evidence of its damage.

It's easy to downplay the lessons of Enron (and WorldCom, Tyco, ImClone, Adelphia, and Rite Aid) because some of the actions of executives in those companies went over the line. We know the vast majority of executives won't stretch the rules so much that they break the law. But some of the same strategic, cultural, organizational, and leadership breakdowns that created the Enron debacle also appeared at Motorola, and J&J, and Rubbermaid, and Mattel, and Cabletron, and Wang, and the Boston Red Sox, and Schwinn. Rather than turn to indictable illegal activities, the executives in these other firms turned to "indictable" strategies and paid the price with bankruptcies, billion-dollar losses, and ruined careers.

The purpose of this book has been to document these mistakes and the destructive syndromes that are behind them so that we can understand the causes of failure, and to suggest ways to avoid falling into the same traps and learn from the experiences of others. Each of the previous chapters has offered some of the answers that we need to avoid the critical mistakes that bring down enterprises. In Part I, we read about executives who faltered while navigating their companies through some of the most challenging corporate passages, from creating new ventures to managing innovation and change, growing via mergers and acquisitions, and dealing with new competitive pressures. Not only do these stories provide insight into the perils of making it in business, they also point us toward a deeper understanding of what does and can go wrong along the way. The lessons from Part I are important, and they tell us how we can learn from the mistakes of others, but they are not the whole story.

Part II taught us a different set of lessons. Looking across a wide spectrum of business breakdowns, we identified the underlying reasons for why smart executives fail: executive mind-set failures that create mistaken pictures of reality; zombie businesses that encourage, rather than challenge, a company's skewed reality; breakdowns in how vital information is identified, disseminated, and utilized; and leadership pathologies that not only thwart attempts to address each of these breakdowns, but actually accelerate their potential to do damage. That these critical mistakes emerged as common patterns across many different types of companies and industries makes it all the more compelling that we heed these lessons of failure.

In the previous chapter we paid particular attention to the warning signs that indicate potential trouble. With an ear to the ground and a critical eye, an astute and cautious manager or investor can pick up at least some of the signals with time to react.

But what if you want to be proactive instead of reactive? What if you want to strengthen your organization's immune system against major management failures? You'd need to know how great corporate mistakes evolve, accelerate, and then overrun the typical corporate defenses and the best intentions of smart executives, so you could think about when to intervene. And you would especially want to know what you could do to avoid, and learn from, major corporate mistakes. This chapter tackles all of these issues as we try to understand how smart executives learn.

What Do We Know About Mistakes?

Imagine that you are buying a house. You researched the neighborhood, the schools, and recent sales of similar properties. You drove your commute route in rush-hour traffic. You figured out how far it is to the grocery store and the local swimming pool. The house has been inspected (twice) and you're confident in your decision to buy it. There is certainly more information you could collect, but the expense of gathering the information is greater than how much you value the information. No doubt you have friends who would gather more data. But at some point, you draw the line, accept the unknowns, and make a decision. You accept a certain level of risk. It happens when you buy a house, and it happens every day in business. What's the result? Mistakes.

It wasn't worth taking the time to talk to the neighbors and meet their kids. Maybe you didn't investigate the plans for the empty lot at the end of the block. A week after you move in, it's pretty clear that the neighborhood kids are brats and the lot is empty by day, but supports a bustling drug trade by night. Now it's unlikely that you would misread a neighborhood so drastically. Surely there were warning signs. But in the struggle to balance decision making, expense, and risk, we make choices that can lead to mistakes. These mistakes are avoidable, but let's face it, we're never going to rid ourselves of all mistakes, nor should we even try. Why? Because risk is inherent in business. If you never took risks, you'd never chart new ground. You would never revolutionize a market or a product or an industry.

When it comes right down to it, you can't afford *not* to take risks. Calculated risks are essential to successful business. And, by definition, where there are risks, there are mistakes. Ingvar Kamprad, the founder of IKEA, said, "Only those who are asleep make no mistakes,"[8] and one of the key values at the New York Times Company is to "take risks and innovate, recognizing that failure occasionally occurs."[9]

A mistake is an experiment to learn from. Many people are familiar with the development of Post-it notes, designed by a scientist at 3M who developed an adhesive with not enough "stick" to do that job, but perfect for its eventual use. The same type of thing happened to William Perkins, a British chemist, who invented artificial dyes when he discovered that a failed experiment to make synthetic quinine left a colored stain.[10] Neither of these things could happen without some acceptance of failure within organizations.

So, some mistakes are unavoidable and understandable—beneficial at best, an ordinary cost of doing business at worst. You can minimize the likelihood and the potential downside, but eliminating them entirely is an exercise in futility.

But not all mistakes are inevitable and understandable. In fact, the mistakes profiled in this book are not only unacceptable, they are legion. No matter how you cut it, it's not possible to justify losing more than 90 percent of your market share in just months because you were unable to offer customers what they wanted, as J&J did in the stent business. It is unacceptable to continue making billion-dollar investments in the face of clear evidence that those investments aren't paying off, as Iridium and General Motors both did. And it is mind-boggling to develop and implement outlandish visions that require buying most any company you can find in the service sector, like Saatchi & Saatchi did, or that justifies spending billions of dollars in the auto business because the CEO likes cars, as Samsung did.

General Motors, Motorola, Saatchi & Saatchi, Samsung, Johnson & Johnson—in each case and in virtually all of the others we studied, there was an opportunity to learn, and derail the freight train bearing down on the company. No, all mistakes are not created equal. Some mistakes just should not happen, not only because of their momentous import, but also because there are so often critical inflection points when intervention can make a difference. To understand how this is so, and what you can do about it, requires a closer look at how mistakes evolve in organizations.

How Mistakes Evolve

There is no "big bang" theory of corporate failure. In the end, an autopsy may indicate that everything broke down within a failing company, but these failures are seldom simultaneous. Mistakes evolve over time, and the reality is that there is no company that can avoid the effects of (1) the company's history and (2) change. Combined, these two factors inevitably bring about shifts in the status quo, which opens a company up to making mistakes.

But if the nature of business and of people running businesses is such that there are inherent flaws within, then why don't all organizations stumble and sometimes die, as the companies profiled in this book have? The answer is that just because organizations possess vulnerabilities and are marked by history does not mean that some sort of failure is preordained. Rather, organizations and executives inevitably have opportunities to take action to avoid disaster; the companies that fail are those where the strategic, cultural, organizational, and leadership breakdowns we described in Part II of this book exacerbate the inherent weaknesses at critical times.

Think about Mattel. Jill Barad parlayed her stunning promotion of the Barbie brand to the CEO's job, taking with her an inherent belief that marketing's importance trumped all other capabilities for Mattel. At the same time, the company's M&A capability was atrophying with the retirement of Barad's successful predecessor and the revolving door in the executive suite. But it was only with the acquisition of the Learning Company that these vulnerabilities came into stark relief. Mattel bought the wrong company, missed the boat on due diligence, and began a string of missed earnings targets. The inability to make the acquisition work, along with Barad's overpromising and underdelivering, combined to create a crisis of confidence in the market. When the dust settled, Barad was gone, the Learning Company was gone, and a new management team led by Bob Eckert was working on the turnaround. If Barad hadn't bought the Learning Company and had managed to retain high-quality executives at the top, she might still be at the helm.

For many firms following the Internet boom years, the bubble that had protected a myriad of latent defects (for example, inexperienced management, lack of financial discipline, and questionable assumptions about strategy) burst to reveal a seascape of hobbled companies. When the winds shifted and the "old economy" economy reemerged, the natural "slack" from good times was gone, and failure occurred much more quickly. Latent defects can't be suppressed when the economy is not on your side.

These examples highlight how inherent vulnerabilities rise to the surface when some trigger strips away the status quo.

When we go back and look at a company after it has fallen apart, it's usually the case that all four destructive syndromes have taken hold. For example, the view of reality at Wang Labs was badly mistaken about the rise of personal computers and what it could do to the market for word processors, Wang's major product at the time. An Wang—despite, or perhaps because of, his animosity toward IBM—stoked a *culture of superiority* with respect not just to competitors but also to customers. These attitudes reinforced the *mistaken picture of reality;* after all, how could IBM bring a better product to market than Wang? At the same time, *information breakdowns* occurred, both because the company relied on An Wang as the central node in the flow of information (he knew everything, and if he didn't, watch out!) and because the board of directors let the benevolent dictator do as he pleased. Finally, the personal hubris and fixation on control that drove An Wang was a classic *illusion of preeminence;* there was no separation of personal and business concerns; and early interactions with IBM defined almost all subsequent behavior.

But in the midst of a breakdown, do strategic, cultural, organizational, and leadership malfunctions occur simultaneously? No. The autopsy reveals massive and multiple failures, as in Wang, but it wasn't until IBM came out with the PC that the benevolent dictator's approach to running his business became so detrimental. There are some natural self-correcting mechanisms in healthy companies that help rein in ill-conceived strategies. Unfortunately, not all companies have a good system of checks and balances, so when several breakdowns occur it becomes increasingly difficult to recover.

Two critical lessons emerge from this section. First, because every company has a history, it is virtually impossible to pinpoint every single potential vulnerability. Rather, companies depend on a culture that thrives on asking questions, staying alert, and being open-minded. The ability to constantly recalibrate in real time is a capability executives must nurture.

Second, when they see conditions changing, executives need to pay special attention to all four underlying forces for failure. Just as people tend to get colds when the seasons change, so too does the level of risk shift for organizations when the status quo is upset. It is at precisely these times when an assessment of potential executive mind-set failures, delusional attitudes, information breakdowns, and leadership pathologies is absolutely needed. While Part II provided a blueprint for just this type of assessment, there are powerful forces at work to insulate an organization from the truth. Our job now is to see through that barrier.

How Smart Executives Create Close-Minded Organizations

So many forces buffet business that it's hard for executives to know which way to turn. In the midst of turmoil, employees, suppliers, partners, and the media all turn their lonely eyes to the top, to the executive class and especially the CEO, for answers. Yet, how can one man or one woman know what is unknowable, what is emerging, forming, and changing virtually every week? Is it leadership to point the direction forward in the midst of confusion? Yes, and no. Leaders define the game that is being played, and set in motion an agenda to win that game, but they cannot, and should not, try to play every position on the field.

Perhaps it is the pressure felt by leaders to have the right answers that directs them to try, in an attempt to validate the heroic dimensions we have placed on the CEO's job. Rather than relying on one person to foretell the future, however, wouldn't companies be better off if the entire organization was built, challenged, and empowered to create the future? When two of the most celebrated CEOs of the past twenty years—Jack Welch of GE and Microsoft's Bill Gates—are unable to see the potential of the Internet until many others already have, is it reasonable to expect CEOs to have the right answers to highly uncertain problems? Rather than expecting CEOs to know, we should be expecting CEOs to create an organization that will know. Rather than turning to the CEO for a vision of the future, we should be turning to the CEO to define the purpose of the organization, and to create an organization that will have the energy, resilience, culture, and talent to manage the unknowable.

It's a huge challenge, creating an organization with the capability to take on the world, and the capability to learn from its mistakes and the mistakes of others and adapt, but at least it is a realistic—and not inevitably futile—challenge. The heroic CEO is not one who can predict the future, for in the uncertain environment that dominates business today such a forecast is surely more luck than talent. The heroic CEO is one who creates an organization capable of meeting the challenges that are constantly emerging, who builds creativity, open-mindedness, a disdain for bureaucracy, and honesty into the DNA of organizational life.

Shifting from a heroic model of all-knowing and powerful CEOs to organizations of open-minded people who ask questions and learn from mistakes is one of the most challenging of all transitions. Heroic CEOs don't really need other people, except to do what they want them to do. And don't think for a second that this message doesn't get through. The formula for apathy—and sometimes worse—starts with the CEO who believes that he or she has all the answers.

What happens next is a story we've seen repeated throughout this book. At Barings Bank in Singapore, people knew; when Rite Aid was hemorrhaging under Martin Grass, people knew (though their fear of retribution was such that they even refused to speak to us off the record); at Snow Brands, numerous people knew; at Enron, dozens if not hundreds of people knew. Whether they were managers, employees, or senior executives, there were always people who knew when the bad stuff was happening. But no one told.

In one of the very few instances when people who knew actually acted on the knowledge—WorldCom—by the time next-level managers such as Cynthia Cooper discovered the $9 billion-plus fraud, it was too late. Some of the people who knew what was happening at WorldCom chose not to reveal what they knew, a choice that may well cost them jail time. The excuse that you were ordered to do something illegal, that you actually had no choice, is not only morally repugnant, it is also a sad commentary on how little many people think of themselves and the power they have to influence decision making.

Surely, there is something you can do that will make it much less likely that your company will fall prey to the same cancer that has destroyed once-great firms. Well, the good news is, there is. The bad news is, what is needed is rather messy, rather slow, and not at all easy. There is no silver bullet. To paraphrase a well-known slogan from just a few years ago, "It's the people, stupid."

Smart Executives Step Up to Learning and Open-Mindedness

Many of the mistakes we've seen in this book were of spectacular magnitude, and while Samsung and Sony have been able to absorb their multibillion-dollar losses and move on, most companies cannot. One element of learning is being aware of how companies break down and what those experiences have been like in other organizations, because if they happen to you the game may be over.[11] We've also seen how mistakes tend to evolve, meaning there really is an opportunity for executives to step in before it is too late and take action to disrupt the pattern and avoid ultimate failure.

Throughout this research we have been on the alert to identify attributes of companies that are most likely to recognize what is happening and have the guts to respond, and the one thing that stands out is open-mindedness. Creating an open culture in which mistakes come to light, and learning from them comes easily, requires a certain type of leader, a leader who believes in the importance of a culture of openness and who lives by the tenets that implies.

The transition to a more open-minded organization is not always a smooth ride. At Boeing, one of the key steps along this road was the arrival of Harry Stonecipher, who came over from McDonnell Douglas when Boeing acquired that company. He didn't take long to shake things up. "Our problem is us!" he exclaimed at an executive meeting. The furor that followed speaks volumes about Boeing's insular culture at the time.[12]

So what does a culture of openness look like? Openness means fighting the natural tendency to cover up unfavorable or distasteful information. It requires leaders to set the standard for learning from mistakes—an unnatural act in many organizations. Leaders who are unable or unwilling to build a culture of openness create organizations that almost choose not to learn. They are defensive, not open.

A culture of openness is a culture where people feel safe to say what they really think and to act on it. You have to encourage information flow rather than force it. Boeing CEO Phil Condit put it this way: "If you are trying to find problems rather than encouraging them out of the organization, you build a culture where people try to hide the problem. It gets down to can you find it? Can you see it? As opposed to the dialogue that is, 'Have we got any issues that we need to address? Is there anything festering in the organization?' "[13]

In the venture capital community, people talk of the "humility sweater"—the sweater you were wearing when you made the call on a losing investment. Wear it as a reminder when you get too confident.[14] At Southwest Airlines a powerful people-centered culture means "We're not going to punish each other for mistakes. We're going to learn from them."[15]

When leaders don't acknowledge their mistakes, the signal to the rest of the organization is sometimes "Carry on." That seems to have been the case when Arthur Andersen settled an SEC civil fraud complaint related to Waste Management without admitting or denying the charges. The partners implicated in the case were not publicly reprimanded, and one of them actually wrote the document management policy that David Duncan—the Houston partner fired for shredding Enron documents— cited as support for his actions. When Enron came along, the Department of Justice saw a pattern of apparently cavalier behavior and that was the end.[16]

Executives not only must be prepared to admit when they're wrong, they also need to create opportunities for others to safely provide feedback. How many CEOs have someone who can tell them that they're wrong, that their pet project is really a dumb idea?

Dealing with this challenge requires considerable effort. Consider what the New York Times Company emphasizes in its cultural value statement: "Treat each other with honesty, respect and civility. Take risks and innovate, recognizing that failure occasionally occurs. Give and accept constructive feedback." The company's "Rules of the Road" encourage a "culture that is open-minded as opposed to closed-minded . . . that is civil and honest and respectful as opposed to judgmental and critical or negative."[17] None of this happens without leadership, of course, and this is evident when you look into how companies such as the New York Times, Boeing, Dell, Intel, Southwest Airlines, and Colgate have become "best-practice" stories on how to learn from mistakes. But there are also some specific tools of the trade that can open up opportunities for you to build a learning culture within your own organizations.

Learning from People

The name of the game is to make it as easy as possible for people to count, to be heard, to have a voice; while a culture of open-mindedness is a critical prerequisite, it's important to back it up with multiple avenues of debate, discussion, and data. You might use an open bulletin board in the private elevators between floors to generate feedback and communication. Suggestion boxes in common spaces are another option. Boeing has employed an "Ethics Hotline" for years to provide an outlet for people to speak out. A few years ago, young, Internet-savvy managers at General Electric coached senior executives on the new technology in a "reverse mentoring" program. Aside from the straightforward benefit of teaching senior managers about the Internet, this approach reinforced GE's antihierarchy ethos and provided a two-way window for senior and junior managers to interact. A company in Australia requires each person to talk to his or her boss for one hour a month about what he or she is doing well and what mistakes are being made.

While the specific type of opportunities an organization creates for dialogue and feedback is less important, the fact that there are such opportunities is very important indeed. People have to believe that their contributions matter and that no one will shoot the messenger. They have to trust that honesty, good intentions, and well–thought-out decisions will be valued and respected. With this culture, insights and criticism are not covered up. With this culture, blaming others in classic scapegoating fashion is not acceptable.

Companies can try to create forums for conversation about mistakes in different ways. At Starbucks, "Senior managers meet with all interested employees to update them on the company's performance, answer questions, and allow them to air grievances."[18] Similarly, at Home Depot, founder Bernie Marcus was known for his "Bernie Road Shows" where he would travel to divisions across the country and encourage managers to give direct feedback. He would grant "immunity" during these meeting so "Managers can ask any type of question no matter how blunt, invasive, or even offensive it might be."[19] In more structured meetings, it can help to appoint a "chief jerk" to argue the counterpoint. By opening the door to criticism and critical thinking, people will feel more comfortable speaking out.

Get to "Worst Practices," Not Just Best Practices

It's intuitive that people learn from exceptions and mistakes, yet businesses, and business schools for that matter, seldom emphasize the value of learning from worst practices. One exception is Boeing, which uses Process Councils to "look at where did people have problems and what worked and what didn't work. Clearly, the emphasis is on trying to share best practices, but you can't do that without talking about what didn't work."[20] These Process Councils presume that you won't be jumped on for bringing up the bad news. To create this feeling in your company, you need to communicate regularly, support people, demonstrate respect, treat people fairly, and keep your promises.

At the Children's Hospital and Clinics in Minneapolis, reporting on safety violations and breakdowns is a scary proposition. There are issues of liability and quality of care. But the importance of knowing what's going on and what is behind it outweighs the "danger" of admitting to violations. Julie Morath, the COO at Children's Hospital, told us, "One of the things we did here was to really amplify the aspects of the culture that focus on safety—to increase awareness, to educate and engage people in learning about safety, and to help people feel safe to report on errors."[21] In order for the hospital to improve its safety record, *errors must be reported*. A company cannot succeed if people fear for their jobs should a mistake become known.

The Air Force has a very particular way of collecting important, and negative, information in a "safe" atmosphere. Immediately after a mission is completed, the team meets to debrief. The debrief is mandatory and involves every single member of the team. No one outside of the team is allowed in the room, including higher-level managers who are not already on the team. Debriefs are nameless and rankless. To help depersonalize the process, actual names are replaced with Lead, Number One, Number Two, and so on. Critically, the formal leader of the group is just another team member during the debrief. To encourage open discussion, the leader typically starts off the debrief by acknowledging his or her own mistakes in detail and then asks others to provide their own feedback on the leader's performance.

Each person is expected to admit what he or she did wrong, and to probe for the reasons behind any performance shortfall. No reprimands are allowed. You admit what you did wrong, others point out what else you may have done wrong, and together you seek to understand why these mistakes took place, and that's the end of it. If this process were the norm in your organization, you could provide a natural incentive for everyone to self-assess and acknowledge their mistakes.[22]

Spread the News

What happens with this information is just as important as the information itself. At Colgate, lessons learned from investigating mistakes are integrated into the company in two ways: sharing them with similar projects and using them as a list of potential failures when starting up new projects. Project teams review the list of past mistakes, pick out the ones most likely to resurface, and create "Continuous Improvement Plans" to avoid or mitigate the problem. Companywide, a team reviews all the data from Continuous Improvement Reviews (CIRs), pulls out the common themes, and develops plans to fix the trouble spots that continuously lead to the problems. For example, if there are weak spots in project management or decision making, they are not only identified through a debriefing process; the CIR process allows Colgate to address the issue on an enterprisewide basis.

Colgate also does a more abbreviated version on the shop floor. It looks at the production data for the day, picks out three issues (machine downtime, maintenance, etc.), goes to the shop floor, and has a short meeting with the leaders and supervisors who then have their own CIR with the machine operators.

Boeing, like a number of other companies, uses its Leadership Center to spread the knowledge gleaned from mistakes. It is the central repository of information. The constant flow of executives through the programs increases the odds that the information is carried back to the company. As CEO Phil Condit puts it, "One of the things we did there intentionally was try to create an environment in which two things would happen. One of them was that people would make mistakes and, two, it didn't matter so that you could learn from them far more easily."[23]

Disseminating information in an accessible way is a challenge all companies face. But communicating the lessons learned from mistakes is the most important piece of the process. It's one thing to admit that you've made a mistake; it's quite another to make sure that everyone can learn from the experience. By acknowledging mistakes and talking about them, the mistakes and their lessons become company legends. Stories of mistakes and the lessons from those mistakes play a critical role in ensuring that people learn from them. It's through stories that people remember events and situations. Stories are the currency of culture.

For stories to work as a learning mechanism, you have to be looking for them. You have to be aware enough to capture stories as they happen and find ways to disseminate them. The best companies share these stories in orientation programs for new employees, during on-going training, and in company publications and speeches. The CEO of a construction company has a wooden plaque on his wall with a doorknob on it. The brass plate beneath it reads, "The $10 million Doorknob." Funny thing to have on your office wall. But he doesn't think it's funny at all. He sees it as essential to the company's success.

A few years ago, the company completed a project for a prominent private school. It was a small project at the beginning of a multimillion-dollar master plan that had not yet been awarded. The project went off without a hitch. Deadlines and budgets were met and the client was ecstatic. The only problem was the school was having some trouble with a doorknob. Workmen went out a couple of times in response to complaints and attempted to fix the doorknob, but never replaced it. The last shoe dropped when the doorknob came off in someone's hand and locked him in the office. But it wasn't just anyone's hand. The doorknob was in the hands of the person who would award the master plan. That one doorknob cost the company millions of dollars in revenue. The plaque in the office serves as a reminder to tell the story and perpetuate a culture of being fanatical about details and client satisfaction.

Mattel Revisited

Wouldn't it be interesting to apply some of these ideas on open-mindedness and learning from mistakes to one of the companies we profiled that lost millions of dollars by doing something quite the opposite? We have that opportunity, in the case of Mattel and the Learning Company. In Chapter 4 we noted how the toy giant under CEO Jill Barad paid $3.5 billion (4.5 times *sales*) for the maker of such interactive CD-ROMs as Reader Rabbit and Carmen Sandiego, despite numerous signs of the company's poor health. In fact, when Mattel made the deal, the Learning Company was still struggling to integrate its own acquisitions while its brands were in decline, resulting in depressed sales and profitability. As it turned out, Mattel never recognized or appreciated how troubled the Learning Company was, and an anticipated Q3 1999 $50 million profit turned into a loss of $105 million.

While a lack of due diligence and appropriate integration in the acquisition were her first mistakes, that is just the beginning. The shortfall in Q3 of 1999 is brushed aside and Barad continues to be confident about the opportunity. She stands by her expected earnings figure of seventy to eighty cents per share. When Q4 comes along, she announces another loss. This time it's $184 million. Yet she remains optimistic. Unfortunately, she repeats the same mistake again (four times in all).[24] Earnings guidance may be a dangerous game, but once you enter to play, the penalty for not mastering the rules is severe. The bottom line: Consistently missing on earnings is a strong signal that a company's view of reality is off. And consistently missing on earnings means a company is not learning from its mistakes.

When the dust settles, Barad is gone and new CEO Bob Eckert sells the Learning Company to buyout firm Gores Technology Group for nothing but a share of the upside should Gores be successful in turning around the losing operation. In contrast to the old Mattel that kept missing earnings targets but always had an explanation for the shortfall, Gores is a company dedicated to not only learning from mistakes, but capitalizing on the mistakes of others. Here's how Chairman Alec Gores describes what he encountered the day after his group took over the Learning Company:

> We called for an "all-hands town hall"–type meeting to openly communicate with employees and set the pace for our management style and plans. We were amazed at how upset and negative the attitudes of the employees were. They had been involved with something that had gone from billions of value to being an industry scar. . . . Frustrations with the parent and the process had left the employees extremely disillusioned.[25]

What Alec Gores and his team did next provides a terrific antidote to the prevailing customs not only at Mattel and the Learning Company, but at so many of the other companies discussed in this book. What's more, it points out how one company can learn from the mistakes of another.

Change the Mind-set to Accurately Reflect Reality

After Gores took over, he challenged traditional mind-sets about what customers wanted and how the company invested capital: "A lot of these very, very smart people were never challenged to say, 'Well, how many customers have endorsed this concept or how many customers have signed up to purchase that enhancement or that product?' There were millions of dollars being spent on projects that absolutely had no validation in reality. . . . It was just amazing. . . . The fundamental basis for return on investment [was] not being tested."

Challenge Delusions That Keep People from Facing Reality

Where the organization is complacent and seemingly content, you challenge people in a way they haven't been challenged before. Part of it is honesty, and part of it is good business practice. "What [employees] do is keep burying the problems instead of saying, 'Let's stop this madness.' . . . One of the things that we do—and it's very subtle—is to change the culture of the company . . . the way people think . . . the way employees think." So the emphasis shifts to critical thinking, innovation, and challenging the status quo. Rather than assume that people are not capable of facing reality, challenge them. The net result is a more honest and open culture.

Start Managing Information More Effectively

Where people in an organization are unfocused, you drill down into the numbers and figure out just what is going on. While many would be content to rest easy when everything appears to be going just as planned, complacency is often the result of ignorance and lack of information. Gores drills to the core. He seeks hard data and reliable information. And he recognizes that it's not easy to do: "People have a difficult time understanding what's underneath the covers. They just don't know how to get deep enough inside the company and figure the problem out."

Change Unsuccessful Leadership Habits

Where there is no communication across groups and little collaboration, Gores builds teams. "We called a meeting with all the various managers in various divisions and some of these people have been there for two, three, four years and had never met. They were never in the same room." The lack of communication across the company was largely due to the particular and heavy-handed leadership of Barad. She is known as someone who "had an ego and who pretty much took the position of 'her way or the highway.' There was minimal communication down below with that regime." The only way to tackle that is to change the leadership. Which is precisely what Gores had done.

Gores brought the company back to profitability in seventy-five days. Much of what he did is exactly what we discussed earlier in this chapter. With his "town hall"–type meeting he created a forum for dialogue and began opening up the culture. He recognized that ideas weren't being challenged and decisions were being made without sufficient consideration. As he empowered people, he coupled it with a sense of responsibility. It's a balancing act—you welcome ideas and action, but with the understanding that there is an expectation of a high level of performance.

In the end, one of the most vital of all executive roles is to create a learning organization. By studying mistakes and failures, we open up a window to learn not just what we shouldn't do but also what we should do. *Smart executives succeed* by learning from the mistakes of others, by understanding the underlying causes of failure and how to be alert to them, and by creating organizations that are open-minded enough to acknowledge and learn from their own mistakes.

Final Words: Where Are They Now?

How well have the companies profiled in this book learned from their mistakes? In truth, many never had the chance. There are those companies that entered Chapter 11 or equivalent and never reemerged, including Webvan, PowerAgent, Barings Bank, and, it appears, Enron. Then there are some companies—General Magic, for one—that seem just a bad day away from joining them. And there are several companies that ended up being acquired by rivals—Rubbermaid by Newell, Boston Market by McDonald's, and Quaker by PepsiCo—and another acquired out of bankruptcy (Boo.com by Fashion.com). Quaker's nemesis, Snapple, has now found itself a thriving home at Cadbury Schweppes via a successful turnaround engineered by Triarc.[26]

Other companies, including Wang Labs, Schwinn, and eToys, came out of bankruptcy a shadow of their former glory. Insurance giant Conseco and telecom heavyweights Adelphia and WorldCom are sure to emerge in some form from bankruptcy as different entities, though you can't help but regret that it took a bankruptcy to get off the path of wooden-headedness and irresponsible leadership. In all of these surviving companies, however, the senior executives at the helm during the failing years have not had a hand in the recovery.

Three companies we studied found themselves up against industry heavyweights, and none fared all that well. Cabletron never did manage to catch up to Cisco during the 1990s and instead adopted almost the polar-opposite strategy—it split up into different companies to focus on narrower segments of the market. The one thing that didn't change? They're still struggling. Advanced Micro Devices continues to battle Intel, staying in the game despite numerous mistakes largely because its absence would leave virtually the entire market to Intel, something that PC makers, federal regulators, and Intel itself probably would not wish for. And Encyclopedia Britannica, while much improved after its mid-1990s swoon, is finding out what life is like when Microsoft is your primary competitor. Britannica's CD-ROM product remains far behind Microsoft's Encarta in market share and product quality.

For some companies, big mistakes didn't cause lasting damage. Coca-Cola's troubles in Belgium were only a blip on the radar for that brand powerhouse, and Marks & Spencer, after a disastrous run in the late 1990s, is on a big upswing under new senior leadership. Toro, the company that makes snow blowers and related products, suffered through a rough stretch in the 1980s when it seemed to believe that it could sell snow blowers even if there was no snow. Today, Toro is doing just fine under longtime CEO Kendrick Melrose.

Perhaps the same can be said about Bankers Trust, Food Lion, RJ Reynolds (remember Project Spa in Chapter 9?), Sony, and Firestone, all of which absorbed their losses and moved on. But let's not forget that most of these companies lost hundreds of millions, sometimes even billions, of dollars.

Also in the billion-dollar–loser department is Samsung Motors, which went out of business after a five-year sojourn trying to make money from Chairman Kun-Hee Lee's love of cars. Samsung the corporation, however, has never done better, as it raises its aspirations to become a global giant rivaling Sony. How Samsung comes to terms with the need for professional management in what is still a classic Korean chaebol remains to be seen.

Johnson & Johnson took years to gain back market share lost after companies such as Guidant, Medtronics, and Boston Scientific entered the stent business with the next-generation products that J&J refused to introduce itself. Now, as we noted in Chapter 3, J&J is poised to shake up the industry once again with a path-breaking drug-eluting stent. Just what the company learned from the earlier debacle will become clear to cardiologists and hospitals—and investors—rather quickly.

Not all organizations are resilient enough to recover from some of the break-the-company mistakes we saw, but there have been some major success stories. The one thing they all have in common, interestingly enough, is that the turnarounds were spearheaded by newly appointed CEOs. Bob Eckert at Mattel quickly sold off the Learning Company, cut costs, added some humility at the top, and started focusing on core brands and products once again. Fruit of the Loom brought back former COO Bob Holland (he had resigned when Fruit was still run by former CEO William Farley) to work with Lazard Freres, finally completed its offshore move, and managed a $400 million swing from positive to negative earnings. As a reward for reorganizing out of bankruptcy, Warren Buffett's Berkshire Hathaway bought the company for $930 million in 2002. Oxford Health Plans brought in veteran executive Norm Payson to fix the mess left by computer glitches, upset customers, and indignant regulators.[27] Carlos Ghosn brought Nissan back from the brink in what is widely seen as one of the most impressive global turnarounds of recent years. Finally, Saatchi & Saatchi had a succession of CEOs following the ouster of the Saatchi brothers, with current CEO Kevin Roberts sitting atop a global advertising powerhouse once again.

Several companies are still immersed in a turnaround, and the jury is out on how successful they will be. In five of these companies—Rite

Aid, Tyco, Snow Brand Milk, AMP, and Ford—new CEOs are leading the recovery, with the first two spending much of their early months on the job trying to get the accounting ledgers back to a semblance of what passes for generally accepted accounting principles, and the latter three fighting to gain back credibility with customers.

In addition to Ford, there are two other car companies still playing catch-up. While it's been many years since Roger Smith was beating up on workers at General Motors, the broad market trend toward competitors' products hasn't changed. Despite some newfound stability under CEO Richard Wagoner, the slow downward spiral of GM continues to this day. The other turnaround story in the car business is at Daimler-Chrysler, where CEO Jürgen Schrempp continues to hold court. The unanswered question here is whether the Chrysler acquisition will ever turn out to be a financial winner given the initial cost and big-time losses that greeted the Germans in the aftermath of the deal.

After the ImClone debacle, which resulted in a $1.1 billion write-off in 2002, Bristol-Myers Squibb continued to get bad press, most recently about inventory games and alleged accounting manipulations designed to help the company hit the aggressive earnings growth targets set by former CEO Charles Heimbold Jr.[28] As for ImClone, there is still considerable uncertainty about whether Erbitux will get FDA approval. Meanwhile, former CEO Sam Waksal has pleaded guilty to a variety of charges.

Sometimes, even when a company is back as a major player in its core marketplace, the effects of past failings linger on. Motorola is a perfect example. With market share in the cell phone business hovering under 20 percent for the past five years—remember that its share was as high as 60 percent in the mid-1990s—the company continues to pay the price for past mistakes. While it remains far behind industry leader Nokia in global share, it's finally close to pulling even in the U.S. Motorola has tried to avoid the mistakes of the past by building greater strength and oversight at the corporate level, going back to basics by focusing on what customers really want, and rebuilding what was once an important element of how the company operated—a healthy spirit of discontent.[29]

Motorola's other venture that went up in smoke provides a rather different lesson. As we noted in Chapter 2, Iridium now lives as a newly capitalized company specializing in satellite-based cell phone service for customers in the marine, military, oil, and aviation industries that really don't have ready access to now virtually ubiquitous land-based telecom. After paying $25 million for assets originally worth a couple of hundred times that amount, Iridium's new owners may have finally found the winning formula. It is now conceivable that there will be sufficient customers to justify this investment as the business model can shift from the hegemony of scale to a targeted focus on a niche market.

The fortunes of Levi Strauss are a little more shrouded as a private company, but the lingering effects of family owners have not been positive. Yet, the family is still in the game. The same can't be said of the third-generation Pressman clan who took Barneys to the cleaners in the mid-1990s. After being ousted in the 1996 bankruptcy, they've taken up fighting each other for the remaining spoils. When Fred Pressman, the father of Bob and Gene—the two brothers who saw the company go bankrupt under their watch—died, he specifically stipulated, "I make no provision hereunder for my son Robert L. Pressman, for good and sufficient reason." Late in 2000 Fred's daughters won an $11 million judgment against their brother Bob, who countered with a suit of his own. This is one case that doesn't appear to have an ending coming anytime soon.[30]

DeLorean's run as auto industry impresario, on the other hand, ended when he was arrested for money laundering and drug trafficking, although he was acquitted in 1986 when federal agents were found to have violated guidelines for sting operations. Legal troubles have been almost continuous since then, however, resulting in a declaration of personal bankruptcy in 1999. DeLorean is apparently planning to sell high-end watches, and rumors of a return to the sports car business of his fame continue to this day.

In a different twist on this theme, sometimes the executives survived but the company didn't. For example, LTCM is no longer in business, but at least two of the firm's principals have started up new hedge funds. And in a fascinating turnabout, Mossimo Giannulli is back as CEO of his namesake company even though the company is barely recognizable with just eight employees. Mossimo eventually learned that he really didn't have any competencies in manufacturing or distributing clothes, no matter how trendy, and reincarnated his company as a licensor to companies such as Target in the United States and the Hudson's Bay Company in Canada. This is turning out to be something of a happy ending because the company simply designs apparel to meet Target's needs, playing off some of the leftover hype around the Mossimo name from the earlier days. Perhaps unsurprisingly, its older Southern California "cousin," L.A. Gear, adopted much the same strategy after it emerged from bankruptcy in the mid-1990s, though L.A. Gear, unlike Mossimo, is no longer run by the people who presided over its failure.

Finally, we have the Boston Red Sox. The story of integration is now long past, and there is no one left in the organization who was part of that period of history. Despite occasional insinuations that vestiges of the past remain, the team is fully integrated. The Red Sox's history stands out as a powerful example of irrational behavior, one that was repeated in totally different guises but repeated nonetheless, in many of the companies we studied.

When our research began some six years ago, few would have predicted that the failure of the Boston Red Sox to integrate with African-American baseball players could stand as a symbol for the critical mistakes made by companies in widely different industries and even different countries. And of course no one could have predicted that the major scandals of the new century in companies such as Enron, WorldCom, Tyco, Adelphia, and ImClone would have roots similar in nature to not only the Boston Red Sox but also to such reputable companies as Johnson & Johnson, Motorola, Rubbermaid, Sony, and Mattel. But in each one of these cases, the same destructive syndromes emerged, cascaded through the organization, and left a trail of breakdowns and failure.

Why do smart executives fail? Because they create and live in organizations where mistaken pictures of reality take hold, delusional policies and attitudes protect that skewed reality from careful scrutiny, organizational procedures designed to manage information, risk, and people break down, and leaders who adopt spectacularly unsuccessful habits magnify all of these problems. What looks irrational from the outside becomes perfectly sensible to executives on the inside who fall into each of these traps. The smart executives profiled in this book did not intend for disaster to strike, but it did, because they weren't aware of the insidious and sometimes complex ways in which failure emerges in organizations. If this book helps to provide a template for smart executives to avoid making these mistakes, much will be accomplished. If this book helps investors to see why some of their investments go wrong, much will be accomplished. And if this book helps people in organizations and in everyday life to better understand how organizations work, much will be accomplished. Who knows? Maybe the Red Sox will win it all next year.

Notes

CHAPTER 1. WHY SMART EXECUTIVES FAIL

1. The one IBM PC critique that might have legs is the idea that the company could have negotiated an exclusive supplier arrangement with Microsoft, or even taken equity in Microsoft in return for handing over the operating system franchise. IBM did neither, despite reports that Bill Gates expected to hand over some equity to get this contract.

2. Boo.com had offices in several European cities, but most of its employees worked in the U.K.

CHAPTER 2. NEW BUSINESS BREAKDOWNS

1. Burnstein, Daniel, and Kline, David, *Superhighway Road Warriors*, New York: Dutton/Plume, 1995.

2. Hill, G. Christian, and Yamada, Ken, "High-Tech Stakes: Five Electronics Giants Hope General Magic Will Turn the trick." *The Wall Street Journal*, February 8, 1993. p. A1.

3. Hill, G. Christian, and Yamada, Ken, "High-Tech Stakes: Five Electronics Giants Hope General Magic Will Turn the Trick," *The Wall Street Journal*, February 8, 1993, p. A1.

4. Futrelle, David, "Down and Out," *UPSIDE Today,* August 2, 1999, p. 40.

5. Futrelle, David, "Down and Out," *UPSIDE Today,* August 2, 1999, p. 40. The hype machine has not disappeared. As recently as 2001 one senior manager told us, "If you are known to be the best technically, that does breed arrogance. We need to harness it and target it. We know we are the best."

6. PR Newswire, Palm press release, December 18, 2002, http://pressroom.palm.com/InvestorRelations/PubNewsStory.aspx?partner=Mzg0T1RMU1BPT10JFkEQUALSTO&product=MzgwU1ZJPVAkWOEQUALSTOEQUALSTO&storyId=77961.

7. Interview with Herschel Shosteck, chairman and president of Herschel Shosteck Associates, a telecommunications consulting firm, February 6, 2002.

8. Cauley, Leslie, "Iridium's Downfall: The Marketing Took a Back Seat to Science," *The Wall Street Journal*, August 18, 1999, p. A3. Interviews with Herschel Shosteck, chairman and president of Herschel Shosteck Associates, a telecommunications consulting firm, February 19, 2001, and February 6, 2002.

9. Interview with George Fisher, former chairman and CEO of Motorola and retired chairman and CEO of Eastman Kodak Company, July 12, 2001.

10. Hardy, Quentin, "Iridium's Orbit: To Sell a World Phone, Play to Executive Fears of Being Out of Touch," *The Wall Street Journal*, June 4, 1998, p. A1.

11. Interviews were conducted with eight Korean managers, three of whom worked for Samsung, May 2000.

12. The number of total employees was actually down significantly from 267,000 in 1997 due to the Asian economic crisis and subsequent corporate restructuring.

13. "Making Its Mark on History," *Business Korea,* 1997, pp. 35–36.

14. Lee, Charles S., "Collision Course," *Far Eastern Economic Review,* 1998, pp. 51–52.

15. Sohn, Young-Ju, "Samsung's Myth of Invincibility Crashes," *Business Korea,* August 1999, pp. 20–23.

16. Kim, Chong-Tae, "Samsung's Report Rattles the Auto Industry," *Business Korea,* July 1997, pp. 30–31.

17. Treece, James, "Renault to Pump $300 Million in Ailing Samsung," *Automotive News,* June 19, 2000, p. 65.

18. Kim, Hee-Seop, "Samsung Carries Out Largest-Ever Promotion," *Chosun Ilbo,* March 11, 2001, http://english.chosun.com/w21data/html/news/200103/200103110304.html.

19. Anders, George, "Co-Founder of Borders to Launch Online Megagrocer," *The Wall Street Journal,* April 22, 1999, p. B1.

20. Shaheen was granted options on fifteen million shares at $8 each. On the first day of trading the stock followed form and went up 65 percent from the IPO price of $15. At close of trading that day the company had a market cap of $7.9 billion. "Bagging groceries," Forbes.com, October 18, 1999, http://www.forbes.com/forbes/1999/1018/6410080a.print.html.

21. Helft, Miguel, "A Long, Strange Trip for Webvan," in *Naples Daily News,* July 29, 2001, http://www.naplesnews.com/01/07/business/d658623a.htm.

22. Some insiders at Webvan believe that if, instead of taking on greater complexity, it had radically retrenched and simplified, the company could have survived. This is uncertain, but the grand vision behind Webvan, though consistent with the boom times of the Internet, called for a heroic business model that had much to do with the constant search for a new angle on growth.

23. Rhine, Jon, "Webvan Chairman, CEO Resigns," *San Francisco Business Times,* April 13, 2001, http://sanfrancisco.bcentral.com/sanfrancisco/stories/2001/04/09/daily50.html.

24. Interview with Leonard Riggio, founder and chairman, Barnes & Noble, January 30, 2002.

25. Interviews were conducted with eight Korean managers, three of whom worked for Samsung, May 2000.

26. As quoted in Sohn, Young-Ju, "Samsung's Myth of Invincibility Crashes," *Business Korea,* August 1999, pp. 20–23. Perhaps not surprisingly, research also suggests that companies run by founders or their descendents are more likely to have weaker boards. See Ranft, Annette L., and O'Neill, Hugh M., "Board Composition and High-Flying Founders: Hints of Trouble to Come?" *Academy of Management Executive,* 2001, 15(1), pp. 126–138.

27. Interviews were conducted with eight Korean managers, three of whom worked for Samsung, May 2000.

28. It is not the case that all companies where CEOs own dominant shareholdings fall into this trap, only that this pattern was overrepresented among the mistake-ridden companies we studied. So, if the CEO in your company is also a major shareholder, there's no certainty that disaster is imminent; but the risk does go up. In Chapter 7 we describe what you can do to manage this risk.

29. Interview with Tony Huffman, former CEO, Huffy Bicycle Company, April 14, 2000.

30. Tilson, Whitney, "Stock Options' Perserve Incentives," *The Motley Fool,* April 3, 2002, http://www.fool.com/news/foth/2002/foth020403.htm.

31. Interview with Mike Stern, former VP and general counsel, General Magic, February 7, 2001.

32. Interview with Marc Porat, former chairman and CEO, General Magic, April 16, 2001.

33. Five United Nations translators were needed at board meetings so directors could understand one another.

34. Actually, Iridium is with us today. A group of private investors acquired the company's assets, satellites and all, for a bargain-basement price of $25 million. Playing the game is completely different when your capital investment is about ⅟₂₀₀th of the original. Rather than worry about five hundred thousand customers, the new Iridium Satellite is targeting large companies in the maritime, oil, and aviation industries, along with the U.S. military, all customers that can't rely on traditional cell phones in the inhospitable environments in which they work.

35. Buck, Pearl S., *What America Means to Me,* London: Meuthen, 1994, p. 101. This quote came from Nierenberg, Gerard I., *Do It Right the First Time: A Short Guide to Learning from Your Most Memorable Errors, Mistakes, and Blunders,* New York: John Wiley & Sons, 1996.

36. As the primary supplier to Iridium, Motorola had an incentive to keep the venture afloat. Even after booking these revenues, however, analysts estimated that Motorola still ended up losing more than $1 billion in the Iridium adventure.

37. Taylor III, Alex, "Boeing's Amazing Sonic Cruiser," *Fortune,* December 9, 2002, pp. 169–76.

38. "Bagging groceries," Forbes.com, October 18, 1999, http://www.forbes.com/forbes/1999/1018/6410080a_print.html.

39. Keller, John, and Hooper, Lawrence, "General Magic Gives AT&T Edge, Despite Touting 'Open' Standard," *The Wall Street Journal,* February 9, 1993, p. B6.

40. Interview with Mike Stern, former VP and general counsel, General Magic, February 7, 2001.

41. Excerpted from "Read the World, with Your Own Thinking" (November 1997), the biographical essay by Kun-Hee Lee, chairman of Samsung.

CHAPTER 3. INNOVATION AND CHANGE

1. Farnham, Alan, "America's Most Admired Company," *Fortune,* February 7, 1994, pp. 50–54.

2. By 1998 stents were used in three-quarters of all angioplasty operations (more than six hundred thousand that year).

3. Cassak, David, "In Stents, How the Mighty Are Falling—Fast," *In Vivo,* January 1998, p. 1.

4. Interview with Robert Croce, company group chairman and worldwide chairman of Cordis, Johnson & Johnson, April 27, 2001.

5. Interview with Ronald Dollens, CEO, Guidant, February 16, 2000.

6. J&J later won large patent infringement suits against Boston Scientific and A.V.E. (now part of Medtronics), but it never did against Guidant, the most powerful competitor it faced then, and now, in this marketplace.

7. Interview with Robert Croce, company group chairman, Johnson & Johnson, worldwide chairman, Cordis Franchise, September 17, 2001.

8. Interview with Stanton Rowe, former senior executive, JJIS (Cordis), June 13, 2000.

9. Mitchell, Will, and Karim, Samina, "Reconfiguring Business Resources Following Acquisitions in the U.S. Medical Sector," 1978–1995. Working paper, University of Michigan, 1999.

10. Interview with Stanton Rowe, former senior executive, JJIS (Cordis), August 30, 2002.

11. Interview with Stanton Rowe, former senior executive, JJIS (Cordis), June 13, 2000.

12. Interview with Ronald Dollens, president and CEO, Guidant, February 16, 2000.

13. Interview with Dr. Eric Topol, chairman, Department of Cardiovascular Medicine, The Cleveland Clinic Foundation, August 19, 2002.

14. Interview with Robert Croce, company group chairman and worldwide chairman of Cordis, Johnson & Johnson, April 27, 2001.

15. Ralph Larsen, former CEO, Johnson & Johnson, in response to a question at the annual shareholders meeting, April 22, 1999.

16. Interview with Robert Croce, company group chairman and worldwide chairman of Cordis, and Johnson & Johnson, September 17, 2001.

17. Interview with Marvin Woodall, former president, JJIS (Cordis), October 1, 2002.

18. Interview with Dr. Eric Topol, chairman, Department of Cardiovascular Medicine, The Cleveland Clinic Foundation, August 19, 2002.

19. Interview with Dr. Eric Topol, chairman, Department of Cardiovascular Medicine, The Cleveland Clinic Foundation, August 19, 2002.

20. Pieper, Lynn C., "Guidant Corporation—Market Perform," Thomas Weisel Partners, October 22, 2002, p. 2.

21. Interview with Dr. Brian Firth, VP medical affairs & health economics worldwide, Cordis Corporation, September 6, 2002.

22. Warren Flick, senior manager at Kmart, quoted in Deutsch, Claudia, "A Giant Awakens to Yawns," *The New York Times,* December 22, 1996, p. C1.

23. Yerak, Becky, "Superstar Stumbles," *Cleveland Plain Dealer,* July 9, 1995, p. H1.

24. Deutsch, Claudia, "A Giant Awakens to Yawns," *The New York Times,* December 22, 1996, p. C1.

25. David Gibbons, president of Rubbermaid's Home Products Unit, quoted in "Walking a Tightrope," *Cleveland Plain Dealer,* September 15, 1996, p. 11.

26. Colvin, Geoffrey, "How Rubbermaid Managed to Fail," *Fortune,* November 23, 1998, p. 32.

27. Interview with David Klatt, president, The Rubbermaid Group of Newell Corp., October 31, 2001.

28. Interview with Robert Galvin, former CEO, Motorola Corporation, May 21, 1999.

29. Crockett, Roger, "How Motorola Lost Its Way," *BusinessWeek,* May 4, 1998, p. 140.

30. Interview with Emilio Echave, president of Eastern Area, AT&T Wireless Services, October 20, 1999.

31. Interview with Bill Oberlink, former president, Southeast Division, McCaw Cellular Communications, December 1, 1999.

32. Three former Motorola CEOs—Gary Tooker (interviewed July 5, 2001), George Fisher (interviewed July 12, 2001), and Robert Galvin (interviewed May 21, 1999)—told us how the company "was at the forefront of the development of digital technology," making it clear that the cell phone story is not about missing out on the next technology, but on choosing not to innovate and change when you had the capability to do so.

33. Interview with Bill Oberlink, former president, Southeast Division, McCaw Cellular Communications, December 1, 1999.

34. Interview with Robert Galvin, former chairman and CEO, Motorola, May 29, 2001.

35. There is an irony in the use of the term, *warring tribes.* While the lack of cooperation between divisions can be characterized in this way, Robert Galvin, the former CEO, pointed out how it was exactly the absence of such conflict and dissension among executives in the cell phone division, and between Corporate and the division, that was at the heart of the cell phone problems in the mid-1990s. (Interview on December 18, 2002.)

36. Interview with Robert Galvin, former CEO, Motorola, May 21, 1999.

37. Interview with Robert Galvin, former CEO, Motorola, May 21, 1999.

38. Herschel Shosteck Associates, Ltd., Wheaton, Maryland (www.shosteck.com).

39. Motorola's global market share may have hit bottom in 2000 when it clocked a 15 per-

cent share. By the end of 2002 its share was over 20 percent, while Nokia was closing in on 40 percent.

40. Motorola has one other thing going for it. The market leader—Nokia—is already showing signs of making some of the same mistakes Motorola made. Several of the industry insiders we interviewed made a point of telling us how Nokia was becoming arrogant and overconfident as it wallows at the top of the market share rankings.

41. Quotes without attribution were drawn from interviews of people inside and outside of Motorola who requested anonymity.

42. Interview with Gary Tooker, former CEO, Motorola, July 5, 2001.

43. Interview with Robert Galvin, former CEO, Motorola, December 18, 2002.

44. Tuchman, Barbara, W., *The March of Folly,* New York: Ballantine Books, 1984.

45. Jaffe, G., and Ricks, T. E., "Of Men and Money: How the Pentagon Often Wastes Both," *The Wall Street Journal,* September 22, 1999, p. A1.

46. Gruley, Bryan, and Smith, Rebecca, "Anatomy of a Fall: Keys to Success Left Kenneth Lay Open to Disaster," *The Wall Street Journal,* April 26, 2002, p. 1.

47. Pearson, Andrall E., "Tough-Minded Ways to Get Innovative," *Harvard Business Review,* May–June, 1988, p. 100.

48. Interview with Tony Huffman, former CEO, Huffy Bicycle Company, April 14, 2000.

49. Crown, Judith, and Coleman, Glenn, *No Hands: The Rise and Fall of the Schwinn Bicycle Company, an American Institution,* New York: Henry Holt, 1996, pp. 2–3.

50. Atchison, Sandra D., "Pump, Pump, Pump at Schwinn," *BusinessWeek,* August 23, 1993, p. 79.

CHAPTER 4. MERGERS AND ACQUISITIONS

1. Deogun, Nikhil, and Lipin, Steven, "Deals & Deal Makers: Big Mergers of '90s Prove Disappointing to Shareholders," *The Wall Street Journal,* October 30, 2000, p. C1.

2. Rattner, Steven, "Mergers: Windfalls or Pitfalls?" *The Wall Street Journal,* October 11, 1999, p. A22.

3. Hiday, Jeffrey L., "Most Mergers Fail to Add Value, Consultants Find," *The Wall Street Journal,* October 12, 1998, p. B91.

4. Jensen, Michael, and Ruback, Richard, "The Market for Corporate Control: The Scientific Evidence," *Journal of Financial Economics,* (1983), 11, pp. 5–50.

5. Deener, B., "Mega-Deals Stifle Shares, Survey Implies," *Dallas Morning News,* November 30, 1999, pp. D1, D6.

6. Interview with senior manager of large pharmaceutical company, January 11, 2000.

7. It is also true that the major alternatives to growth via acquisition—alliances and internal development—are far from foolproof themselves. Nevertheless, it remains that the M&A track record is not good and, hence, that there is much to be learned about what to do and not do in the M&A game.

8. Interview with Bryan Briggs, division VP of sales & marketing, Colonial Distributors, March 19, 2001.

9. Interview with William Smithburg, former CEO, Quaker Oats, January 18, 2001.

10. Prince, Greg, "Come Together," *Beverage World,* December 1995, pp. 50–54.

11. Interview with William Smithburg, former CEO, Quaker Oats, January 18, 2001.

12. Interviews with Michael Weinstein, former CEO, Triarc Beverage Group, November 10, 1999, and December 21, 2000.

13. Burns, Greg, "Will Quaker Get the Recipe Right?" *BusinessWeek,* February 5, 1996, pp. 140–45.

14. Interview with Bryan Briggs, division VP of sales & marketing, Colonial Distributors, March 19, 2001.

15. Snapple was bought for $1.7 billion and sold for $300 million. Quaker recorded a $350 million tax benefit with the sale (which offset some of the capital gains from the Snapple-related sale of the pet-food and candy businesses). Hence, after two and one-half years, the Snapple mistake cost Quaker somewhere between $1 billion and $1.5 billion, depending on how one chooses to account for tax issues and the opportunity cost of selling the pet-food brands, which doubled in operating profit after being sold to Heinz. Smithburg resigned soon after the sale, and PepsiCo eventually acquired Quaker in December 2000 for $13.4 billion in stock.

16. Interview with Leonard Marsh, cofounder of Snapple Beverage Group, February 1, 2001.

17. Griffin, Nancy, and Kim Masters, *Hit and Run: How Jon Peters and Peter Guber Took Sony for a Ride in Hollywood*, New York: Simon & Schuster, 1996, p. 190.

18. The beta format was actually picked up by broadcasters, where it survives to this day because of its superior special effects and editing features.

19. Griffin, Nancy, and Kim Masters, *Hit and Run: How Jon Peters and Peter Guber Took Sony for a Ride in Hollywood*, New York: Simon & Schuster, 1996, p. 196. In addition, one of the reasons Sony may not have been as aggressive as Matsushita in "building a family" is that many people within Sony believed that Matsushita had copied the original Sony design. See Lardner, J., *Fast Forward*, New York: W. W. Norton, 1987, pp. 151–52.

20. Interview with Peter Guber, former CEO, Sony Pictures, March 7, 2001.

21. "The stories of [Peter's] tempestuous explosions are available on every corner in Hollywood, stories of tantrums and bullying." Boyer, Peter J., "Hollywood Banzai," *Vanity Fair*, February 1990, p. 190.

22. The Academy Award for *Rain Man* was given to producer Mark Johnson, who allowed Guber and Peters to borrow it for the photograph. Klein, Edward, "Lost Tycoon," *Vanity Fair*, May 1995, p. 68.

23. Boyer, Peter J., "Hollywood Banzai," *Vanity Fair*, February 1990, p. 135.

24. $3.4 billion cash plus $1.4 billion in debt for Columbia, $200 million for GPEC, and $500+ million settlement with Time Warner. The $6 billion figure is quoted by Mickey Schulhof in Klein, Edward, "Lost Tycoon," *Vanity Fair*, May 1995, p. 58.

25. In fact, Peters was one of a very small number of people we interviewed who agreed to an interview but refused to allow us to quote what he said.

26. Griffin, Nancy, and Kim Masters, *Hit and Run: How Jon Peters and Peter Guber Took Sony for a Ride in Hollywood*, New York: Simon & Schuster, 1996, p. 320. The distaste with CEO compensation extends to some CEOs. In an interview we did about Mattel with Alan Hassenfeld, chairman and CEO, Hasbro, Inc., on June 28, 2001, he said, "I am sick and tired of people in general being overpaid . . . and you see it happening day in and day out in Hollywood. I want to come back as a failed Hollywood executive. You end up getting more for messing up than for succeeding."

27. Technically, they were not. Guber grouped Columbia and Tri-Star together. If Disney or Warner grouped together all of their production units, they each would have had a higher box-office share than Sony.

28. Interview with Michael (Mickey) P. Schulhof, former CEO, Sony USA, March 28, 2001.

29. Matsushita responded to Sony's deal by acquiring MCA, creating a stalemate in the software control game.

30. British poet Christopher Logue wrote the poem, "Come to the Edge," in 1968 in honor of the fiftieth anniversary of the death of French poet William Apollinaire.

31. Interview with Robert Seelert, chairman, Saatchi & Saatchi, February 25, 1999.

32. Interview with Tamara Ingram, former CEO, Saatchi & Saatchi United Kingdom, January 16, 2001.

33. Interview with Jim Adler, former president & COO, Saatchi & Saatchi Advertising Affiliates, January 20, 1999.

34. Interview with Jim Adler, former president & COO, Saatchi & Saatchi Advertising Affiliates, March 15, 2002.

35. Interview with Robert Seelert, chairman, Saatchi & Saatchi, February 25, 1999.

36. Saatchi & Saatchi had considered bidding for Phillips & Drew before plans were halted in 1985 by Union Bank of Switzerland's acquisition of the British stockbroker. This information was only revealed to the market with the failed Midland Bank bid.

37. Maremont, Mark, "And Now . . . the Saatchi & Saatchi Bank?" *BusinessWeek*, September 28, 1987, p. 92.

38. Melcher, Richard, "A Deal That May Finally Satisfy the Saatchis," *BusinessWeek*, May 26, 1986, p. 60.

39. Interview with Jim Adler, former president & COO, Saatchi & Saatchi Advertising Affiliates, March 15, 2002.

40. Interview with Maurice Saatchi, reported in Sanai, Darius, "M of M&C: An Interview with the Saatchi Who Talks (and Some Thoughts About the One Who Doesn't)," *The Independent*, April 12, 2000, http://www.independent.co.uk/story.jsp?story=40152.

41. These comments were made by interviewees who preferred to remain anonymous.

42. These comments were made by interviewees who preferred to remain anonymous.

43. That year was particularly momentous for Maurice, who was named a peer (call him Lord Saatchi) by then British Prime Minister John Major.

44. Wentz, Laurel, "After a Stormy Beginning, M&C Saatchi Has Crafted Success in London, but the U.S. Remains Elusive," *Advertising Age*, February 28, 2000, p. 24.

45. Sanai, Darius, "M of M&C: An Interview with the Saatchi Who Talks (and Some Thoughts About the One Who Doesn't)," *The Independent*, April 12, 2000, http://www.independent.co.uk/story.jsp?story=40152.

46. Hansell, Saul, "Dot-Com Era Notions Guided a Huge Merger," *The New York Times*, July 19, 2002, http://www.nytimes.com/2002/07/19/business/19MERG.html.

47. Burns, Greg, "Will Quaker Get the Recipe Right?" *BusinessWeek* February 5, 1996, pp. 140–45.

48. Interview with William Smithburg, former CEO, Quaker Oats, January 18, 2001.

49. Interview with Michael Weinstein, former CEO, Triarc Beverage Group, November 10, 1999.

50. Interview with William Smithburg, former CEO, Quaker Oats, January 18, 2001.

51. Lagnado, Lucette, "Hospital Mergers: Indications of Severe Trauma," *The Wall Street Journal*, May 14, 1999, p. B1.

52. Andrews, Edmund L., "DaimlerChrysler's Chief Defends His Strategy," *The New York Times*, December 2, 2000 (http://www.nytimes.com/2000/12/02/business/02DAIM.html).

53. Grubb, Thomas M., and Lamb, Robert B., "Exploiting Opportunities When Your Rivals Merge," *Across the Board*, 36(1), p. 22.

54. Nathan, John, *Sony: The Private Life*, Boston: Houghton Mifflin, 1999, pp. 214–15.

55. Hayward, Mathew L. A., and Hambrick, Donald C., "Explaining Premiums Paid for Large Acquisitions: Evidence of CEO Hubris," *Administrative Science Quarterly* (1997), 42, pp. 103–27.

CHAPTER 5. STRATEGY GONE BAD: DOING THE WRONG THINGS

1. This point came out in at least two interviews with former senior executives at Wang Labs.

2. Kenney, Charles, *Riding the Runaway Horse: The Rise and Decline of Wang Laboratories*, Boston: Little, Brown, 1997, pp. 103–4.

3. Interview with Fred Wang, former president & COO, Wang Labs, August 7, 2001.

4. Interview with a former manager, Wang Labs, March 26, 2001. Kenney, Charles, *Riding the Runaway Horse: The Rise and Decline of Wang Laboratories*, Boston: Little, Brown, 1992.

5. Nash, Kim S., "Not Fred's Fault," *Computer World*, February 17, 1992, p. 69.

6. In fact, he even delisted Wang stock off the NYSE and switched to the ASE when the exchange officers in New York refused to allow a special nonvoting class of Wang shares to be sold.

7. Bulkeley, William M., "Wang Labs Unveils Debt Restructuring, Can Begin to Deal with Other Crises," *The Wall Street Journal*, August 22, 1989, p. 1.

8. "Why Have the Brands Been Falling?—Snow Brand and Sogo," *Sankei Shimbun*, 2000, http://www1.plala.or.jp/hico-net/docu/documet.htm.

9. "Why Have the Brands Been Falling?—Snow Brand and Sogo," *Sankei Shimbun*, 2000, http://www1.plala.or.jp/hico-net/docu/documet.htm.

10. "Snow Brand Low-Fat Milk; *Staphylococcus Aureus* Was Found in the Manufacturing Process," *Mainichi Shimbun Daily*, July 1, 2000, http://www12.mainichi.co.jp/news/search news/860298/90e188f393fb8bc6814090bb91a28dH92f682c982a082e9-¢«4html.

11. Golden, Daniel, Maremont, Mark, and Armstrong, David, "How Tyco Pushed ADT Dealers into Poor Areas to Boost Growth," *The Wall Street Journal*, November 15, 2002, http://online.wsj.com/article/0,,SB1037311502971480828,00.html?mod=home%5Fpage%5Fone%5Fus.

12. Honig, Donald, *Baseball America*, New York: Macmillan Publishing, 1985, p. 250.

13. Rader, Benjamin G., *Baseball: A History of America's Game*, Urbana, IL: University of Illinois Press, 1992, p. 149.

14. Marshall, William, *Baseball's Pivotal Era: 1945–1951*, Lexington, KY: University Press of Kentucky, 1999, p. 123.

15. Halberstam, David, *Summer of '49*, New York: William Morrow and Company, 1989, pp. 184–85.

16. In a fascinating conversation with John Harrington, former CEO of the Boston Red Sox (October 25, 2000), he told us that "the owners decided they would try to do it right," and "the decision was made that the Dodgers would sign Robinson and that he would go to their farm team in Montreal" to avoid the expected hostile reception he would get in a place such as Louisville. Glen Stout and Richard Johnson, however, note in their recent book (*Red Sox Century*, New York: Houghton Mifflin, 2000, pp. 290–91) that the Red Sox did have other minor league teams and could also have loaned these players to other teams, a common practice at the time.

17. Halberstam, David, *Summer of '49*, New York: William Morrow, 1989, pp. 185–86.

18. The Red Sox did sign other African-American players, but none were ever brought up to the major league team.

19. Quoted in Edes, Gordon, "Final Frontier—He Broke Last Color Line: Boston's," *Boston Globe*, February 23, 1997, p. C1.

20. These results also statistically controlled for other factors influencing a team's won–lost percentage, meaning that our finding on black players held regardless of such factors as attendance at home games (as a proxy for a team's pay scale), local population (to account for differences between big-market and small-market teams), and the team's won–lost record the previous year (a statistical control that minimizes historical performance differences among teams).

21. In *Red Sox Century* (New York: Houghton Mifflin, 2000) baseball historians Glenn Stout and Richard A. Johnson make a compelling case that the Red Sox's resistance to baseball integration has had a considerably longer and more harmful effect on the team than even the famous sale of the Babe (Ruth) in 1918.

22. Stout, Glenn, and Johnson, Richard, *Red Sox Century*, New York: Houghton Mifflin,

2000. This view is not universally held, however, a point we heard frequently in our interviews with baseball experts.

23. Edes, Gordon, "Historian Rewrites Story of Sox 'Curse': Stout Says It's Race, Not Ruth," *Boston Globe*, November 26, 2000, p. C12.

24. Interview with Phil Benton, retired president, Ford Motor, February 12, 1999.

25. Interview with Charles McElyea, product manager, General Motors, February 18, 1999.

26. Interview with Joseph Spielman, VP and general manager, Metal Fabrication Division, General Motors, May 10, 1999.

27. Interview with Robert Lutz, vice-chairman, General Motors, and former senior executive at Chrysler and Ford, February 23, 2001.

28. Lee, Albert, *Call Me Roger*, Chicago: Contemporary Books, 1988, p. 130.

29. Lieberman, Marvin B., and Dhawan, Rajeev, "Assessing the Resource Base of U.S. and Japanese Auto Producers: A Stochastic Frontier Production Function Approach," working paper, UCLA, August, 1999.

30. Wiersema, Margarethe, "Holes at the Top: Why CEO Firings Backfire," *Harvard Business Review*, December 2002, pp. 70–77.

CHAPTER 6. BRILLIANTLY FULFILLING THE WRONG VISION

1. This vignette is a fictional representation of events that are often reported during military campaigns. While the details vary from case to case, the basic story line has repeated itself numerous times.

2. Jorion, Philippe, "How Long-Term Lost Its Capital," *Risk Magazine*, September 1999, pp. 31–36.

3. Warner, Alison, "Behind the Hedges," *The Banker*, November 1998, p. 24.

4. Lieberman, Marvin B. and Montgomery, David B., "First-Mover Advantages," *Strategic Management Journal*, 1988, 9, pp. 41–58.

5. Mount, Ian, "Toys 'R' Us: Beware the Giraffe," www.ecompany.com, September 2000, p. 162.

6. Ante, Spencer, E., and Weintraub, Arlene, "Why B2B Is a Scary Place to Be," *BusinessWeek*, September 11, 2000, p. 34.

7. Gurley, J. William, "If iWon Wins, Do Portals Lose?" *Fortune*, February 7, 2000, p. 190.

8. Perhaps the best single source for the intellectual underpinnings of this philosophy can be found in James Brian Quinn's *Intelligent Enterprise* (New York: The Free Press, 1992).

9. Levine, Joshua, *The Rise and Fall of the House of Barneys*, New York: William Morrow, 1999, p. 58.

10. Interview with David McLaughlin, former CEO, The Toro Company, January 13, 1999.

11. Dess, Gregory G., and Picken, Joseph C., "Creating Competitive (Dis)advantage: Learning from Food Lion's Freefall," *Academy of Management Executive* (1999), 13(3), pp. 97–111.

12. Barnett, Chris, "Success on a Shoestring; L. A. Gear; Company Profile," *California Business*, October, 1988, p. 44.

13. Darlin, Damon, "Getting Beyond a Market Niche," *Forbes*, November 22, 1993, p. 106.

14. Deogun, Nikhil, and Lipin, Steven, "Cautionary Tales: When Big Deals Turn Bad," *The Wall Street Journal*, December 8, 1999, p. C1.

15. Bowe, Christopher, "Merck Withdraws from IPO of Unit," *Financial Times*, July 31, 2002, p. 22.

16. Labich, Kenneth, "Is Herb Kelleher America's Best CEO?" *Fortune*, May 2, 1994, p. 44.

17. Interview with Herschel Shosteck, president and chairman, Herschel Shosteck Associates, a telecommunications consulting firm, February 19, 2001.

18. Steinhauer, Jennifer, "Hip but Not Haughty at Barneys New York," *The New York Times*, August 25, 1998, p. D1.

19. Interview with Tom Travers, VP medical delivery systems, Oxford Health Plans, January 19, 1999.

20. Lowenstein, Roger, *When Genius Failed*, New York: Random House, 2000.

21. Winslow, Ron, and Anders, George, "How New Technology Was Oxford's Nemesis," *The Wall Street Journal*, December 11, 1997, p. B1.

22. Sanders, Lisa, "Wall Street's Designer Dud," *BusinessWeek*, January 20, 1997, p. 6.

23. Ball, Jeffrey, White, Joseph B., and Miller, Scott, "Earnings at DaimlerChrysler Fall as Trouble at U.S. Division Piles Up," *The Wall Street Journal*, October 27, 2000, http://interactive.wsj.com/articles/SB97260864082844555.htm.

24. Morrison, David C., "Starburst," *The New Republic*, April 27, 1992, p. 21; Nimroody, Rosy, "Star Wars' brain drain," *Financial World*, May 27, 1986, p. 72.

25. Squeo, Anne Marie, "Army Places Gigantic Wager on Revamped Patriot Missile," *The Wall Street Journal*, January 31, 2003, p. A1.

26. Interview with Bryan Briggs, former division VP of sales & marketing, Colonial Distributors, March 19, 2001.

27. Andrews, Edmund L., "DaimlerChrysler's Chief Defends His Strategy," *The New York Times*, December 2, 2000, http://www.nytimes.com/2000/12/02/business/02DAIM.html.

28. Finkelstein, S., "Internet Startups in the New Economy: So Why Can't They Win?" *Journal of Business Strategy* (July/August 2001), 22(4), pp. 16–21.

29. Franklin, Stephen, "Farley's Fruit: A Firm in Ruins," *Chicago Tribune*, January 9, 2000, p. 1.

CHAPTER 7. DELUSIONS OF A DREAM COMPANY

1. Lowenstein, Roger, *When Genius Failed*, New York: Random House, 2000, pp. 33–34.

2. Crown, Judith, and Coleman, Glenn, *No Hands: The Rise and Fall of the Schwinn Bicycle Company, an American Institution*, New York: Henry Holt, 1996, pp. 2–3.

3. Munk, Nina, "How Levi's Trashed a Great American Brand," *Fortune*, April 12, 1999, p. 85.

4. Hill, Suzette, "Levi Strauss: The American Icon Revolution," *Apparel Industry Magazine*, January 1999, pp. 66–69.

5. Lant, T. K., Milliken, F. J., and Batra, B., "The Role of Managerial Learning and Interpretation in Strategic Persistence and Reorientation: An Empirical Investigation," *Strategic Management Journal* (1992), 13, pp. 585–608; Meyer, A. D., Goes, J. B., and Brooks, G. R., "Organizations reacting to hyperturbulence," in G. P. Huber and W. H. Glick (Eds.), *Organizational Change and Redesign*, New York: Oxford University Press, 1993, pp. 66–111; Miller, D., and Chen, M-J, "Sources and Consequences of Competitive Inertia," *Administrative Science Quarterly*, 1994, 39, pp. 1–23.

6. Greve, H. R., "Performance, Aspirations, and Risky Organizational Change," *Administrative Science Quarterly* (1998), 43, pp. 58–86.

7. Levine, Joshua, *The Rise and Fall of the House of Barneys*, New York: William Morrow, 1999, p. 201.

8. Schultz, Howard, and Yang, Dori Jones, *Pour Your Heart into It: How Starbucks Built a Company One Cup at a Time*, New York: Hyperion, 1997, p. 167.

9. Zaleznik, Abraham, *The Managerial Mystique*, New York: Harper & Row, 1989.

10. Britt, Russ, and DeTar, James, "Sanders' Reign at AMD: Tales of Merriment, Woe," *Investor's Business Daily*, June 30, 1999, pp. A6ff.

11. Fialka, John J., "Fear of a Different Sort of Infiltrator Paralyzes U.S. Nuclear Project," *Wall Street Journal*, December 20, 1999, p. A1.

12. Strom, Stephanie, and Steinhauer, Jennifer, "Haughty Couture," *The New York Times*, January 21, 1996, section 3, p. 1.

13. Stevens, Tim, "Deja Blue," *Industry Week*, November 17, 1997, p. 82.

14. Sitkin, Sim B., "Learning Through Failure: The Strategy of Small Losses," *Research in Organizational Behavior*, 14, pp. 231–66.

15. Stein, Nicholas, "The Rise and Fall of Chiquita Banana: How a Great American Brand Lost Its Way," *Fortune*, November 26, 2001, p. 182.

16. Yates, Brock, *The Decline and Fall of the American Automobile Industry*, New York: Empire Books, 1983, p. 80.

17. Parietti, Jeff, *The Book of Truly Stupid Business Quotes*, New York: Harper-Collins, 1997, p. 87.

18. Rob Baskin, Coca-Cola spokesman, quoted in Hays, Constance L., Cowell, Alan, and Whitney, Craig R., "A Sputter in the Coke Machine," *The New York Times*, June 30, 1999, p. C1.

19. Marcus, Bernie, and Blank, Arthur, with Bob Andelman, *Built from Scratch: How a Couple of Regular Guys Grew the Home Depot from Nothing to $30 Billion*, New York: Times Business, 1999. As Home Depot has grown and the founders have stepped down, these values have become a little harder to maintain. While the jury is still out on whether the company can continue its ethic of humility, this attitude has played a big part in the emergence of Home Depot as a big-box powerhouse.

20. Verespej, Michael A., "Michael Dell's Magic," *Industry Week*, November 16, 1998, p. 57.

21. Interview with Bill Gates in "Visionary-in-Chief: A Talk with Chairman Bill Gates," *BusinessWeek*, May 17, 1999, p. 114.

22. MacCormack, George, "Zeroing in on Safety Excellence—It's Good Business," May 27, 1999, http://www.dupont.com.

23. Interview with David Klatt, president, Rubbermaid Group of Newell Corp., October 31, 2001.

24. Stevens, Tim, "Deja Blue," *Industry Week*, November 17, 1997, p. 86.

25. Eisenhardt, Kathleen M., "Survival of the Swiftest," *Red Herring*, April, 2000, p. 380.

26. In contrast to Iridium, we should note, once it became apparent that FAX machines would be standard office equipment, ZapMail was quickly canceled. Interview with Fred Smith, CEO, FedEx, October 20, 1999.

27. Labarre, Polly, "Screw Up, and Get Smart," *Fast Company*, November, 1998, p. 58.

28. Argote, Linda, *Organizational Learning: Creating, Retaining and Transferring Knowledge*, Boston: Kluwer Academic Publishers, 1999.

CHAPTER 8. TRACKING DOWN THE LOST SIGNALS

1. Kletz, Trevor, *Lessons from Disaster: How Organizations Have No Memory and Accidents Recur*, Houston: Gulf, 1993.

2. Public Broadcasting System, "Triumph of the Nerds: The Rise of Accidental Empires," December 30, 1999, http://www.pbs.org/nerds/index.html.

3. PR Newswire, "Nissan Charts Course for Global Turnaround Centered on U.S. Product Onslaught," January 11, 1999.

4. Kletz, Trevor, *Learning from Accidents*, 2nd ed., Oxford, England: Butterworth-Heineman Ltd., 1994.

5. Mount, Ian, "Out of Control," *Business 2.0*, August 2002, pp. 38–44.

6. Berner, Robert, and Maremont, Mark, "Fall of Rite Aid Chief Has Critics Wondering: Where Was the Board?" *The Wall Street Journal*, October 20, 1999, p. A1.

7. Rite Aid proxy statement, Global Disclosure Online, June 30, 1999.

8. Ed Comeau, research analyst for Donaldson, Lufkin & Jenrette, quoted in Berner, Robert, and Maremont, Mark, "Fall of Rite Aid Chief Has Critics Wondering: Where Was the Board?" *The Wall Street Journal*, October 20, 1999, p. A1.

9. Hill, Miriam, "Irresponsible Accounting Foibles Create Dire Situation for Rite-Aid," *Knight Ridder Tribune Business News*, July 15, 2000.

10. Fay, S., *The Collapse of Barings: Panic, Ignorance and Greed*, London: Arrow Business Books, 1996.

11. Stein, Mark, "The Risk Taker as Shadow: A Psychoanalytic View of the Collapse of Barings Bank," *Journal of Management Studies* (2000), 37, pp. 1215–29.

12. Ferris, Stephen P., Jagannathan, Murali, and Pritchard, Adam C., "Monitoring by Directors with Multiple Board Appointments: Corporate Performance and the Incidence of Securities Fraud," working paper #99–013, University of Michigan, 1999.

13. Mollenkamp, Carrick, "How Money Store Inspired a Big Change at First Union," *The Wall Street Journal*, July 25, 2000, http://interactive.wsj.com/articles/SB96447611043364 2881.htm.

14. Interview with Kevin Roberts, CEO, Worldwide, Saatchi & Saatchi, August 27, 2001.

15. Interview with Stanley Gault, retired chairman and CEO, Rubbermaid, Inc., and the Goodyear Tire & Rubber Co., May 15, 2001.

16. Copley, Frank B., *Taylor, Frederick W.: Father of Scientific Management*, New York: Harper & Brothers, 1923.

17. Keller, Maryann, *Rude Awakening: The Rise, Fall and Struggle for Recovery of General Motors*, New York: William Morrow, 1989, p. 65.

18. Taylor, Alex, "Can GM Remodel Itself?" *Fortune*, January 13, 1992, p. 32.

19. Keller, Maryann, *Rude Awakening: The Rise, Fall and Struggle for Recovery of General Motors*, New York: William Morrow, 1989, p. 106.

20. Lee, Albert, *Call Me Roger*, Chicago: Contemporary Books, 1988.

21. Crockett, Roger, "How Motorola Lost Its Way," *BusinessWeek*, May 4, 1998, p. 140.

22. Jackson, Sally, "Bruises in Barbieland," *The Australian*, December 7, 1999, p. 32.

23. Bannon, Lisa, "Goodbye Dolly: Mattel Tries to Adjust as 'Holiday Barbie' Leaves Under a Cloud," *The Wall Street Journal*, June 7, 1999, p. A1.

24. Lockheed Martin Astronautics, which designed and manufactured the spacecraft, provided data to the navigation team at NASA's Jet Propulsion Lab in pounds and inches, while NASA assumed that the data were metric-system measurements of kilograms and centimeters. In spite of countless checks and rigorous quality control, the slip-up was never discovered and caused the *Orbiter* to drift to its death in Mars's atmosphere. Hotz, Robert Lee, "Mars Probe Lost Due to Simple Math Error," *Los Angeles Times*, October 1, 1999, p. A1.

25. Torekull, Bertil, *Leading by Design: The IKEA Story*, New York: HarperBusiness, 1999, p. 35.

26. Dillon, Nancy, and Siemaszko, Corky, "The Little Piggies Went to Market," *New York Daily News*, June 9, 2002, p. 4.

27. Spiegel, Peter, "Enron Collapse: The Fastow Factor," *Financial Times*, May 21, 2002, p. 32.

28. Piskora, Beth, "Art of the Steal: Dumped Tyco Chief Kozlowski Indicted," *New York Post*, June 5, 2002, p. 35.

29. Markon, Jerry, and Anand, Geeta, "ImClone's Former CEO Pleads Guilty to Charges," *The Wall Street Journal*, October 16, 2002, http://online.wsj.com/article/0,,SB1034692313 191762636,00.html?mod=article-outset-box.

30. Dugas, Christine, "Employees' Faith in Enron Cost Them Dearly," *USA Today*, January 21, 2002, p. 1B.

31. Interview with senior executive, DaimlerChrysler, September 24, 2001.

32. Interview with Robert Lutz, vice chairman, General Motors, and former senior executive at Chrysler and Ford, February 23, 2001.

33. Interview with Bary Bertiger, former senior VP, Motorola, July 13, 2001.

CHAPTER 9. SEVEN HABITS OF SPECTACULARLY UNSUCCESSFUL PEOPLE

1. Hass, Nancy, "The Ups and Downs of Mossimo," *Los Angeles Magazine*, June 1997, p. 60.

2. Sandoval, Greg, "Shaheen Defends Webvan Tenure," cNetNews.Com, April 23, 2001, http: news.cnet.com/news/0-1007-200-5702575.html.

3. Hatlestad, Luc, "How Cabletron Failed," *Red Herring*, October 1999, pp. 98–104.

4. Levin, Doron, *Irreconcilable Differences: Ross Perot versus General Motors*, New York: Penguin Group, 1992, p. 238.

5. Britt, Russ, and DeTar, James, "Sanders' Reign at AMD: Tales of Merriment, Woe," *Investor's Business Daily*, June 30, 1999, p. A6.

6. Hamburger, Tom, "Enron Official Tells of 'Arrogant' Culture," *The Wall Street Journal*, February 15, 2002, p. A3.

7. Riley Chartered Accountants, "The Changing Retail World," February 11, 2000, http://www.rileycom.co.uk/rileycom/data/document.nsf/ID+View/B34A2B6F52A0605F802569.

8. Interview with former executive, Rubbermaid, August 30, 2002.

9. Hatlestad, Luc, "How Cabletron Failed," *Red Herring*, October 1999, pp. 98–104.

10. Interview with Samsung managers, May 2000.

11. Deutsch, Claudia, "A Giant Awakens to Yawns," *The New York Times*, December 22, 1996, p. C1.

12. Atchison, Sandra D., "Pump, Pump, Pump at Schwinn," *BusinessWeek*, August 23, 1993, p. 79.

13. Smith, Lee, "Can Oxford Heal Itself?" *Fortune*, December 29, 1997, p. 238.

14. Britt, Russ, and DeTar, James, "Sanders' Reign at AMD: Tales of Merriment, Woe," *Investor's Business Daily*, June 30, 1999, p. A6.

15. For example, one Bankers Trust employee was caught on tape saying, "Funny business, you know? Lure people into the calm and just totally f— 'em." Holland, Kelley, Himmelstein, Linda, and Schiller, Zachary, "The Bankers Trust Tapes," *BusinessWeek*, October 16, 1995, p. 106.

16. Serwer, Andy, and Harrington, Ann, "Frank Newman Feels the Heat," *Fortune*, October 26, 1998, p. 121.

17. McCleary, Carol, "Fruit of the Loom Wants to Examine Former CEO's Donations," *Dow Jones Business News*, June 8, 2000.

18. Fallon, Ivan, and Srodes, James, *Dream Maker: The Rise and Fall of John Z. DeLorean*, New York: Putnam, 1985.

19. Kozlowski spent more than $2 million of company money on a birthday party in Sardinia for his wife, commissioned a yacht that would have cost the company millions more, and regularly poured millions of dollars of company money into decorating his houses and apartments. The details of what was charged to Tyco were stunning: $6,000 for a shower curtain, $2,900 for coat hangers, $17,100 for a toiletry kit, $15,000 for a poodle-shaped umbrella stand, $6,300 for a sewing kit, $5,960 for two sets of sheets. Kuczynski, Alex, "Lifestyles of the Rich and Red-Faced," *The New York Times*, September 22, 2002, section 9, p. 1; Ross, Barbara, "Tyco Pig Ducks Pen," *New York Daily News*, September 20, 2002, p. 3.

20. Strom, Stephanie, and Steinhauer, Jennifer, "Haughty Couture," *The New York Times*, January 21, 1996, section 3, p. 1.

21. Levine, Joshua, *The Rise and Fall of the House of Barneys*, New York: William Morrow, 1999.

22. Interview with former executive, Rubbermaid, April 12, 1999.

23. Yerak, Becky, "Superstar Stumbles," *Cleveland Plain Dealer*, July 9, 1995, p. H1.

24. Interview with Stanley Gault, retired chairman and CEO, Rubbermaid, Inc., and The Goodyear Tire & Rubber Co., May 15, 2001.

25. Interview with Wolfgang Schmitt, former chairman and CEO, Rubbermaid, June 12, 2001.

26. Interview with former employee, Wang Labs, April 6, 2001.

27. Johnson, Greg, "Moss the Boss; Red-Hot Designer Mossimo Giannulli Shoots for Fashion's Big Leagues," *Los Angeles Times*, September 8, 1996, p. D1.

28. Johnson, Greg, "Trying Public on for Size; Corona Del Mar Grad Will Offer Mossimo Shares for Sale on Stock Exchange," *Los Angeles Times* (Orange County edition), December 21, 1995, p. D1.

29. Interview with Barry Ridings, Managing director, Lazard Frères, May 9, 2002.

30. Crown, J., and Coleman, G., *No Hands: The Rise and Fall of the Schwinn Bicycle Company, an American Institution*, New York: Henry Holt, 1996, p. 246.

31. Greising, David, "A Man of Many Faces Gets in over his Head," *Chicago Tribune*, September 1, 1999, p. 1.

32. Levin, Doron, *Irreconcilable Differences: Ross Perot Versus General Motors*, New York: Penguin Group, 1992, p. 267.

33. Miller, James P., "Fruit of the Loom's Farley Gives Up CEO Post, as Firm Warns on 2nd Half," *The Wall Street Journal*, August 31, 1999, p. B6.

34. Stanton, Russ, "The Rise and Fall of Mossimo Giannulli," *Los Angeles Times*, March 8, 1998, p. 1.

35. Norris, Floyd, "Steve Hilbert Made $172 Million, and Ran out of Cash," *The New York Times*, May 26, 2000, p. C1.

36. Interview with Irving Gutin, senior VP, Tyco International, November 27, 2001.

37. Lee, Albert, *Call Me Roger*, Chicago: Contemporary Books, 1988.

38. Smith, Lee, "Can Oxford Heal Itself?" *Fortune*, December 29, 1997.

39. Kuczynski, Alex, "Lifestyles of the Rich and Red-Faced," *The New York Times*, September 22, 2002, section 9, p. 1.

40. Brockner, J., "The Escalation of Commitment to a Failing Course of Action: Toward Theoretical Progress," *Academy of Management Review* (1992), 17, pp. 39–61.

41. Burrough, Bryan, *Barbarians at the Gate*, New York: Harper & Row, 1990, p. 112.

42. Interview with former RJ Reynolds executive, October 6, 1999.

43. Burns, Greg, "Crunch Time at Quaker Oats," *BusinessWeek*, September 23, 1996, p. 70.

44. Hammonds, Keith H., and Jackson, Susan, "Behind Oxford's Billing Nightmare," *BusinessWeek*, November 17, 1997, p. 98.

45. Interview with Alan Hassenfeld, chairman and CEO, Hasbro, June 28, 2001.

46. There is a related academic literature that emphasizes how an executive's background and experiences influence the types of decisions he or she makes. For a wide-ranging elaboration of this idea, see Finkelstein, S., and Hambrick, D.C., *Strategic Leadership: Top Executives and Their Effects on Organizations*, St. Paul, MN: West, 1996.

CHAPTER 10. LEARNING FROM MISTAKES

1. Snook, Scott A., *Friendly Fire: The Accidental Shootdown of U.S. Black Hawks over Northern Iraq*, Princeton, NJ: Princeton University Press, 2000.

2. Latane, B., and Darley, J. M., *The Unresponsive Bystander: Why Doesn't He Help?* New York: Appleton-Century-Crofts, 1970.

3. While there is an occasional success story of co-CEOs, they are almost always in situations that result from internal development and growth, and not external acquisition. For example, Bob Daly and Terry Semel at Time Warner successfully shared the top job for years; Goldman Sachs also relies on more than one person at the top to direct the firm. What's different is that such co-CEOs typically developed a working relationship that emerged over years, and were not thrust together in the high-stakes, high-ego game of mergers and acquisitions.

4. Interview with Marc Porat, former chairman & CEO, General Magic, April 16, 2001.

5. Jeter, Debra, and Chaney, Paul, "How Internet Companies Play Games with Their Numbers," *Bridge News*, December 7, 2000.

6. Stewart, Sinclair, "Investors Misled over Earnings: Regulators Warn of 'Widespread Use' of Unconventional Financial Reporting," *National Post*, January 15, 2002, p. FP1.

7. Warner, Melanie, "A Tale from the Dark Side of Silicon Valley," *Fortune*, April 13, 1998, pp. 92–96.

8. One of the two venture capitalists on the board actually did take a stand against management, but in classic fashion resigned in protest rather than stay on to fight for change.

9. Cooper, Christopher, and Portanger, Erik, "Flashy Clothing Site Had Good Ideas, but Financial Controls Were Lacking," *The Wall Street Journal*, June 27, 2000, http://interactive.wsj.com/articles/SB962060900205288660.htm.

10. Porretto, John, "Overbilling May Be the Next Issue to Plague WorldCom," Associated Press State & Local Wire, July 3, 2002, http://web.lexis-nexis.com/universal/document?_m=abb9fa5e78e8a7867d1 a22f68abd2932&_docnum=2&wchp=dGLbVlz-1S1A1&_md5=f829d11e83dac9a9 7abeb0122e171dla

11. Wallack, Todd, "WorldCom to Ante Up $8.5 Million; State Lawsuit Accused Long-Distance Phone Company of Slamming, Abusive Billing," *San Francisco Chronicle*, March 8, 2002, p. B1.

12. PlanetFeedBack is an online feedback services company that allows companies to collect and analyze customer feedback in real time.

13. PR Newswire, "PlanetFeedback Releases Consumer Data Findings on WorldCom; Thumbs Down from Consumers on Billing Practices, Customer Service and More," May 2, 2002, http://web.lexis-nexis.com/universe/document?_m=1e36d778cc6a81df16163b4eb513 119a&_docnum=wchp=dGLbVlz-1S1A1&_md5=7407197a0f88921ba4a 1b3d1a6f6e1e5.

14. Interview with John Keogh, president and COO, National Union Fire Insurance Co. of Pittsburg, PA, October 25, 2002.

15. Van Natta Jr., Don, and Berenson, Alex, "Enron's Chairman Received Warning about Accounting," *The New York Times*, January 15, 2002, http://www.nytimes.com/2002/01/15/politics/15ENRO.html.

16. Interview with John Keogh, president, National Union Fire Insurance Company, October 25, 2002.

17. Machiavelli, Niccolo, *The Prince*, translated and edited by Mark Musa, New York: St. Martin's Press, 1946, p. 151.

18. These insights owe much to a student project at Tuck by Jason Adair, Joe Bachman, Tracy Brown, Andrew McBrien, and Laura Scott.

19. Caruso, David, "For Years, Rigas Treated Adelphia Like a Family Business," Associated Press State & Local Wire, May 27, 2002, http://web.lexis-nexis/com/universe/document?_m=505b7137b8ae91c79bf4 0c18972ce022&_docnum=2&wchp=dGLbVtbp1S1A1&_md 5=548bfe56a03943f501a9774b38980acf.

20. Robinson, D, "The Company That Lies Built," *Buffalo News*, July 28, 2002, p. B13.

21. Zremski, Jerry, "Rigas Indictments Outlined; Founder, 4 Others Face Charges," *Buffalo News*, September 24, 2002, p. A1.

22. Gaither, Chris, "Top Ranks Are Thinned at Sun as No. 2 Executive Joins Exodus," *The New York Times*, May 2, 2002, http://web.lexis-nexis.com/universe/document?_m=337 5507b77dd541164ed807675ddea36&_docnum=23&wchp=dGLbVlz-1S1zV&_md5=51 01a7d87a3f5bfc 99f23794e51fc903; Clark, Don, "Sun to Lay Off 11% of Workers, Posts Loss Amid Weak Revenue," *The Wall Street Journal*, October 18, 2002, http://online.wsj.com/article/0.,SB1034789952448161308,00.html?mod=home ome_whats_news_us.

23. Byron, Christopher, "The Story of ImClone," *New York Post*, January 14, 2002, p. 31.

24. Anand, Geeta, "In Waksal's Past, Repeated Ousters—at Four Prestigious Labs ImClone Founder Faced Questions about Work," *The Wall Street Journal*, September 27, 2002, p. A1.

25. A study of over three hundred Fortune 500 companies found essentially the same result: Those companies run by founders had significantly greater variability in return on assets and stock returns than companies run by nonfounder "professional executives." See Adams, Renee B., Almeida, Heitor, and Ferreira, Daniel, "Powerful CEOs and Their Impact on Corporate Performance," working paper, Federal Reserve Bank of New York, November 27, 2002.

26. Mollenkamp, Carrick, "Subprime Asset: How Money Store Inspired a Big Change in First Union's Course," *The Wall Street Journal*, July 25, 2000, p. A1.

27. CMGI gave up the rights to the Patriots new football stadium two years after acquiring them, and took a $21 million write-off. The team will now play at "Gillette Stadium."

28. PSINet gave up its naming rights in early 2002 (a prudent move given the company was bankrupt), as did Enron (now called Minute Maid Park).

29. Interview with Russell Lewis, president and CEO, The New York Times Co., November 6, 2002.

30. Doward, Jaime, "Day the WorldCom World Was Turned Upside Down: The Giant's Fall," *The Observer*, June 30, 2002, Business section, p. 4; Dreazen, Yochi, and Solomon, Deborah, "WorldCom Aide Conceded Flaws—Controller Said Company Was Forced to Disguise Expenses, Ignore Warnings," *The Wall Street Journal*, July 16, 2002, p. A3; Sloan, Alan, "WorldCom's Wrong Numbers," *Newsweek*, July 8, 2002, p. 44; Economist.Com, "From Bad to Worse; WorldCom," July 1, 2002, http:/web.lexis-nexis.com/universe/document?_m=6ce 47e557b6f026369b64 e4e4485a9ba&_docnum=1*wchp=dGLbVlzp1S1A1&_md5=02386 0sf6c297a03d5 4c1a00175c6146; Dreazen, Yochi, "Push for Sales Fostered Abuses at WorldCom," *The Wall Street Journal*, May 16, 2002, p. B1.

31. Fowler, Tom, "The Fall of Enron; A Year Ago, Enron's Crumbling Foundation Was Revealed to All When the Company Reported Its Disastrous Third-Quarter Numbers," *Houston Chronicle*, October 20, 2002, p. A1.

32. *The American Heritage® Dictionary of the English Language*, 4th ed., New York: Houghton Mifflin, 2000.

33. Serwer, Andy, "The Socialite Scientist," *Fortune*, April 15, 2002, p. 152.

34. Schultz, Stacey, "The Drug That Could Have Been," *U.S. News & World Report*, August 19, 2002, p. 23.

35. Deogun, Nikhil, and Lipin, Steven, "Cautionary Tales: When Big Deals Turn Bad," *The Wall Street Journal*, December 8, 1999, p. C1.

36. Goldman, Abigail, "Mattel CEO's Report Fails to Ease Investors' Doubts . . . but Barad Says the Worst Is Over," *Los Angeles Times*, October 22, 1999, p. 1.

37. Hof, Robert, and Peter Burrows, "Intel Won't Feel the Heat from This Fusion," *BusinessWeek*, November 5, 1995, p. 40.

38. Interview with Tony Galban, vice president, D&O underwriting manager, Chubb Group of Insurance Companies, June 26, 2002.

39. Interview with Tony Galban, vice president, D&O underwriting manager, Chubb Group of Insurance Companies, June 26, 2002.

40. Interview with John Keogh, president and COO, National Union Fire Insurance Co. of Pittsburg, PA, October 25, 2002.

41. Interview with Tony Galban, vice president, D&O underwriting manager, Chubb Group of Insurance Companies, June 26, 2002.

CHAPTER 11. HOW SMART EXECUTIVES LEARN

1. Hamburger, Tom, "Enron Official Tells of 'Arrogant' Culture," *The Wall Street Journal*, February 15, 2002, p. A3.

2. Van Natta Jr., Don, and Berenson, Alex, "Enron's Chairman Received Warning about Accounting," *The New York Times*, January 15, 2002, http://www.nytimes.com/2002/01/15/politics/15ENRO.html.

3. Eichenwald, Kurt, "Company Hobbled Investigation by Its Law Firm, Report Says," *The New York Times*, February 4, 2002, http://www.nytimes.com/2002/02/04/business/04WATK.html.

4. McLean, Bethany, "Why Enron Went Bust," *Fortune*, December 24, 2001, p. 62.

5. Hamburger, Tom, and Emshwiller, John, "Enron Executives Wanted a Lawyer Fired for Approach to Partnership Negotiations," *The Wall Street Journal*, February 6, 2002, http://online.wsj.com/article/0_SB101292627612707408.00.html?mod=hom e_whats_news_us.

6. Oppel, Jr., Richard A., "Merrill Replaced Research Analyst Who Upset Enron," *The New York Times*, July 30, 2002, http://www.nytimes.com/2002/07/30/business/30ENRO.html.

7. Bethany McLean, speaking at a conference at the Tuck School of Business at Dartmouth, February 7, 2002.

8. Torekull, Bertil, *Leading by Design: The IKEA Story*, New York; HarperBusiness, 1999, p. 237.

9. Interview with Russell Lewis, President and CEO, The New York Times Co., November 6, 2002.

10. Akbar, Hammad, "The Endogenous Nature of Knowledge Transformation: Towards an Integrated Model of Organizational Learning and Knowledge Levels," working paper, Cambridge University, 2001.

11. There is actually a burgeoning academic literature on the value of studying the mistakes of other organizations. See, for example, Argote, Linda, *Organizational Learning: Creating, Retaining and Transferring Knowledge*, Boston: Kluwer Academic Publishers, 1999; and Weick, K. E., "The Nontraditional Quality of Organizational Learning," *Organization Science* (1991), 2, pp. 116–24.

12. Useem, J., "Boeing vs. Boeing," *Fortune*, October 2, 2000, p. 152.

13. Interview with Phil Condit, chairman and CEO, Boeing, October 22, 2002.

14. Interview with Ernie Parizeau, partner, Norwest Partners, May 15, 2002.

15. Interview with Gary Kelly, executive vice-president and CFO, Southwest Airlines, October 22, 2002.

16. Norris, Floyd, "Execution Before Trial for Andersen," *The New York Times*, March 15, 2002, http://www.nytimes.com/2002/03/15/business/15ASSE.html.

17. Interview with Russell Lewis, president and CEO, The New York Times Co., November 6, 2002.

18. Schultz, Howard, and Yang, Dori Jones, *Pour Your Heart into It: How Starbucks Built a Company One Cup at a Time*, New York: Hyperion, 1997, pp. 158–9.

19. Marcus, Bernie, and Blank, Arthur, with Bob Andelman, *Built from Scratch: How a Couple of Regular Guys Grew the Home Depot from Nothing to $30 Billion*, New York: Times Business, 1999, p. 252.

20. Interview with Phil Condit, chairman and CEO, Boeing, October 22, 2002.

21. Interview with Julie Morath, COO, Children's Hospitals and Clinics, Minneapolis, February 21, 2001.

22. More on how the military conducts debriefing can be found in Murphy, James D., *Business Is Combat*, New York: Regan Books, 2000.

23. Interview with Phil Condit, chairman and CEO, Boeing, October 22, 2002.

24. Bannon, Lisa; "Mattel's New Profit Shortfall Punishes Stock and Raises Questions About CEO," *The Wall Street Journal*, October 5, 1999, p. A3.

25. All quotes in this section are taken from interviews with Alec Gores, chairman, and Vance Diggins, CEO, Gores Technology Group, April 12, 2002.

26. The $300 million Triarc paid for Snapple turned into a $1.3 billion windfall, the price Cadbury Schweppes paid for Snapple in October 2000 when it bought the company.

27. After a successful turnaround, Norm Payson retired as CEO at the end of 2002.

28. Harris, Gardiner, "Ex-Executives Tell How Bristol Burnished Its Financial Results," *The Wall Street Journal*, December 12, 2002, http://online.wsj.com/article/0..SB1039655849 651935353.00.html?mod=home%5Fpage%5Fone%5Fus.

29. Interview with Robert Galvin, former CEO, Motorola, December 18, 2002. The expression "healthy spirit of discontent" actually was coined by Robert Sr. (present CEO Chris Galvin's grandfather) decades ago.

30. Moin, David, and Young, Vicki M., "Barneys' Former Co-Chairman Was Bob Pressman," *Women's Wear Daily*, August 27, 2002, p. 3.

Index

Toyota, 127–28, 184, 188–89
Toys "R" Us, 141
track records, 49, 51, 206–7, 235–37, 255
Triarc Company, 79, 82
Tuchman, Barbara, 71
Tyco, 2–8, 6, 118, 130, 231, 287–88

ungovernable organizations, 202
unheeded warnings, 250–51
Unilever, 95
United Airlines, 150–51
unlikely events, 157–59, 163, 180
Upjohn and Pharmacia, 104, 244

Venetis, 252
Vivendi Universal, 94, 95

Waksal, Harlan, 255
Waksal, Sam, 208–9, 228, 254–55, 256,
    260, 288
Walker, Moses Fleetwood, 120
Wall Street Journal, The, 261
Wal-Mart, 61–62
Walsh, Bill, 101
Wang, An, 3, 109–13, 215, 219, 220–21,
    226, 232, 236
Wang, Fred, 111–12
Wang Labs, 3, 9, 109–13, 124, 274, 286;
    culture of, 129; debt of, 113;
    delusions of, 170; as family
    business, 112; strategic errors of,
    126; structure of, 111–12, 113
Warner Brothers, 85
Watkins, Sherron, 267
Wealth of Nations, The (Smith), 41
Webvan, 21, 35–40, 248, 285; alliances
    of, 39; bankruptcy of, 36, 40;
    competitors for, 38, 46;
    HomeGrocer.com and, 39–40;
    hub-and-spoke system of, 36, 40;
    investors in, 36; IPO of, 38;
    productivity model of, 36–37

Weill, Sandy, 244
Weinstein, Michael, 81, 98
Weisel, Tom, 105
Welch, Jack, 185
Westinghouse, 101
What America Means to Me (Buck), 47
White, Jim, 23
Wiggins, Stephen, 155, 220, 221,
    231–32, 235, 237
Windolph, John, 30–31
wireless technology, 23
WorldCom, 43, 131, 249, 251, 258, 276,
    286
World Trade Center attack (2001), 109,
    192–93

Xerox, 196

Yates, Brock, 181
Yawkey, Tom, 124–25, 200
"yesterday's answer." *See* outdated
    beliefs
Young-Sam Kim, 34

Zander, Edward, 253–54
"zombie" companies, 166–91, 205,
    212; customers of, 173–75,
    176; employees of, 168, 170,
    175–76; information at, 191;
    negative feedback lacking at,
    176–78; perfectionism of,
    178–81, 186–87, 190; positive
    attitudes at, 175–77, 185–86,
    189–90; preventing, 182–90;
    pride and sense of superiority at,
    168–70, 183–84, 189, 274;
    public relations of, 181–82;
    suppliers of, 174; team spirit
    of, 180–81; as thriving,
    168–70
Zwain, Larry, 178

Note from the Author

I hope that the stories of failure and the insights that come from them have been helpful as you think about your own life in and out of organizations. Even though the book is dedicated to understanding mistakes and failure, my goal throughout has really been to help people and companies be more successful. It is when we study what goes wrong that we gain a fresh window to what could go right. Toward that end, I invite readers to visit my Web site (http://www.whysmartexecutivesfail.com), where you can find some related materials from our research project. In addition, the Web site will give you an opportunity to share your own stories of mistakes and failures, and especially what you and the people around you learned from those experiences. I hope you'll continue the dialogue.